"Thank you, Paula, for inviting women back to live-fire cooking, and for this incredibly informative and beautiful book. *Thank You for Smoking* proves that almost anything we've enjoyed without smoke may be enjoyed—subtly or boldly—with smoke. There's nothing gimmicky about the dishes. I'm so excited to cook from this book!"

—Carla Hall, TV chef and author of *Carla Hall's Soul Food*

"Paula Disbrowe and I go way back. I recall her excitement about these smoky flavors (and how to achieve them) from decades ago. As I sip one of her simple, delightfully smoky cocktails, I marvel at how this book offers so many tasty ways to look at food!"

—Alex Guarnaschelli, author of *The Home Cook* and executive chef at Butter Restaurant

"*Thank You for Smoking* gives grillers the confidence to take backyard cooking to the next level. Whether you're experienced on the smoker or lighting wood for the first time, this book provides the tools to master the most flavorful part of barbecue. Paula offers clear and creative explanations of how to apply smoking techniques to even the most unexpected ingredients, with recipes for everything from cocktails to dessert."

—Rodney Scott, pit master at Rodney Scott's BBQ

THANK YOU FOR
SMOKING

THANK YOU FOR
SMOKING

Fun and Fearless Recipes Cooked with a Whiff of Wood Fire on Your Grill or Smoker

PAULA DISBROWE

Photographs by Johnny Autry

TEN SPEED PRESS
California | New York

Contents

WHERE THERE'S SMOKE, THERE'S FLAVOR

"Evolutionarily speaking, fire and smoke signal meat roasting, so we may have been programmed to find them desirable in expectation of what is to come."
—CHARLES SPENCE, PROFESSOR OF EXPERIMENTAL PSYCHOLOGY, OXFORD UNIVERSITY

Where there's smoke, there's dinner. At least that's what I learned—and enthusiastically embraced—while developing my last cookbook, *Any Night Grilling*, for Food52. The project gave me the lucky charge of several months of backyard cooking, cementing a lifelong friendship with my gas and charcoal grills. In addition to developing recipes that made the unique satisfaction of grilled foods possible *any* night of the week, I explored ways to infuse foods with a subtle smoky flavor using various forms of hardwood (chips, chunks, or logs). Along the way, I discovered how easy it is to infuse just about any ingredient—from dried lentils to lacinato kale—with a seductive whiff of smoke. The delicious results fueled a strong desire to keep the fires burning—and the book you're holding in your hands.

In *Thank You for Smoking*, smoke is part of the seasoning process, adding character and complexity to every dish. Lightly smoked oats and pecans form the base of your new favorite granola, smoked peppercorns and spices perfume sweet and savory tarts, and smoked Marcona almonds become a silky nut butter that you want to slather on everything. Following the same general formula (grilling + wood smoke) for all recipes, this book shows you how to infuse weeknight staples like salads, soups, and pasta with more intrigue (and the deep, satisfying flavors you associate with your favorite wood-fired restaurant) and how to create an updated larder of smoked ingredients (such as dried legumes, grains, smoked seasonings, and enticing condiments) that will add flair to future meals.

The irony of my smoking obsession isn't lost on me. Before embarking on this journey, I wasn't a fan of "smoked" flavors, because it often implies something that's artificially produced or heavy-handed (think of the smoked cheeses in holiday gift baskets or smoked soups at your local supermarket). Even though I love the influence of natural wood smoke, I don't like too much of it (a rare case of when my usual "more is more" enthusiasm doesn't apply). That's why this method was such a delicious revelation: Grill-smoking items for thirty or so minutes, or simply grilling them over a fire that incorporates wood, creates a subtler form of smoke flavor. Then it's a matter of balance. When I use smoked ingredients in a meal, I team them up with other fresh and vivid flavors. For instance, if I'm making a carrot-quinoa salad, I won't smoke both the grain and the vegetables, because the smokiness would be overpowering. Instead, I prefer to begin with one or two key smoked elements and partner them with other fresh, bright, and acidic supporting players (for example, herbs, citrus juice, pickled vegetables, and the like) that anchor the smokiness.

To celebrate occasions when you can kick back and enjoy extended time around a fire (with friends and cold libations), there are longer smokes: larger cuts of meat tagged with a ✿ icon that require longer cook times. These recipes result in sumptuous feasts and festive fare for a crowd, like a holiday ham or a smoked duck cooked atop white beans that absorb the flavorful drippings. Smoke also drifts into desserts to create playful, surprising treats such as Krispie squares made with burnt marshmallows, as well as sophisticated endings like a velvety chocolate cake with smoked pears.

Like many people, I'd always associated the seductive flavor of smoke with low-and-slow barbecue (a process that requires eight to twelve hours of babysitting a fire). But when I began grilling on a regular basis, I discovered that adding a smoky flavor doesn't need to take any longer than grilling your favorite foods—because my method essentially *is* grilling, with the influence of a smoke source. The recipes in this book primarily begin on hot grates (after all, cooking over a live fire provides its own smoky nuance). It doesn't require more than a few minutes of additional time to add a packet of chips, a few chunks, or a log of hardwood to hot coals (or wood chips to a smoker box for gas grills) that will generate a steady stream of smoke to perfume anything you're cooking.

In the following chapters, you'll find recipes devoted to smoking ingredients like grains, nuts, seeds, and dried beans that create an inspired larder and the springboard for countless meals. The process is highly enjoyable, but you can also think of the time investment as replacing the need for a lengthy marinade or long braise, because it creates a foundation of foods that are deeply flavored from the get-go.

SMOKING 101

Like most passionate backyard grillers, I've bonded with my particular grill because it's the model that works for me. The PK 360 Grill and Smoker's oblong shape makes it particularly easy to create two heat zones (more on this to follow), the airflow is easy to control, and there's enough room in the expansive cooking chamber to handle larger items like whole chickens or a spatchcocked turkey. However, you can use any grill or smoker for the recipes in this book; just keep in mind that because your setup may be different than mine, temperatures and cooking times may vary slightly. But if you follow the same general guidelines and adjust according to the visual and other cues I give you in the recipes, an enticing array of foods seasoned with a whiff of wood smoke are in your future.

In this section, I'll cover the fundamentals of how smoking is defined in this book, including rigging your grill as a smoker, operating a variety of smokers, and the best way to deploy wood (and other items) as smoke sources.

How to Rig Your Grill as a Smoker

A two-zone cooking setup is my preferred way to cook almost everything. To create two cooking zones in your grill, you simply bank the coals on one side. The area directly over the coals is your hot "direct heat" zone, where you will sear steaks and burgers, develop deeply flavored char marks, and crisp chicken skin. The adjacent area without coals becomes your cooler "indirect heat" zone, where food cooks from the grill's ambient heat and the convection airflow created by venting your grill. The indirect heat zone also provides a safety net— an area that allows you to move foods to avoid flare-ups or burnt exteriors, and to cook through the interior of foods (such as chicken thighs or carrots) more slowly and gently.

The following method is the basic setup for most of the recipes in this book. Foods that are "grill-smoked," or grilled over direct heat with a smoke source added to the fire, do not require a drip pan.

The Smoking Setup:

1. Prepare a charcoal grill for two-zone cooking and build a medium-high fire, or heat a gas grill to high. **2.** When the coals are glowing red and covered with a fine gray ash, use tongs to remove the cooking grate and place a drip pan with ½ to 1 inch (1.3 to 2.5 cm) of warm water on the side with no coals (see sidebar, page 5), then add a smoke source (see page 7). **3.** Return the cooking grate to its position, then carefully wipe the grates with a lightly oiled paper towel (I use a basic vegetable oil—there's no need to use your best extra-virgin oil here). Using a grill brush, scrape the grill grates clean, and then carefully

HARNESS THE HEAT

Traditional "low and slow" barbecue relies on a smoking temperature between 225°F (107°C) and 250°F (121°C). For my approach to this book— infusing foods with a whiff of wood smoke—I rely on a slightly higher heat. Throughout my field tests, after emptying chimneys of hot charcoal and adding a drip pan of water to the grill, I found the internal temperature to consistently hover around 300°F (150°C). This higher (but still gentle) heat worked beautifully for seasoning various ingredients with a smoky flavor in a short time. So, unless the recipe states otherwise, assume that I'm smoking or grill-roasting foods at around 300°F (150°C). Don't freak out if your grill is running a bit off in either direction. If the temperature is too high, use the vents to reduce the oxygen in the cooking chamber to lower the heat. If the heat is too low, use the vents to stoke the fire with more air, or add a couple of chunks of charcoal on the periphery of the glowing embers (you don't want fresh fuel directly under the food, because it will get too hot).

wipe the grates with a lightly oiled towel again. Technically you don't have to oil the grates if you're only smoking in containers, but you don't want your food to pick up sooty flavors from previous meals. I habitually clean the grates because I'm usually multitasking, smoking something on indirect heat and perhaps firing up a pork chop or a few vegetables for dinner. It's a good habit to get into to avoid a sooty buildup on your grates. **4.** When the fire begins to produce a steady stream of smoke, place the item you're cooking directly on the grate above the drip pan or, for smaller items like grains, in a disposable aluminum pan or in a foil packet (crimp the edges of the foil upward to create a rim that prevents the items from sliding off). Close the grill, vent the grill for smoking, and smoke for the time suggested in the recipe. Again, you won't use a drip pan for quicker-cooking items (like kale, shrimp, or burgers) that are simply grilled over a wood-infused fire.

Guide to Smokers

Although I do the majority of my smoking on my charcoal grill, if you rely on a smoker (or have your heart set on buying one), here's a look at the many types on the market. A growing interest in live-fire cooking (in restaurants, at food festivals, and with backyard pit masters) means increasingly sophisticated models of smokers are now available for home cooks. The ideal model should be adept at both high-temperature searing and smoking at a lower heat, and perhaps most importantly, suit the style of grilling that you're comfortable with (do you like the sport of managing a live fire or would you rather set it and forget it?). The truth is, you can adapt any grill for smoking, and many smokers can grill and sear, but few of them do both well.

Kamado, Ceramic, and Egg Smokers As modern incarnations of the Japanese *kamado*, an earthenware cooking urn whose original design is at least three thousand years old (Indian tandoori models are similar), these egg-shaped, charcoal-fueled devices can be made of ceramic, cement, terra-cotta, and other materials that are excellent insulators. The Big Green Egg has a cult following (and has spawned a flurry of branded accessories); it and the beautifully designed Komodo Kamado are two leading examples of high-end ceramic cookers. These smokers have thick sides that retain and radiate heat evenly, making them excellent smokers and roasters (because they use less charcoal and oxygen, there's very little airflow so they help preserve moisture in meats). They're also excellent for pizza, bread, and paella because the sides and domes absorb and radiate heat like a brick oven. The downside of these cookers is that with their round (and sometimes narrow) cooking surface and heavily insulated construction, it's harder to create two temperature zones (even with the dividers and deflectors that many of them sell).

A disposable aluminum pan (or a small narrow steam table pan from a restaurant supply store) filled with ½ to 1 inch (1.3 to 2.5 cm) of warm water is an important element in smoking—even for the relatively quick smoking methods in this book. That's because the water tempers the heat and radiates it back evenly, which helps prevent temperature fluctuations and creates humidity that helps the smoke "stick" to whatever you're cooking (this is especially important for dried ingredients like beans and grains). The added humidity helps prevent meats and vegetables from drying out, allowing them to retain their flavorful juices. The water also helps generate flavor: as the moisture melds with the fire's combustion gases, those unique "barbecued" flavor notes are created—the kind of satisfying results that entice us all to fire up the grill in the first place.

Two important details: Always add the water pan after your grill is hot and at a stable temperature, and use warm water so it doesn't usurp the heat and bring the temperature down.

Bullet Smokers There are a number of bullet-shaped smokers on the market. When I wrote an article on how to smoke a brisket, I took the advice of a pit master friend and got a Weber Smokey Mountain (available in three sizes), a model popular on the competitive barbecue circuit and considered the best. Bullet smokers are great for creating the low-and-slow heat for cuts like brisket and ribs. For the best results, new models need to be seasoned and calibrated before use (a helpful way to learn how to regulate the temperature).

The Weber Smokey Mountain series grills have plated steel cooking grates, heavy-gauge steel charcoal grates, and built-in lid thermometers. But for the most accurate results, you'll still want to rely on a good digital oven thermometer, because the built-in dial metal thermometer sits in the dome lid, where it's typically 10 to 20 degrees hotter than on the cooking grate where your meat cooks. Once you get rolling with these cookers, make sure you empty the grease from the foiled water pan (to avoid fires and a rancid oil smell), and clean out the ash from the bottom before lighting a new fire, so the remnants of your last endeavor doesn't disrupt the air intake and absorb the heat. Bullet cookers come with two cooking grates positioned above the water pan. If you use both grates simultaneously, place the faster cooking meat on top so it's easier to remove (major bonus: as it cooks, the dripping juices will flavor the meat or pan of beans cooking below). To maintain your cooking temperature and a steady stream of smoke and even temperature, you'll need to add a couple chunks of wood every 30 minutes or so, and more hot water to the drip pan every couple hours.

Offset Smokers If offset smokers—like the ones made by Char-Broil, Broil King, or Oklahoma Joe's—were trucks, they'd be a jacked-up diesel with dualies (eight tires) because these macho, massive machines show others that you're a force to be reckoned with. But are they the most efficient for your needs? The general consensus among pros is that you should steer clear of cheap models, because they're made from thin metal, so heat retention is poor and they often leak air. If you're committed to this style of cooking, invest ($700 or more) in a model made from thick metal with tight doors and dampers that will distributes heat more evenly from end to end. But keep in mind that it's more difficult to wrangle a steady temperature from offset smokers, even for the pros. If you do use one, pit masters suggest cooking with charcoal (not wood), preheating the cooking chamber well before adding meat, only adding fully lit coals, and using a reliable thermometer on each end.

Pellet Smokers If your style of grilling involves a lawn chair, a cold beer snuggled into a Koozie, and zero stress, pellet smokers, like the ones manufactured by Traeger or Z Grills, are for you. Comprised of an auger to feed in compressed wood pellets, a blower to help them burn, and digital temperature controls, these "set it and forget it" machines are all about convenience and control, and a subtle wood smoke flavor. Because pellet smokers primarily rely on an ambient heat, they're best for smoking turkey, duck, ribs, pork chops, brisket, and salmon, but they don't generate the high heat prized for searing steaks.

Stovetop Smokers Stovetop models like KitchenQue (the one I use at home) are great for people who don't have the space to cook outdoors, or when you want to smoke small quantities (say, mushrooms for an appetizer) that don't warrant firing up a larger grill or smoker. Stovetop smokers are also fun for camping trips because they can be used on a rustic grate set-up or small gas burners, and they're particularly adept at smoking fish and fowl. The procedure is generally the same: you place a small amount of a smoke source (food-grade sawdust or shavings) in the bottom, add a drip pan and replace the grate top, put the food on the rack, and then keep the food covered so only a small amount of smoke escapes. Models with an integrated thermometer make it easy to regulate heat.

Smoke Sources

Here's where the magic happens. Incorporating hardwood in any of the following forms creates the stream of aromatic smoke to infuse whatever you're cooking. If you're using a gas grill, your only option is to rely on wood chips (soaked in water beforehand so they'll slowly smolder) placed in a smoker box or foil packet that's placed directly on the grates over a flame. You can also use soaked chips in a charcoal grill, either wrapped in a foil packet or scattered directly on the coals. Chips burn much more quickly than wood chunks, so consider the latter for recipes that require longer cook times. I love wood chunks because I can place a couple directly on a bed of hot coals (no soaking required), where they'll light quickly and smolder steadily, and they're easy to move with tongs if I need to balance the heat. Wood chunks are a great way to build heat if your temperature begins to drop midway through cooking and you don't have hot coals at the ready. Once the chunks ignite, you can control the speed at which they burn by moving them around the fire and venting your grill to control the amount of air the fire is receiving.

A log of hardwood is another great option for generating flavorful smoke and extending the life of a fire. When I use a log, I place it adjacent to the bed of hot coals (between the coals and the drip pan, if I'm using one). I prefer to use wood that's been split, so I can tilt the log at a 45-degree angle, with the thinner edge over the hot embers. When my only option is a round log, I simply nestle it into the fire and allow it to burn down to about half its size before grilling. Logs can take a bit longer to ignite and produce smoke, so to speed up that process, I often add them as soon as I empty the charcoal chimney. But once a log is smoldering, it will burn steadily for a longer amount of time (if the temperature drops, you may need to rearrange the coals and reposition the wood over the hottest embers). You can also reuse a log for several more fires; just close all the vents to snuff out the oxygen when you're done cooking so it doesn't continue to burn.

Wood Chips I primarily use hickory and oak chips, because their flavors (more on that, below) complement everything. Before using, soak the chips in water for at least 30 minutes, or up to one hour. When you're ready to smoke, drain the chips, double-wrap them in heavy-duty aluminum foil, use a sharp knife to perforate the top of the foil packet, then place it directly on top of hot coals. For a gas grill, place the chips in a smoker box or a foil packet and position it directly over the flame. When the chips begin to produce a steady stream of smoke, you're ready to cook. Alternately, scatter the soaked chips around the periphery of the hot coals; obviously they'll burn more quickly than they do when insulated in foil, so this is a good approach when you want to generate smoke quickly, for a shorter cook.

Wood Chunks Commonly available in the grilling aisle of markets and sold in net bags alongside charcoal, chunks of hardwood (tennis ball–size pieces of oak, hickory, and mesquite) are a smoker's best ally. When the coals are glowing red and covered with a fine gray ash, place two or three chunks around the fire (close enough to the coals that they begin to smolder). When they ignite and begin to produce a steady stream of smoke, you're ready to cook. If the chunks flare up too vigorously, adjust the air vents in your grill (closing them slightly or completely to reduce airflow) to coax them back to a steady smolder.

Hardwood Logs Seek out dry or "cured" hardwood ("green" wood that's still moist and heavy will produce a sooty smoke), and make sure it's untreated and safe for cooking. When you empty your charcoal chimney, place the log in the center of the grill and nestle it against the fire (in two-zone cooking, the opposite side of the grill will have no coals). When the log begins to burn and produce a steady stream of smoke, you're ready to cook.

Hardwood Pellets Pellets are made from sawdust that has been compressed into little rabbit pellet–size cylinders, each less than $1/2$ inch (1.3 cm) long. They're used in pellet smokers, where they're poured into a burn pot and ignited. The number of pellets added to the fire and the oxygen supply are regulated by a digital controller that maintains a steady temperature. Although pellets can also be used in charcoal and gas grills, they'll flare and finish quickly, so I don't recommend them there.

Cooking with Wood

The following varieties of wood are commonly available (in stores and online) in all forms of the smoke sources described above. Although each kind of wood imparts its own nuance, for the shorter smoking times in this book, you'd be hard-pressed to taste a significant difference. (In a blind tasting, I'm not sure many of us could distinguish between applewood and maple wood, for instance.) The exception is mesquite, which produces a strong, distinct flavor—I reserve it for beef, lamb, and other recipes that benefit from its heady perfume. Wood preferences vary regionally throughout the country, typically based on what's grown and available in the area. Never attempt to smoke with softwood or pressure-treated lumber.

Oak Massive live oak trees define the Central Texas landscape (and provide shade for grazing cattle, goats, and the rest of us during the sweltering summers). It's no coincidence that oak (specifically post oak) is the most common variety used in Central Texas barbecue. It burns evenly and has a sweet, mellow flavor that enhances anything, from cheese to pork.

Hickory The most popular wood for smoking (particularly in the Southeast), hickory has a robust presence and subtly sweet flavor that's a natural with pork, beef, game, and poultry (particularly dark meat).

Apple, Cherry, Persimmon, and Other Fruitwoods Because these varieties burn relatively quickly and produce a delicate flavor, they're best used to produce a burst of smoke for milder foods cooked quickly over direct heat, like chicken breasts, fish, and vegetables.

Pecan Our yard in Austin is framed by towering pecan trees, and windstorms leave me plenty of branches to use for cooking (once they're dried). Pecan burns more quickly than oak, so I use it to enhance mushrooms, fish, thin pork chops, chicken breasts, and other quick-cooking foods that will benefit from its delicate perfume.

Maple This is another quicker-burning variety that produces a subtle flavor that's good with chicken, small game birds, cheese, corn on the cob, mushrooms, and chiles.

Mesquite As one of the hottest burning woods, mesquite generates an assertive, earthy aroma that's best saved for beef or lamb, or when you want a particularly pronounced character to permeate a dish, as with the Mesquite-Smoked Pecan Rolls (page 76).

Other Sources of Smoke

In addition to hardwood, you can use hearty herb sprigs and branches, dried tea leaves, corn husks, hay, and other "smoky" ingredients to create a flavorful nuance and/or enhance a wood-fueled fire. The following sources won't produce enough cooking heat to replace a charcoal fire, so think of them as enhancements that will add an additional layer of intrigue to the results.

Fresh Herb Sprigs Place sturdy sprigs or small branches of fresh rosemary or bay leaves on the periphery of glowing embers (or in a perforated foil packet over direct heat in gas grills), where they'll burn more slowly. I don't soak the herbs because I place them strategically (*not* directly on the hottest part of the fire) so that I don't dilute their fragrant oils. I also love to place herb sprigs (including thyme, oregano, and marjoram) on top of fish, poultry, pork chops and steaks as they cook so their herbaceous fragrance mingles with the sizzling meat fat and olive oil and perfumes the meat.

Tea Dried green or black tea leaves are often combined with other spices and seasonings (coriander, star anise, peppercorns, brown sugar) to infuse chicken and duck. Place the leaves in a perforated foil packet directly over coals.

Corn Husks Like their smell, fresh corn husks impart a sweet, grassy aroma to the cooking chamber. Use them with foods that need shorter cooking times, like fish (they're delicious with salmon). After shucking the corn, discard the silk and soak the husks in water for 20 minutes. Then place the husks over hot coals, directly under whatever you're cooking.

Hay Hay-smoking meat is common in Italy, and the method has been embraced by celebrity chefs here in the United States. Seek out fresh-cut varieties (such as alfalfa or timothy from local farms or garden or feed stores, and ensure it hasn't been treated with chemicals) to infuse food with a grassy, wheat-field flavor. To use it, place an armful directly onto glowing embers. You can also use the hay to grill-smoke over direct heat—place an inch or so layer of hay in a disposable aluminum pan, top it with, say, a porterhouse pork chop or ham steaks, cover the meat with more hay, and cook to the desired doneness.

Essential Equipment

Smoking doesn't require a bunch of fancy gadgets, but having a few key items close at hand will keep you organized, avoid scrambling for necessary tools while your food is cooking, and help you Keep Calm and Smoke On (the process is more fun when you're relaxed).

BECOME A SMOKE CHARMER

The best flavor comes from producing a plume of clean, white smoke—not dark, sooty smoke. Attention to a few key details will help you produce the right results.

- Keep your grill clean: a buildup of soot and ash will usurp heat and inhibit airflow, two things that can choke a fire and create fits and spurts of uneven smoke.

- Never use "green" or moist wood. Seek out dry, cured hardwood that's meant for cooking from a trusted source.

- Excess moisture can snuff out a fire and cause temperature fluctuations. Make sure you drain soaked chips and scatter them around the periphery of a stable fire.

Aluminum drip pans (disposable) These are available in a wide range of sizes (from loaf pans to rectangles deep enough to hold a chicken) to suit whatever you're smoking. For dry ingredients, such as nuts or dried beans, choose a size that allows the items to be no deeper than ½ inch (1.3 cm), so they'll absorb smoke evenly.

Apron Essential for keeping your clothes from becoming soot-smudged and ash-dusted. I feel more on my game with an apron cinched around my waist. I particularly love aprons with pockets to hold matches, a digital thermometer, my iPhone and my Burt's Bees lip gloss (hey, we've all got our quirky proclivities). Don't forget to tuck a kitchen towel through your apron strap, so it's there when you need to wipe your hands (trust me, you'll need it).

Cleaning brush or broom I prefer an old-school corn fiber whisk brush for sweeping out cooled ashes from the grill and keeping surfaces (like side tables) clean, but there are several grill-specific varieties available.

Digital thermometer A good digital thermometer is a small investment to ensure that the meat you're serving family and friends is cooked enough to kill disease-causing bacteria (and to prevent you from overcooking that splurge steak or pork chop you're anticipating). Buy a rapid-read, handheld model with a rotating display that's easy to read from any angle, and take the guesswork out of gauging doneness. Two reliable options are the Thermapin Mk4 and the Thermoworks Super-Fast ThermoPop.

Grill brush (metal) Use this tool to scrape sooty buildup and debris from the grates, something you should do each and every time you fire up the grill.

Metal spatula (long-handled) A decisive thrust of a metal spatula helps you flip foods and maintain their browned crust. A spatula is also helpful in supporting larger items (a whole snapper, for example) when you turn them. The thin edge of a slotted fish spatula is particularly adept at releasing the skin of delicate foods (like swordfish steaks, fish fillets, chicken breasts) from grates.

Perforated baskets, grids, or wok pans Sometimes called a fish or vegetable basket, these allow you to cook and manipulate smaller foods (green beans, asparagus, shrimp) that might slip through the cracks of standard cooking grates. Preheating these pans creates an instant sizzle and sear. I use a stainless-steel tray model that sits on the grates, so I can flip the ingredients with tongs (or shake the basket as I would a skillet) while they cook. Stainless-steel mesh roasting pans with two handles make it easy to slide them on and off the grill.

Poultry shears A sturdy, spring-loaded model, like the one by OXO, makes quick work of spatchcocking chickens or even turkeys. You'll also reach for them to open bags of charcoal, slice pizza, and snip fresh herbs from the garden. The soft-grip handle makes them comfortable, and the stainless-steel blades are dishwasher-safe (take them apart at the hinge to ensure they get really clean).

Rimmed baking sheets These are super handy for transporting bowls of ingredients, tools, and seasonings to and from the grill; you can also transfer the baking sheets to a low oven to keep the grilled items warm before serving, if necessary. If I use them for raw meats, I line them with parchment or foil that I change out before pulling the finished product off the grill.

Tongs (long-handled) I'd be lost without them. Tongs help you place food on the grill and flip it during cooking, rearrange a bed of hot coals, and lift the grates to add more charcoal. I keep two at the ready for heavy lifting (and wipe off any ashes before using them on food). The long-handled variety helps you work comfortably over a hot fire. Look for spring-loaded models, as they give you one less thing to manipulate.

Trash cans (small, metal) These are handy for storing and protecting charcoal, wood chunks, and chips (and even the paper bags for the charcoal chimney) from the elements.

Wooden matches Plenty of folks rely on plastic utility lighters, but I think the simple gesture of striking a match to create a flame is more gratifying. I fiddled around with flimsy restaurant varieties a couple of times before realizing life (and lighting charcoal chimneys) is much easier with sturdy wooden kitchen matches.

And Some Nonessential but Fun-to-Have Tools

Will the results of your dinner depend on the extras that follow? Absolutely not—but they're fun to have, especially if you're a music lover or fan of cooking after dark.

Grill light with Bluetooth speaker Necessary? Nope. Fun? You bet, so I can stream Austin stations like KUTX while I'm out back with tongs in hand. The Bluetooth capability plays music from your phone or radio, and a handy clamp allows you to position the light precisely where it's most handy (like on the sizzling rib eye that you don't want to overcook).

LED headlamp Don't be shy about gearing up *Mission Impossible*–style for cooking after dark. The best headlamps are small in size, with eight LED bulbs that make nighttime cooking, last-minute bread toasting, and beverage opening (insert: sound of popping wine cork) easier.

Remote digital thermometer A wireless digital meat thermometer with a dual probe monitors food and/or the temperature of your grill or smoker from up to 300 feet away, enabling you juggle tasks and enjoy your company without continuously excusing yourself (hold that thought, be right back) to monitor the heat. That said, I still prefer to remain close to the fire and engaged in the process.

Smoking gun If you don't have access to outdoor cooking, using a hand-held smoke infuser is an easy and fun way to infuse just about anything (including cocktails!) with the flavor of wood smoke—without adding extra heat. I've had excellent results with the Breville smoking gun, because it's intuitive to manipulate and it allows you to add applewood or hickory flavors (the two varieties included with the gun) to food before or after cooking. It's compact and lightweight enough to wield with only one hand, and the 18-inch (46 cm) hose allows you to direct the smoke into anything from resealable plastic bags to a cocktail shaker. All you do is place a pinch of the wood chips (no soaking required) in the burn chamber, turn on the fan as you ignite them, and then use the flexible hose to direct the smoke into a sealed container. The heat is contained in the anodized-aluminum smoking chamber, so the smoke that's released is cool, making it gentle enough for use on foods like butter, oils, creamy fillings, and delicate fruits and vegetables without changing their texture or temperature.

Smoke pouches and mesh grilling bags They look like a disco handbag or fancy mailing envelope, and work like a charm over heat. You fill silver smoking pouches with wood chips or wood pellets and place them over the heat in your gas grill for plenty of steady, long-lasting smoke. The fine-mesh stainless steel limits the airflow into the pouch, so the wood smolders slowly and never bursts into flame. Mesh grilling bags (like those made by Companion Group) hold small items like cherry tomatoes, snap peas, and garlic cloves, and allow you to flip the entire thing at once, so you're not chasing around each tiny bit of food.

CHAPTER ONE

THE SMOKED LARDER

Even though I'm a fan of firing up my grill any night of the week, it's typically not realistic to tackle two cooking methods—say, smoking lentils and then simmering them for a salad—before a family-friendly dinner hour. That's why I rely on a larder of smoked ingredients that inspire and expedite meals. The process of building that larder is actually quite time efficient: devote a couple of pleasant hours to smoking a variety of items (e.g., dried beans, grains, seeds, spices, and nuts) all at once, and then be armed with an enticing array of options to pull from all week or month long. The thick cast-aluminum body of my PK Grill holds heat extremely well, so one chimney of charcoal (and a few additional wood chunks to keep the smoke streaming) typically provides enough heat for two 30- to 40-minute "bulk" smoking sessions that produce a bounty of options for the recipes in this book or your own inspirations.

The ability to reach for fragrant condiments, like Smoked Arbol Honey (page 25) or Smoked Garlic Aioli (page 33), that instantly elevate a simple grilled chicken breast or lamb burger, makes menu planning more fun. The smoked components bring so much character that you don't need much else to make the dish shine— one bite of smoked chickpeas dressed with nothing more than extra-virgin olive oil and a sprinkling of salt, and you'll know exactly what I mean.

This chapter is devoted to basics with a shelf life that complement everything from cocktails to dessert. I've given you recipes that rely on the smoked larder ingredients, but you'll also have leftovers that can be incorporated into your go-to meals. You can crumble smoked rosemary in tomato sauce, or use smoked cumin and fennel seeds in beef or vegetarian chili. Flavor enhancers like smoked condiments, salsas, syrup, and dried fruits are great to have on hand for granola, baked goods, charcuterie platters, and more.

SMOKED SPICES, HERBS, SALTS, DRIED FRUIT & DRIED CHILES

USE THIS METHOD TO SMOKE:

Dried chiles: ancho, arbol, guajillo, pasilla

Dried fruit: cherries, coconut, cranberries, dates, figs, nectarines, peaches, pears, prunes, raisins

Herbs (hearty sprigs or branches): bay leaves, marjoram, oregano, rosemary, thyme

Salts

Spices

Vanilla beans

Depending on their weight and density, most larder ingredients will smoke for 10 to 40 minutes over a drip pan of water that provides humidity to mitigate heat and help the smoky flavor "stick." (Note: Smoking dried chiles is really a matter of toasting them over a wood-infused fire for as little as 5 minutes, because they will darken very quickly.) Once your grill or smoker is at temperature, the process is mostly unattended, although you'll want to stir and/or rotate the ingredients after 5 to 15 minutes to ensure all items (every dried bean, for instance) receive a uniform level of smoke.

Note that foods with a higher fat content will react to heat more quickly, so keep a close eye on them toward the end of the process and continue to stir as necessary (items around the perimeter of the pan will darken first) to prevent them from becoming too dark and tasting acrid. Fresh herbs like rosemary, with its essential oils and sticky, finger-coating resin, can do the same, so you may need to pull them off the heat sooner than dried spices like fennel seeds or peppercorns. In other words, for the best results, pay attention—to the temperature and the way the process is playing out (see the before-and-after photo on page 20).

To smoke spices, herbs, salts, or dried fruit, prepare a charcoal grill for two-zone cooking and build a medium-high fire, or heat a gas grill to high.

When the coals are glowing red and covered with a fine gray ash, use tongs to remove the cooking grate and place a drip pan with 1 inch (2.5 cm) of warm water on the side with no coals, and add your smoke source (chips, chunks, or log). Return the cooking grate to its position, allow it to preheat, and then carefully wipe the preheated grates with a lightly oiled paper towel. Using a grill brush, scrape the grill grates clean, then carefully wipe with a lightly oiled towel again.

Place the ingredients in a disposable aluminum pan or atop two sheets of heavy-duty aluminum foil (crimp the edges of the foil upward to create a rim to prevent the ingredients from sliding off).

When the fire begins to produce a steady stream of smoke, place the ingredients over indirect heat, close the grill, vent the grill for smoking, and smoke for 10 to 30 minutes for spices, herbs, and salt and 30 to 40 minutes for dried fruits. To smoke dried chiles, preheat a grill basket or heavy cast-iron skillet over direct heat for 5 minutes. Place the chiles in the skillet and smoke until they are puffed and slightly darkened, about 1 to 2 minutes per side.

Remove the ingredients from the grill and let them cool and dry completely. Store in an airtight container in a cool, dry place for up to 3 months (dried fruits will last for 4 months).

Left: Ingredients shown before and after smoking reveal the subtle color changes that smoking creates. Above: Smoked Arbol Honey (page 25), smoked pink peppercorns, Cowgirl Salt (page 24), Smoked Castelvetrano Olives (page 39), and Charred Jalapeño-Rosemary Syrup (page 36).

SMOKED OLIVE OIL, MAPLE SYRUP & HONEY

I'm mostly a purist when it comes to olive oil (I prefer extra-virgin to the heavily scented varieties sold in oil boutiques). However, oil that's cold smoked with natural elements (heat can degrade a cold-pressed oil) creates a fragrant finish for grilled bread, hummus, hard-cooked eggs, roasted vegetables, grilled fish, or soup. That's why I rely on a smoking gun to flavor oil and other viscous syrups. I don't use smoked oil for cooking; I prefer it as a garnish, so I can appreciate its distinct flavor in small amounts. You can also use smoked olive oil to marinate olives (with herbs, citrus zest, and chile flakes) or fresh cheeses. Smoked maple syrup and smoked honey are both delicious drizzles over aged cheeses, grilled sausages, bacon, or pizza. See also Smoked Arbol Honey (page 25).

To smoke olive oil (use extra-virgin), maple syrup, or honey, pour the desired amount into a glass jar (it shouldn't be more than half full to allow room for the smoke).

Add a pinch of wood chips to the burn chamber of a smoking gun, place the hose in the jar with the end above the liquid, and cover the jar with plastic wrap. Follow the manufacturer's instructions to ignite the wood chips and smoke for a few seconds, until the jar is filled with a dense smoke. Remove the hose and reseal the plastic wrap. Let the smoke infuse for 3 minutes, then remove the plastic wrap.

Taste, and if you want smokier results, repeat the process, stirring in between smoking to distribute the flavor. Cover the jar and store in a cool, dark place for up to 2 months.

MASTER RECIPE

SMOKED GARLIC

Whether the entire head is slow roasted in glowing embers or a few cloves are blistered in a basket, skillet, or mesh bag over moderate heat, smoked garlic is easy to prepare while you're firing up something else on the grill. And its aroma and texture are luxuriously rich—something that's great to have on hand to add a smoky sweetness to tomato sauce, emulsified salad dressings, or soups. See also Smoked Garlic Aioli (page 33).

To smoke garlic, prepare a charcoal grill for two-zone cooking and build a medium fire, or heat a gas grill to medium-high.

Trim the tops from 3 heads garlic (just enough to reveal the cloves), place the heads cut side up in an aluminum foil packet, drizzle with enough olive oil to lightly coat, and toss to combine. Partially close each packet but do not seal.

When the coals are glowing red and covered with a fine gray ash, add your smoke source (chips, chunks, or log). Carefully wipe the preheated grill grates with a lightly oiled paper towel. Using a grill brush, scrape the grill grates clean, then carefully wipe with a lightly oiled towel again.

When the fire begins to produce a steady stream of smoke, place the packet directly over the heat on the cooking grate, if using a gas grill. Otherwise, place the garlic packet on the periphery of the coals, or place it on the cooking grate if the heat feels particularly intense (you want the temperature moderate enough that the garlic softens and caramelizes before it gets overly black). Cook until the garlic is tender, 30 to 40 minutes.

Cool slightly, then transfer the garlic to a sealable glass jar. Add enough olive oil to cover the garlic halfway, then seal the jar and store it in the fridge for up to 1 month.

COWGIRL SALT

MAKES ABOUT ¾ CUP
(150 G)

¼ cup (50 g) smoked pink
peppercorns (see page 18)

2 teaspoons smoked fennel
seeds (see page 18)

2 teaspoons smoked
rosemary leaves (see page 18)
or chopped fresh rosemary

¼ cup (50 g) kosher salt

½ teaspoon minced dried
orange peel

Pinch of red pepper flakes
or crumbled chile pequin

This pretty and aromatic blend (see the photo on page 21) reminds me of the fragrance of the sunbaked Texas Hill Country. Use it to season steaks or pork tenderloins, or to sprinkle over fresh goat cheese (along with a drizzle of olive oil) or poached eggs. The colors—pink peppercorns and red chile—make it pretty enough to give as a gift when packaged in a small glass jar and tied with rustic twine and a sprig of fresh rosemary. My favorite chile is chile pequin, a bright red chile the size of a small jelly bean that has a fiery heat. Feel free to use an equal amount of any crushed or crumbled red chile.

Using a mortar and pestle, lightly crush the peppercorns, fennel seeds, and rosemary. Transfer the seasonings to a small mixing bowl, add the salt, orange peel, and red pepper flakes and stir to combine. Store in a sealed container in a cool, dark place for up to 2 months.

PICKLED MUSTARD SEEDS

MAKES ABOUT 1¼ CUPS
(425 G)

¾ cup (140 g) yellow
mustard seeds

1 cup (240 ml) distilled
white vinegar

⅓ cup (65 g) sugar

1 dried arbol chile

½ teaspoon kosher salt

A quick simmer and a bit of soaking transforms dried mustard seeds into tender golden orbs that deliver a "pop" of vinegary heat. Consider them flavor bombs in any salad (they're particularly good with peppery greens (see Smoked Salmon with Wild Pepper, page 134) or as condiments for burgers or grilled sausages.

Rinse the mustard seeds in a fine-mesh sieve, pat dry with paper towels, and place in an 8-ounce (240 ml) glass jar or heatproof bowl. In a small heavy saucepan, combine the vinegar, sugar, chile, and salt. Bring the mixture to a boil over medium heat, stirring to dissolve the sugar. Pour the hot liquid over the mustard seeds and let them soak at room temperature until softened, 3 to 4 hours. Store the pickled mustard seeds in a sealed jar in the refrigerator for up to 4 months.

SMOKED ARBOL HONEY

The bright heat of arbol chiles infuse honey with a fiery kick and pretty red hue. Drizzle this kicky condiment over grilled chicken wings, fresh cheeses, pizza, and ribs. To achieve the right texture and consistency, use pasteurized honey (raw honey can crystallize when heated and is often not pourable at room temperature). After steeping, the chiles soften in the amber syrup, giving the condiment an appealing texture, so there's no need to strain the mixture. Because dried chiles toast quickly and I want the garlic to cook gently, I don't preheat the grill basket in this method.

Prepare a charcoal grill for two-zone cooking and build a medium fire, or heat a gas grill to medium-high.

When the coals are glowing red and covered with a fine gray ash, add your smoke source (chips, chunks, or log). Carefully wipe the preheated grill grates with a lightly oiled paper towel. Using a grill brush, scrape the grill grates clean, then carefully wipe with a lightly oiled towel again.

When the fire begins to produce a steady stream of smoke, place chiles and garlic in a grill basket or cast-iron skillet over direct heat and cook, turning occasionally, until the chiles smell rich and toasty, 2 to 3 minutes total, and the garlic has blackened in spots and its interior has softened, 12 to 15 minutes. Watch them closely, as they can turn from toasted to black and acrid in seconds. Remove each chile and garlic clove from the heat as it finishes cooking and set aside to cool.

Stem and seed the chiles and peel the garlic. Crumble the chiles into pieces and place them in a food processor with the garlic, oregano, salt, and pepper and process into a coarse paste.

In a small saucepan, combine the honey and chile paste over medium-low heat until the mixture just barely comes to a simmer. Remove the pan from the heat, cool briefly, and use a rubber spatula to transfer the mixture into a clean quart jar (do not strain). Allow the honey to cool completely, then seal with the lid and steep at room temperature for at least 1 day before using. After steeping, store the honey in the refrigerator for up to 2 months.

MAKES ABOUT 2 CUPS (475 ML)

3 smoked pasilla chiles (about 1 ounce/28 g total)

2 cloves garlic, unpeeled

2 teaspoons smoked oregano or marjoram (see page 18), or fresh oregano or marjoram

1 teaspoon kosher salt

½ teaspoon freshly ground black pepper

2 cups (475 ml) pasteurized honey

SPICY CURRY SALT

MAKES ½ CUP (100 G)

¼ cup (50 g) Madras curry

¼ cup (60 ml) kosher salt

2 tablespoons Korean red pepper flakes (gochugaru)

1 teaspoon red pepper flakes or crumbled chile pequin

1 teaspoon smoked marjoram or oregano (see page 18)

Meet your new salt and pepper. Used as a base seasoning (for meats or vegetables headed toward the grill), this earthy blend adds depth and a subtle but alluring flavor in everything you make. I also love it as a finishing salt, tossed with smoked cashews and a bit of olive oil, or sprinkled over herb-roasted potatoes or soft scrambled eggs.

Place the curry powder, salt, Korean chile flakes, red pepper flakes, and marjoram in a bowl and stir to combine. Store in a sealed container in a cool, dark place for up to 2 months.

GREEN OLIVE TAPENADE

MAKES ABOUT 2½ CUPS (590 G)

1 clove garlic, thinly sliced

Pinch of kosher salt

Pinch of red pepper flakes

5 oil-packed anchovy fillets, finely chopped

2 tablespoons drained capers

1½ tablespoons finely grated lemon zest

2 tablespoons freshly squeezed lemon juice

2 tablespoons fresh oregano or marjoram leaves

2 cups pitted Smoked Castelvetrano Olives (see page 39)

¾ cup (180 ml) extra-virgin olive oil

Freshly ground black pepper

With its savory backbone of anchovies and capers, tapenade has been a favorite condiment of mine since I cooked in the South of France (where it's a staple). It is equally delicious with green or black olives (see the leg of lamb on page 204), and wildly intriguing when the olives are smoked (either all or half of them, as you prefer for intensity). You only need a portion of this tapenade for the chicken thighs on page 157, so slather leftovers on toasted bread, grilled vegetable sandwiches, hard-cooked eggs, or any grilled meat (it's divine with dry-aged steak).

Combine the garlic, salt, and red pepper flakes in the bowl of a food processor and pulse into a coarse paste. Add the anchovies, capers, lemon zest and juice, oregano, and olives and process until smooth. With the machine running, gradually add the olive oil and process until the mixture is very smooth. Taste the puree and season with pepper as desired. Store in a sealed container in the refrigerator for up to 3 weeks.

SMOKED ANCHOVY BUTTER

Infusing a temperature-sensitive ingredient like butter with a smoky nuance requires a cold-smoking method, so I use my smoking gun. Here anchovies give the sweet, smoky butter a salty depth that's delicious with grilled vegetables or fresh pasta, like Pappardelle with Smoked Anchovy Butter & Herbs (page 133), or slathered on grilled bread or fish steaks like tuna or swordfish.

Place the butter, anchovies, lemon zest, parsley, fish sauce, salt, and pepper in the bowl of a food processor and process until combined.

Using a rubber spatula, transfer the butter to a mixing bowl and cover with plastic wrap. Add a pinch of wood chips to the burn chamber of a smoking gun, place the hose under the plastic wrap with the end sitting above the butter, and reseal the plastic wrap. Follow the manufacturer's instructions to ignite the wood chips and smoke for a few seconds, until the bowl is filled with a dense smoke. Remove the hose and reseal the plastic wrap. Let the butter infuse for 3 minutes. Taste, and if you want smokier results, repeat the process, stirring in between smoking to distribute the flavor.

Cut a piece of parchment paper into an 11-inch (28 cm) square. Remove the plastic wrap from the bowl and transfer the smoked butter to the center of the parchment square. Roll the butter into a log and twist or fold the ends to seal. Store the butter in the refrigerator for up to 2 weeks.

VARIATION

To make other flavors of cold-smoked butter, use the smoking gun to infuse room-temperature unsalted butter as instructed above, then stir in other aromatics (such as minced garlic or chopped fresh herbs) and slather it on corn on the cob, potatoes, haricots verts, or grilled oysters or fish, or toss it with fresh pasta.

MAKES 1½ CUPS (340 G)

1 cup (225 g) unsalted butter, at room temperature

4 or 5 anchovy fillets, drained of excess oil (do not rinse)

Finely grated zest of 1 lemon

2 tablespoons chopped fresh flat-leaf parsley

½ teaspoon fish sauce

½ teaspoon kosher salt

Freshly ground black pepper

GREEN CHILE SALSA

I crave green chile salsa all year long—as a topping for tacos or nachos, or at happy hour with guacamole, tortilla chips, and an agave beverage (contender for last meal request). But the desire is especially strong in late summer, when Hatch chiles from New Mexico arrive in Austin. These chiles are celebrated at festivals, fire-roasted outside of supermarkets, and incorporated into everything from burgers to pimento cheese. When Hatch chiles aren't in season, I use Anaheim or chilaca chiles (the fresh version of pasillas, with a sweet, floral flavor). Because Anaheim chiles don't have the same depth (or heat) as Hatch, I often add a charred jalapeño or serrano for a bit more fire. To turn this salsa into a sauce for enchiladas or huevos rancheros, sizzle it in a skillet with a couple tablespoons of olive oil and then thin it to your desired consistency with chicken broth.

MAKES ABOUT 3 CUPS (900 G)

1½ pounds (680 g) Hatch green chiles (or Anaheim chiles)

8 ounces (225 g) tomatillos, husked and rinsed

½ white onion (115 g), quartered

2 cloves garlic, unpeeled

Olive oil, for drizzling

1½ tablespoons freshly squeezed lime juice, plus more as desired

½ teaspoon dried oregano (preferably Mexican) or 1 tablespoon chopped fresh oregano

Kosher salt

Prepare a charcoal grill for two-zone cooking and build a medium-high fire, or heat a gas grill to high.

When the coals are glowing red and covered with a fine gray ash, add your smoke source (chips, chunks, or log). Carefully wipe the preheated grill grates with a lightly oiled paper towel. Using a grill brush, scrape the grill grates clean, then carefully wipe with a lightly oiled towel again and place a grill basket over direct heat.

Place the chiles in the grill basket and grill, using tongs to turn, until the chiles are charred and blistered on both sides, 1 to 2 minutes total. Transfer the chiles to a bowl, cover with a kitchen towel, and steam for 10 minutes. Return the grill basket to the heat.

Meanwhile, combine the tomatillos, onion, and garlic in a bowl and drizzle with enough olive oil to lightly coat, toss to combine, and place them on the preheated grill basket. Use tongs to flip and rotate as needed, until each is blackened and blistered on all sides, 3 to 5 minutes for the tomatillos, and a few minutes longer for the onion and garlic. Remove each item from the heat as it finishes cooking and set aside to cool.

Wearing rubber gloves, use your hands to remove the stem, skin, and seeds from the chiles. Do not rinse the chiles under water, or you'll rinse away their charred flavor! Combine the chiles, tomatillos, onion, garlic, lime juice, and oregano in a food processor or blender and process to your desired consistency. Taste and season with salt or more lime juice to taste. Store in a sealed container in the refrigerator for up to 5 days, or in the freezer for up to 4 months.

RANCH HAND SALSA

MAKES ABOUT 2 CUPS (600 G)

3 or 4 dried chiles (such as guajillo, cascabel, or pasilla; about ½ ounce/15 g total)

4 cloves garlic, unpeeled

1 pound (450 g) tomatillos, husked and rinsed

2 serrano chiles

Extra-virgin olive oil, for drizzling

½ teaspoon kosher salt, plus more as needed

1 to 2 teaspoons honey (optional)

This is my favorite salsa—the combination of toasted dried chiles and charred tomatillos creates a tangy, brick-red mixture with an addictive heat and wonderful complexity. As a general rule, smaller dried red chiles like arbol tend to be hotter and more brightly flavored, while wrinkly, darker dried chiles (that range from burgundy to black) like the ones I suggest here have an earthy, fruity fragrance. When in doubt, trust your nose; a chile's aroma is the best indicator of the flavor it will impart.

Prepare a charcoal grill for two-zone cooking and build a medium fire, or heat a gas grill to medium-high.

When the coals are glowing red and covered with a fine gray ash, add your smoke source (chips, chunks, or log). Carefully wipe the preheated grill grates with a lightly oiled paper towel. Using a grill brush, scrape the grill grates clean, then carefully wipe with a lightly oiled towel again.

When the fire begins to produce a steady stream of smoke, place the chiles and garlic in a grill basket or cast-iron skillet over direct heat, cook until the chiles darken slightly and smell toasty, 1 to 3 minutes (flip after a minute), and the garlic has blackened in spots and its interior has softened, 10 to 12 minutes. Watch the chiles closely, as they can turn from toasted to black and acrid in seconds. Remove each chile and garlic clove from the heat as it finishes cooking and set aside to cool. Return the grill basket to the heat.

Stem and seed the chiles, then place them in a bowl and cover with hot water (weigh them down with a small plate to keep them fully submersed). Soak until softened, about 20 minutes.

Meanwhile, place the tomatillos and serranos in a bowl, drizzle with enough olive oil to lightly coat, toss to combine, and place them on the preheated grill basket. Use tongs to flip and rotate the tomatillos and serranos around the heat as needed, until the serranos are evenly blistered, about 4 to 5 minutes, and the tomatillos are charred and their juices are beginning to bubble, 8 to 10 minutes. Remove each item from the heat as it finishes cooking (returning them to the same bowl). Stem the serranos and slice them into a few sections.

Drain the softened chiles and peel the garlic. Place them in a food processor with the serranos and salt and process into a coarse paste. Add the tomatillos (and any juices and olive oil in the bowl) and process until smooth. Taste the salsa and add additional salt and the honey, if you want to soften the tangy, acrid edges. Store in a sealed container in the refrigerator for up to 5 days.

GRILLED PICKLED JALAPEÑOS

A quick spin on a hot grill adds charred flavors and diffuses the bracing bite (just enough!) of pickled jalapeños. The chiles will hold up better if you grill and pickle them whole, then you can slice as needed. Your nachos, scrambled eggs, and martinis will thank you.

Prepare a charcoal grill for two-zone cooking and build a medium-high fire, or heat a gas grill to high.

When the coals are glowing red and covered with a fine gray ash, use tongs to remove the cooking grate and place a drip pan with 1 inch (2.5 cm) of warm water on the side with no coals, and add your smoke source (chips, chunks, or log). Return the cooking grate to its position, allow it to preheat, and then carefully wipe the preheated grill grates with a lightly oiled paper towel. Using a grill brush, scrape the grill grates clean, then carefully wipe with a lightly oiled towel again.

Place the jalapeños in a mixing bowl, drizzle with enough olive oil to lightly coat, and toss to combine. When the fire begins to produce a steady stream of smoke, place the jalapeños over direct heat, close the grill, vent the grill for smoking, and smoke for 4 to 5 minutes, until charred and blistered on all sides (flipping and rotating the jalapeños around the heat every couple minutes for even cooking). Remove the jalapeños from the heat and set aside to cool.

Combine the vinegar, garlic, bay leaves, salt, peppercorns, and coriander seeds in a saucepan and bring to a boil over medium-high heat on the stovetop. Lower the heat and simmer for about 4 minutes, stirring to infuse the brine with the aromatics, then remove from the heat. Place the grilled jalapeños and carrot slices in a clean quart jar and pour in enough hot brine to cover. Allow the mixture to cool completely and then refrigerate until cold and crisp; they will keep for up to 2 months.

MAKES 1 QUART (420 G)

1½ pounds (680 g) jalapeño chiles

Extra-virgin olive oil, for drizzling

2 cups (475 ml) distilled white vinegar

4 garlic cloves, lightly crushed and peeled

6 bay leaves (preferably fresh)

2 tablespoons kosher salt

1 tablespoon smoked black peppercorns (see page 18) or regular black peppercorns

1 tablespoon coriander seeds

8 ounces (225 g) carrots, peeled and thinly sliced

SMOKED ONION MARMALADE

MAKES 1¼ CUPS (400 G)

2 pounds (900 g) sweet onions, thinly sliced

2 cloves garlic, thinly sliced

3 sprigs thyme or rosemary, or a combination

2 tablespoons extra-virgin olive oil, plus more for drizzling

Kosher salt and freshly ground black pepper

½ cup (120 ml) apple cider vinegar

3 tablespoons honey

3 bay leaves, preferably fresh

Pinch of red pepper flakes or crumbled chile pequin

This sweet and sticky condiment is delicious alongside grilled steaks or piled on sandwiches made with a crusty bread, like ciabatta.

Prepare a charcoal grill for two-zone cooking and build a medium fire, or heat a gas grill to medium-high.

While the grill heats, place the onions, garlic, and herb sprigs in a bowl, drizzle with enough olive oil to lightly coat, toss to combine, and place in a disposable aluminum pan.

When the coals are glowing red and covered with a fine gray ash, add your smoke source (chips, chunks, or log). Carefully wipe the preheated grill grates with a lightly oiled paper towel. Using a grill brush, scrape the grill grates clean, then carefully wipe with a lightly oiled towel again.

When the fire begins to produce a steady stream of smoke, place the pan over indirect heat, close the grill, vent the grill for smoking, and smoke for 30 minutes, until the onions have softened and their color has deepened. Add additional hot coals or wood chunks as needed to maintain a steady temperature of 300°F (150°C). Remove the pan from the heat and set it aside to cool slightly.

On the stovetop, heat 2 tablespoons olive oil in a large heavy nonstick skillet over medium heat. Add the onion mixture, any liquid in the pan, a generous pinch of salt, and a few grindings of pepper and cook, stirring frequently, until the onions are fragrant and sizzling, 2 to 3 minutes. Add the vinegar, honey, bay leaves, and pepper flakes and bring the mixture to a simmer, then turn the heat to medium-low. Cook, partially covered, for 15 to 25 minutes, stirring every now and then, until the juices thicken and the mixture is sweet and golden (if there is still liquid in the pan, simmer until most of it is gone). Discard the herb sprigs and use the marmalade immediately, or cool and store in a sealed container in the refrigerator for up to 3 months.

SMOKED GARLIC AIOLI

My favorite way to use smoked garlic is to incorporate its heady, caramelized sweetness into this silky condiment. If time is of the essence, you can simply whisk minced smoked garlic into store-bought mayo for a speedy version of the spread. But you'll get the deepest flavor and the most luxurious texture if you make your own.

Squeeze the smoked garlic from each individual clove and set aside.

Place the egg, yolk, and mustard in the bowl of a food processor and pulse until combined. With the machine on low speed, slowly pour in the oil until the mixture thickens. Add the smoked garlic and lemon juice and process until just combined. Season with salt and pepper. Store in a sealed container in the refrigerator for up to 4 days.

VARIATION

To make cold-smoked aioli using a smoking gun, prepare the recipe using roasted garlic or grate 2 cloves fresh garlic on a Microplane. Place the garlic in the food processor and process with the egg, yolk, and mustard. Finish the aioli, as above, transfer it to a bowl, and cover with plastic wrap. Add a pinch of hickory wood chips to the burn chamber of a smoking gun, place the hose under the plastic wrap with the end sitting above the aioli, and reseal the plastic wrap. Follow the manufacturer's instructions to ignite the wood chips and smoke for a few seconds, until the bowl is filled with a dense smoke. Remove the hose and reseal the plastic wrap. Let the aioli infuse for 3 minutes, then remove the plastic wrap. Taste, and if you want smokier results, repeat the process, stirring in between smoking to distribute the flavor. Use immediately, or store in a sealed container in the refrigerator for up to 4 days.

MAKES ABOUT 1½ CUPS (330 G)

4 cloves Smoked Garlic (page 23), or to taste

1 egg plus 1 yolk

1 teaspoon Dijon mustard

1 cup (240 ml) olive oil, or a mix of olive oil and vegetable oil

2 tablespoons freshly squeezed lemon juice, plus more to taste

Kosher salt and freshly ground black pepper

CHAPTER TWO ———————————

SMOKY COCKTAILS

An herbaceous gin martini served with a whiff of campfire, a chile-infused margarita made with the bittersweet juice of a charred blood orange, or smoked tomato juice for the ultimate Bloody Mathilda (Mary's ill-behaved cousin) . . . who's thirsty? As I'm known to suggest (when the light begins to fade and the snap and crackle of a charcoal fire ushers in the close of another day), let's start with a drink. Adding a smoky nuance to adult beverages is as fun—and seductive—as it is with food. In this chapter, I'll talk about setting up a smoked bar with flavor enhancers that make classic cocktails more thrilling, as well as share a few of my favorite elixirs to keep you refreshed when you're firing up dinner.

My smoked bar primer begins with a collection of fragrant simple syrups that add aroma and just the right amount of sweetness. Then I turn to smoked secret weapons: spicy salt rims, smoky muddled fruits, and homemade liqueurs that make drinks (and everyday occasions) more memorable. To keep your options flexible, some of these recipes rely on ingredients that are already smoky, like molasses, smoked paprika, and spirits like Scotch and mezcal that provide their own bittersweet, burnt, and peaty nuances. The idea here is to stock your smoked bar over time so you can eventually create inspired options on the fly and step up everything from Manhattans to your evening nightcap (the elixir you want to sip while curled up with a hefty novel or, let's be honest, the latest J.Crew catalog). Most of these enhancers can be incorporated into a "bulk smoke" on an afternoon when you're already building your smoked larder (see page 17), and they'll last for months in the refrigerator or pantry. Other accoutrements can be flavored in a flash with the help of a smoking gun.

SMOKED SIMPLE SYRUPS

Think of these as alluring vials in your cocktail laboratory. When swirled into drinks, the following sweet and smoky syrups balance their sharp or spicy counterparts, while adding their own layer of intrigue.

Lapsang Souchong Syrup

Traditionally smoke-dried over a pinewood fire, Lapsang souchong is a black tea (originally from the Chinese province of Fujian) with a strong peaty flavor that translates well into a simple syrup.

In a glass jar, combine the sugar and the tea. Cool, cover, and store in the refrigerator for up to 1 month.

MAKES ABOUT ¾ CUP (175 ML)

½ cup (100 g) demerara sugar

4 ounces (60 ml) hot, strong-brewed Lapsang souchong tea

Charred Jalapeño–Rosemary Syrup

This zippy sweetener is easy to make if you grill an extra jalapeño while firing up dinner.

Prepare a charcoal grill for two-zone cooking and build a medium fire, or heat a gas grill to medium-high. When the coals are glowing red and covered with a fine gray ash, add your smoke source (chips, chunks, or log). Carefully wipe the preheated grill grates with a lightly oiled paper towel. Using a grill brush, scrape the grill grates clean, then carefully wipe with a lightly oiled towel again and place a grill basket over direct heat.

Place the jalapeño in the grill basket and use tongs to turn until char marks appear on all sides, 1 to 2 minutes total. Remove the jalapeño from the heat, let it cool briefly, then remove the stem and slice it into ¼-inch (6 mm) rounds.

Combine the sugar, water, jalapeño, and rosemary in a small saucepan and cook over medium heat on the stovetop, stirring frequently, until the sugar dissolves, about 7 minutes. Remove the pan from the heat and allow the mixture to steep at room temperature for 1 hour. Strain the syrup through a fine-mesh sieve, pressing on the solids to extract as much syrup as possible, before chilling. (Or, for a more pronounced herb flavor and spicier syrup, do not strain before chilling.) Store the syrup in a sealed container in the refrigerator for up to 1 month.

MAKES ¾ CUP (175 ML)

1 jalapeño chile

½ cup (100 g) sugar

½ cup (120 ml) water

1 sprig rosemary

Shooting Star Syrup

A higher ratio of sugar to water creates a thicker, richer syrup that's perfumed with faraway flavors. Try this fragrant sweetener with London dry-style gins or rum drinks.

Combine the sugar, water, star anise, allspice, cloves, coriander, and bay leaves in a small saucepan and cook over medium heat, stirring frequently, until the sugar dissolves, about 7 minutes. Remove the pan from the heat and allow the mixture to steep at room temperature for 1 hour. Strain the syrup through a fine-mesh sieve, pressing on the solids to extract as much syrup as possible, before chilling. (Or, for a more robust flavor and a spicier syrup, do not strain the aromatics before chilling.) Store in a sealed container in the refrigerator for up to 1 month.

continued

1 cup sugar (200 g)

½ cup water (120 ml)

2 smoked star anise pods (see page 18)

3 smoked allspice berries (see page 18)

2 smoked cloves (see page 18)

½ teaspoon coriander seeds

2 fresh bay leaves, torn

**MAKES ABOUT 1½ CUPS
(355 ML)**

1 cup (200 g) demerara sugar

1 cup (240 ml) water

3 smoked cinnamon sticks
(see page 18)

½ smoked vanilla bean
(see page 18)

Strip of orange peel (1 by
4 inches/2.5 by 10 cm)

Smoked Cinnamon Syrup

**The richer, darker flavor of demerara sugar creates a warmly spiced
syrup that's particularly good with rye whiskey, bourbon, and
reposado tequila cocktails.**

Combine the sugar, water, cinnamon sticks, vanilla bean, and orange peel in
a small saucepan and cook over medium heat, stirring frequently, until the
sugar dissolves, about 7 minutes. Remove the pan from the heat and allow the
mixture to steep at room temperature for 1 hour. Strain the syrup through a
fine-mesh sieve, pressing on the solids to extract as much syrup as possible.
(Or, for a stronger spiced flavor, do not strain before chilling.)

Store in a sealed container in the refrigerator for up to 1 month.

**MAKES ABOUT 1 CUP
(240 ML)**

1½ cups (225 g) kumquats

¼ cup (50 g) sugar

1 smoked dried arbol chile
(see page 18)

1 teaspoon smoked pink
peppercorns (see page 18)

⅓ cup (80 ml) Grand Marnier
or other orange liqueur

Smoked Kumquat Syrup

**Bright citrus, a kick of heat, and orange liqueur create an
aromatic syrup that's delicious in sparkling wine, Manhattans,
and tequila drinks.**

Place the kumquats, sugar, arbol chile, and peppercorns in the bowl of a food
processor and pulse into a coarse puree. Transfer the mixture to a glass jar,
add the Grand Marnier, and refrigerate for at least 2 hours, or up to 1 week.
Strain the mixture through a fine-mesh sieve, pressing on the solids to extract
as much syrup as possible.

To smoke the syrup, transfer it to a glass jar. Add a pinch of wood chips to the
burn chamber of a smoking gun, place the hose in the jar with the end above the
syrup, and cover the jar with plastic wrap. Follow the manufacturer's instructions
to ignite the wood chips and smoke for a few seconds, until the jar is filled with
a dense smoke. Remove the hose and reseal the plastic wrap. Let the syrup
infuse for 3 minutes, then remove the plastic wrap, stir the syrup, and repeat
the process once more. Cover the jar with its lid and store the smoked syrup
in the refrigerator for up to 1 month.

SMOKED CASTELVETRANO OLIVES

Yes, these olives and their brine (see the photo on page 21) will make your dirty martini dreams come true, but they're also an inspired addition to grain salads and seafood pastas, or as a savory snack—just marinate them with extra-virgin olive oil, a crushed garlic clove, red pepper flakes, and herbs. In a pinch, you can use dried bay leaves here, but as with most of my recipes, I strongly prefer the distinct "green" flavor that fresh bay leaves impart.

MAKES 1½ QUARTS (570 G)

Two 20-ounce (1.4 kg plus 115 g) jars Castelvetrano olives, with brine

2 sprigs rosemary

2 fresh bay leaves

Prepare a charcoal grill for two-zone cooking and build a medium-high fire, or heat a gas grill to high.

When the coals are glowing red and covered with a fine gray ash, use tongs to remove the cooking grate and place a drip pan with 1 inch (2.5 cm) of warm water on the side with no coals, and add your smoke source (chips, chunks, or log). Return the cooking grate to its position, allow it to preheat, and then carefully wipe the preheated grill grates with a lightly oiled paper towel. Using a grill brush, scrape the grill grates clean, then carefully wipe with a lightly oiled towel again.

Pour the olives and their brine in a disposable aluminum pan and tuck the fresh rosemary and bay leaves into the liquid. When the fire begins to produce a steady stream of smoke, place the olives over indirect heat, close the grill, vent the grill for smoking, and smoke for 30 to 60 minutes, as desired for smokiness (use a spoon to taste an olive and a bit of brine). Remove from the heat and set the olives aside to cool. Transfer the olives, herbs, and brine to clean glass jars and store in the refrigerator for up to 2 months.

SMOKED PICKLED CHERRIES

The piney perfume of fresh rosemary and bay leaves, warmth of peppercorns, and bright sweetness of balsamic vinegar create a fragrant bath for lightly smoked cherries that will perk up cocktails like the Smoked Cherry Old-Fashioned (page 53), grilled lamb chops, pound cake (vanilla or chocolate), and ice cream. Note that the cherries are best enjoyed a couple of days after you make them, to allow the flavors to meld, so plan accordingly.

Prepare a charcoal grill for two-zone cooking and build a medium fire, or heat a gas grill to medium-high.

When the coals are glowing red and covered with a fine gray ash, use tongs to remove the cooking grate and place a drip pan with 1 inch (2.5 cm) of warm water on the side with no coals, and add your smoke source (chips, chunks, or log). Return the cooking grate to its position, allow it to preheat, and then carefully wipe the preheated grill grates with a lightly oiled paper towel. Using a grill brush, scrape the grill grates clean, then carefully wipe with a lightly oiled towel again.

Place the cherries, rosemary, bay leaves, red wine vinegar, and water in a disposable aluminum pan, tucking the herbs under the fruit. When the fire begins to produce a steady stream of smoke, place the cherries over indirect heat, close the grill, vent the grill for smoking, and smoke for 30 to 40 minutes, until the fruit is dark and soft and has reached your desired level of smokiness (use a spoon to taste a cherry and a bit of brine). Set the cherries aside to cool and then use a fine-meshed sieve to strain the liquid into a small saucepan and discard the herbs. Place the drained cherries in a clean glass jar.

Add the balsamic vinegar, sugar, salt, peppercorns, and star anise to the saucepan with the cherry brine and bring the mixture to a boil over medium-high heat on the stovetop, stirring occasionally. Lower the heat and simmer until the sugar dissolves, 3 to 4 minutes, stirring constantly. Remove the pan from the heat and let the brine cool for 10 minutes.

Pour enough brine to cover the cherries into the glass jar, allow the liquid to cool completely, cover with a tight-fitting lid, and refrigerate for 2 days to allow the flavors to meld before serving. Store in the refrigerator for up to 2 months.

**MAKES ABOUT
1½ QUARTS (570 G)**

2 pounds (900 g) sweet cherries, stemmed and pitted, or thawed frozen cherries

2 sprigs rosemary

2 fresh bay leaves

½ cup (120 ml) red wine vinegar

½ cup (120 ml) water

2 tablespoons balsamic vinegar

½ cup (100 g) sugar

1 teaspoon kosher salt

10 to 12 smoked black peppercorns (see page 18) or regular black peppercorns

2 smoked star anise pods (see page 18)

BORDER DUST

MAKES ½ CUP (100 G)

3 tablespoons kosher salt

2 tablespoons sugar

1 tablespoon ground chipotle chile powder

1 tablespoon pure ground chile powder (such as ancho or arbol)

This blend of chile-tinged salt and sugar provides a kiss of heat for margaritas and palomas. While you can use any pure ground chile powder for this recipe, I prefer the bright, high-noon heat of red chiles (like ancho or arbol) and chipotle (made from dried and smoked jalapeños).

Combine the salt, sugar, and chile powders in a glass jar, cover, and store in a cool, dark place for up to 1 month. To use for a cocktail, place the Border Dust on a plate or shallow bowl. Moisten the glass rim with a lime wedge (or dip it in water), dip the rim in the Border Dust, and add your preferred beverage.

BLOODY MATHILDA

SERVES 2

1¼ cups (300 ml) tomato juice

½ cup (120 ml) vodka

2 tablespoons freshly squeezed lemon juice

1 tablespoon prepared horseradish

1 teaspoon Worcestershire sauce

½ teaspoon hot sauce

½ teaspoon fish sauce

½ teaspoon celery salt

Freshly ground black pepper

2 each pickled okra, peperoncini, celery stalks, and beef sticks, for garnish (optional)

4 Smoked Castelvetrano Olives (page 39, optional)

Every summer we escape the Texas heat to spend several weeks with my family in Minnesota. "Up north," Bloody Marys (garnished with celery, a beef stick, olives, and your favorite pickled vegetables) are a weekend tradition. This smoked riff on the classic (I like to imagine Mathilda is Mary's sultry, ill-behaved sister) is easy to love— serve it Midwestern-style, with a short beer chaser.

Combine the tomato juice, vodka, lemon juice, horseradish, Worcestershire, hot sauce, fish sauce, and celery salt in a cocktail shaker filled with ice. To smoke the mixture, add a pinch of wood chips to the burn chamber of a smoking gun. Place the hose in the cocktail shaker with the end above the liquid, and partially cover the shaker with the lid. Follow the manufacturer's instructions to ignite the wood chips and smoke for a few seconds, until the shaker is filled with a dense smoke. Remove the hose, close the shaker, and shake vigorously for 10 seconds. Divide the drink between 2 tall pint glasses (adding more ice as needed) and garnish as desired.

SMOKED KUMQUAT CORDIAL

Bright with citrus notes and a kick of chile, a drizzle of kumquat syrup creates a sophisticated take on a mimosa (meet your new favorite brunch companion). To give this drink a French 75 spin, add ¾ ounce (20 ml) gin along with the syrup.

Pour the smoked kumquat syrup into a Champagne flute, top off the glass with the bubbly, and garnish with the lemon twist.

SERVES 1

2 tablespoons Smoked Kumquat Syrup (page 38)

6 to 10 ounces (180 to 300 ml) Champagne or dry sparkling wine (such as Cava), well chilled

Twist of lemon peel, for garnish

ROMEO'S LIMONATTO

With a floral aroma and less acid than regular lemons, Meyer lemons add a burst of sunny sweetness to any recipe—but their season is fleeting. Paired with lightly charred orange peels (the heat caramelizes their essential oils), this version of the popular Italian digestif delivers a vibrant citrus flavor all year long. (If you like your limonatto on the puckery side, use regular lemons instead.) Be sure to use organic citrus fruits in this recipe to avoid the wax and pesticides sometimes found on the skins of conventional fruits.

Using a vegetable peeler, remove the peels from the lemons and oranges in wide strips, making sure to avoid the bitter white pith. Place the peels in a 1-quart (950 ml) glass jar with a tight-fitting lid and add the alcohol. Tighten the lid and let the mixture steep at room temperature in a cool, dark place, undisturbed, for 12 days. After 12 days, remove the peels and add the syrup. Stir to combine and store in the freezer for up to 6 months.

MAKES ABOUT 3½ CUPS (830 ML)

4 Meyer lemons (preferably organic)

4 navel oranges (preferably organic)

2 cups (475 ml) grain alcohol (such as Everclear 151)

1½ cups (355 ml) Shooting Star Syrup (page 37)

BURNT ORANGE MARGARITA

SERVES 1

2 blood oranges

Border Dust (page 42), to rim

1 ounce (30 ml) silver tequila

¾ ounce (20 ml) Ancho Reyes

1 ounce (30 ml) Cointreau

1 ounce (30 ml) freshly squeezed lime juice

Charred blood oranges and a spicy spirit make this margarita a force to be reckoned with. Alba Huerta, one of the South's most talented mixologists and the owner of Julep in Houston, turned me on to Ancho Reyes, an ancho chile liqueur based on a 1927 recipe from Puebla, Mexico. The unique spirit adds a tingling heat to a traditional margarita (or any other tequila drink).

Prepare a charcoal grill for two-zone cooking and build a medium fire, or heat a gas grill to medium-high.

When the coals are glowing red and covered with a fine gray ash, add your smoke source (chips, chunks, or log). Carefully wipe the preheated grill grates with a lightly oiled paper towel. Using a grill brush, scrape the grill grates clean, then carefully wipe with a lightly oiled towel again.

Halve 1 blood orange horizontally and grill it cut side down over direct heat until dark char marks appear, 2 to 3 minutes. Slice the other blood orange into ¼-inch (6 mm) rounds and grill until charred on one side, about 1 minute. Place the Border Dust on a plate or shallow bowl. Juice the blood orange halves. Moisten the rim of a rocks glass and dip it into the Border Dust to coat. Combine the tequila, Ancho Reyes, Cointreau, 1 ounce (30 ml) juice from the charred blood orange, and the lime juice in a cocktail shaker filled with ice. Shake vigorously. Fill the salt-rimmed glass with ice and strain the margarita into the glass. Garnish with a ½ round of charred blood orange.

Lefty's Mezcal Sting (left; page 46) and Burnt Orange Margarita (right).

LEFTY'S MEZCAL STING

SERVES 1

2 ounces (60 ml) reposado tequila

1 ounce (30 ml) mezcal

½ ounce (15 ml) Charred Jalapeño–Rosemary Syrup (page 36)

2 ounces (60 ml) grapefruit soda (such as Squirt)

Cold sparkling water (such as Topo Chico), as needed

Twist of grapefruit peel, for garnish

If you're not familiar with the exquisite lyrics in Townes Van Zandt's song "Pancho and Lefty," do yourself a favor and download it immediately. Like his song, this drink (see the photo on page 45)— which gets a smoky hit from mezcal and a mule kick of heat from jalapeño-infused syrup—raises a glass to Pancho Villa's trusty sidekick, Lefty.

Combine the tequila, mezcal, and syrup in a cocktail shaker filled with ice. Shake vigorously and strain into a Collins glass filled with ice. Add the grapefruit soda, top off with sparkling water, and garnish with the grapefruit twist.

SMOKE & FLOWERS

SERVES 1

1½ ounces (45 ml) mezcal (preferably Gem and Bolt)

¼ ounce (8 ml) elderflower liqueur (such as St-Germain)

3 or 4 dashes grapefruit bitters

½ ounce (15 ml) freshly squeezed Ruby Red grapefruit juice

½ ounce (15 ml) freshly squeezed lime juice

Twist of grapefruit peel, for garnish

Gem and Bolt is one of my favorite mezcals because it's distilled with damiana, a Mexican herb long revered by the Mayans and Aztecs for its aphrodisiac and mood-elevating properties. I choose to believe in the magic (why not?) and am pretty sure this drink will take you to a higher level of consciousness.

Combine the mezcal, elderflower liqueur, bitters, grapefruit juice, and lime juice in a cocktail shaker filled with ice. Shake vigorously and strain into a chilled coupe glass. Garnish with the grapefruit twist.

BUCK SNORT

My family and friends begin each New Year's Day with a "polar bear plunge" into Barton Springs, a beautiful spring-fed pool in Austin that remains 68°F (20°C) year-round. The water is almost always warmer than the temperature of the air, so the most challenging part of the jump is usually disrobing on the cold concrete and working up the nerve to leap. The adults often arrive in robes and furry hats, clutching thermoses of coffee or hair-of-the-dog beverages like this cocktail, which is as refreshing as the plunge. Of course, you're not likely to fire up your grill just for oranges, but while it's roaring for dinner some night, particularly in cooler weather, sizzle a few orange (or tangerine) slices on the grates or in a grill pan and set them aside (or refrigerate them) to make this drink.

Combine the aquavit, Lillet Blanc, Cointreau, lemon juice, and syrup in a cocktail shaker filled with ice. Shake vigorously and strain into a double rocks glass filled with crushed ice. Garnish with the charred tangerine slice.

SERVES 1

2 ounces (60 ml) Vikre aquavit

¾ ounce (20 ml) Lillet Blanc

½ ounce (15 ml) Cointreau

½ ounce (15 ml) freshly squeezed lemon juice

½ ounce (15 ml) Shooting Star Syrup (page 37)

1 charred tangerine (or orange) slice, for garnish

FIVE O'CLOCK SOMEWHERE

**MAKES ABOUT 2 CUPS
(475 ML)**

2 cups (475 ml) triple-distilled
vodka

3 or 4 smoked hazelnuts
(see page 18)

½ smoked vanilla bean
(see page 18)

3 or 4 dark-roasted coffee
beans

My fondness for a coffee liqueur (something I hadn't really sipped since college) was renewed when our abundantly talented friends gave us a homemade hazelnut liqueur as a holiday present. They used toasted hazelnuts and roasted coffee beans in their version, but of course I needed to try it with smoked nuts and a smoked vanilla bean for added perfume. You can sip this liqueur on its own, serve it with half-and-half White Russian–style, or use it in Carey's cocktail, the Little Chestnut (page 49). Starting with a triple-distilled vodka will create the smoothest results. I don't strain the vanilla or coffee beans because they look pretty in the jar and continue to infuse the liqueur over time.

Pour the vodka into a 1-pint (475 ml) glass jar with a tight-fitting lid and add the hazelnuts, vanilla bean, and coffee beans. Tighten the lid and let the mixture steep at room temperature, undisturbed, for at least 1 week to allow the flavors to develop (then it's ready to enjoy). Remove the hazelnuts, and then store in a cool, dark place at room temperature for up to 6 months.

LITTLE CHESTNUT

Created by my neighbor Carey Eskridge, this beautiful digestif (after dinner drink) is brimming with botanical notes that are balanced by the rich, smooth quality of the hazelnut and coffee liqueur.

Combine the Five O'Clock Somewhere, Fernet Branca, Punt e Mes, and bitters in a cocktail shaker filled with ice. Stir well with a bar spoon and strain into a chilled coupe glass. Garnish with the lemon peel.

VARIATION

To make Carey's aperitif (before dinner) version of this cocktail, combine 2 ounces (60 ml) Five O'Clock Somewhere (page 48), ¾ ounce (22 ml) sweet Vermouth (preferably Del Professore), ½ ounce (15 ml) dry vermouth (preferably Dolin), 3 dashes Angostura bitters, and garnish and serve as instructed above, with a lemon twist.

SERVES 1

2 ounces (60 ml) Five O'Clock Somewhere (page 48)

½ ounce (15 ml) Fernet Branca

½ ounce (15 ml) Punt e Mes

A few dashes bitters (preferably Fee Brothers Whiskey Barrel–Aged)

Strip of lemon peel, for garnish

KERN RAMBLE

In this refreshing drink, warm spices and ginger ale balance the deep flavors of a peaty Scotch (and quite possibly transport you to a heather-covered hillside in the Highlands). For the fullest flavor, use strongly spiced soda, like Blenheim Hot Ginger Ale. Complete the armchair travel by serving with Smoked Scottish Oatcakes (page 60) and a nicely aged Cheddar.

Combine the Scotch, syrup, and bitters in a Collins glass filled with ice cubes and stir to combine. Top off with the ginger ale and garnish with the lemon wedge.

SERVES 1

1½ ounces (45 ml) single-malt Scotch

1 teaspoon Shooting Star Syrup (page 37)

2 dashes Fee Brothers Old-Fashioned bitters or Angostura bitters

2 ounces (60 ml) cold ginger ale, or more as desired

1 lemon wedge, for garnish

DIRTY MARTINI
with Smoked Castelvetrano Olives

SERVES 1

2½ ounces (37.5 ml) London dry-style gin (such as Beefeater or Plymouth) or a triple-distilled vodka

¾ ounce (20 ml) Dolin dry vermouth

½ ounce (15 ml) smoked Castelvetrano brine (page 39)

1 or 2 Smoked Castelvetrano Olives (page 39), for garnish

Twist of lemon peel, for garnish

The Progress restaurant in San Francisco put martinis infused with house-smoked olives on the map. The combination is a salt lover's dream and can be used with either vodka or gin. You can use the smoking method with any variety of brined olives, but meaty, pale green Castelvetranos are particularly delicious, and they're lovely in a martini glass. The bright perfume of lemon zest is the perfect garnish, but if you're feeling fancy, you can top the drink with a few drops of rosemary-infused olive oil, as they do at the Progress.

Combine the gin, vermouth, and olive brine in a mixing glass. Add a handful of ice cubes and stir with a bar spoon. Strain the mixture into a chilled coupe glass and garnish with 1 or 2 smoked olives and the lemon twist.

YUYO'S GIN & TONIC

I swooned even before I took a sip. Garnished with a gutsy number of pink peppercorns and a sprig of thyme, the gin and tonic at Yuyo, a stellar Peruvian restaurant in my neighborhood, punches all my buttons (and gets additional high marks for serving the drink with a just-opened bottle of Fever Tree on the side). When I begged my friend and Yuyo's chef, Maribel Rivera, for the recipe, she explained that Lima very much follows the trends of Spain, which includes the country's G&T obsession. Sweet peppercorns (called *molle* in Spanish) grow abundantly in Lima and throughout South America. Consider serving this drink Spanish-style, in a stemless wine tumbler that concentrates the drink's botanical aromas.

Fill a stemless wine tumbler (or a highball glass) with ice and add the gin. Top with the tonic and garnish with the peppercorns and thyme.

SERVES 1

2 ounces (60 ml) London dry-style gin (preferably Plymouth)

3 to 4 ounces tonic water (preferably Fever Tree)

6 to 8 smoked pink peppercorns (see page 18)

1 or 2 sprigs fresh thyme

SMOKED CHERRY OLD-FASHIONED

Sweet, smoky cherries are easy allies with the spicy bite of rye whiskey. In this version of the classic cocktail, demerara sugar (a less-refined brown sugar with a rich flavor) and a combination of bitters provide added complexity and a robust nut flavor.

Place the sugar cube in an old-fashioned glass. Douse with the bitters and the water. Add the whiskey and stir with a bar spoon until the sugar is dissolved. Add several large ice cubes and stir rapidly to chill. Garnish with the pickled cherries and the orange twist.

SERVES 1

1 demerara sugar cube

2 or 3 dashes Angostura bitters or Fee Brothers Whiskey Barrel–Aged Bitters

2 dashes black walnut bitters

A few drops water

2 ounces (60 ml) rye whiskey

3 to 4 Smoked Pickled Cherries (page 41), for garnish

Twist of orange peel, for garnish

CHAPTER THREE

GRAINS

After just 15 to 30 minutes of absorbing smoke, grains become more complex versions of their former selves. Armed with a pantry of these beauties (I store them in clear glass jars so I can admire their earthy palettes and distinctive shapes), it's easy to assemble granola, a nourishing rice bowl, or a satisfying salad that's already "preseasoned" with a whiff of wood smoke.

When it comes to smoking grains, I prefer to stick with heartier whole grains like thick-cut oats, farro, or barley. You could certainly smoke a long-grain white rice like basmati, but whole-grain flours and grains have an outer layer of bran and germ that provide a heat buffer, and their heartier flavor melds particularly well with smoke. Smoking—and eating—whole grains also means you get more fiber, vitamins, and minerals.

In the interest of time efficiency (and making the most of a hot fire), I typically smoke two or three varieties of grains (and/or other larder ingredients; see pages 18 and 22) at once, placing each item in its own disposable aluminum pan or foil packet. You can smoke any quantity you choose, from a cup to a couple of pounds; just be sure the pan is large enough to hold the grains no deeper than ½ inch (1.3 cm) and stir them a time or two during the smoking process to get even results. Remember that heartier grains like farro will need more time than flour or wheat germ, and you'll also need to fit those pans over the water pan and indirect heat (items placed too close to direct heat are likely to burn), so strategize accordingly.

SMOKED GRAINS

MASTER RECIPE

Prepare a charcoal grill for two-zone cooking and build a medium-high fire, or heat a gas grill to high.

When the coals are glowing red and covered with a fine gray ash, remove the cooking grate and place a drip pan with 1 inch (2.5 cm) of warm water on the side with no coals, and add your smoke source (chips, chunks, or log). Return the cooking grate to its position, allow it to preheat, and then carefully wipe the grates with a lightly oiled paper towel. Using a grill brush, scrape the grill grates clean, then carefully wipe with a lightly oiled towel again.

Place the grains in a disposable aluminum pan or atop two sheets of heavy-duty aluminum foil (crimp the edges of foil upward to create a rim and prevent the grains from sliding off).

When the fire begins to produce a steady stream of smoke, place the grains over indirect heat, close the grill, vent the grill for smoking, and smoke for 15 to 30 minutes (depending on their size, density, and the heat), until they've darkened a few shades, typically from the perimeter of the pan inward (which is why you want to stir them a time or two for even results). The smoking time is a general guide and assumes an internal temperature of around 300°F (150°C), but if the heat in your grill fluctuates, or, say, you're battling the elements, use your eyes and nose as a guide. If the grains are tinged with color and have a rich smoky smell at 20 minutes, pull them. If they're still pale after 30 minutes, give them another 10 minutes over the heat.

Remove the grains from the grill and let them cool and dry completely. At this point, they're ready to be prepared as you normally would—no need to adjust the usual cooking methods. In the meantime, store in a cool, dry place in an airtight container for up to 2 months.

USE THIS METHOD TO SMOKE:

Barley

Bulgur

Cornmeal (blue or yellow, preferably coarsely ground)

Farro

Flours, including buckwheat, semolina, whole-grain rye, and whole wheat

Freekeh

Oats, including thick-cut and steel-cut

Quinoa

Rice, including basmati, black, brown, jasmine, red, and wild rice

Wheat bran or germ

CREAMY STEEL-CUT OATS
with Salted Honey

Calling all lumberjacks—or lovers of leisurely, comforting breakfasts. Creamy, fruity, and perfumed with lightly smoked outs, this hearty oatmeal will be your salvation on a bracing wintry morning. The mixture can be refrigerated for two days; just reheat it gently with more milk or cream to loosen as necessary. My favorite oatmeal topping is a generous drizzle of Bee's Knees Salted Honey, but you can also use regular honey and a pinch of flaky salt, or maple syrup, if you prefer.

In a heavy saucepan, combine the whole milk, almond milk, and water and bring to a boil over medium heat. Stir in the oats, cinnamon, ginger, and the salt. Cover, turn the heat to low, and cook, stirring occasionally, until the oats are al dente and the porridge is creamy, about 20 minutes.

Remove the pan from the heat and stir in the cherries, raisins, prunes, and honey. Cover the pan and let sit for 5 minutes, until the dried fruits have softened. Stir in additional almond milk, if desired, for texture. Serve in bowls, drizzled with honey and topped with almonds.

SERVES 4 TO 6

1 cup (240 ml) whole milk or cream

1 cup (240 ml) unsweetened unflavored almond milk, plus more as needed

1 cup (240 ml) water

1 cup (225 g) smoked steel-cut oats (see page 56)

1 teaspoon ground cinnamon

½ teaspoon ground ginger

¼ teaspoon kosher salt, plus more to taste

¼ cup (30 g) dried tart cherries

¼ cup (30 g) golden raisins

¼ cup (30 g) chopped prunes

1 tablespoon honey (or salted honey or maple syrup), plus more for drizzling

¼ cup (25 g) sliced almonds or chopped smoked almonds (see page 72), for topping

SMOKY GRANOLA
with Chocolate & Cherries

**MAKES ABOUT 12 CUPS
(1.1 KG)**

1 cup (240 ml) pure maple syrup

⅓ cup (75 g) packed dark brown sugar, turbinado sugar, or coconut sugar

⅓ cup (80 ml) canola oil (or a blend of store-bought coconut and sunflower oils)

¾ teaspoon kosher salt, plus more as needed

1 tablespoon pure vanilla extract

4 cups (375 g) smoked thick-cut rolled oats (see page 56)

1 cup (110 g) raw pecan halves or 1 cup (140 g) whole almonds

½ cup (70 g) hulled raw pumpkin seeds

½ cup (70 g) hulled raw sunflower seeds

½ cup (60 g) nonfat dry milk powder

½ cup (60 g) ground flaxseed meal

1 cup (80 g) dried unsweetened coconut flakes

½ cup (60 g) dried cherries

½ cup (60 g) golden raisins

⅓ cup (60 g) dark chocolate chips or chunks

Smoked oats create a grown-up, sophisticated granola with a flavor that's likely to transport you to your favorite campsite. The combination of dried fruit and dark chocolate tilt this version into the sweet treat category—meaning it's delicious with almond milk or yogurt for breakfast, or sprinkled over vanilla bean ice cream for dessert. Using dry milk powder helps the granola clump together and adds a terrific crunch.

Position the oven racks in the upper and lower thirds of the oven and preheat the oven to 300°F (150°C). Line two baking sheets with parchment paper.

Combine the maple syrup, brown sugar, oil, and salt in a small saucepan and cook over medium heat, stirring occasionally, until the sugar is dissolved, about 5 minutes. Remove the pan from the heat and stir in the vanilla.

In a large bowl, combine the smoked oats, nuts, the seeds, milk powder, and flaxseed meal. Pour the warm syrup mixture over the dry ingredients and mix well with a rubber spatula.

Spread the moistened oats evenly between the prepared baking sheets. Bake for 20 minutes, then stir the granola with a metal spatula and switch the baking sheets to the opposite racks to ensure even cooking. Bake for 20 minutes more, then stir and switch the baking sheets again. Continue baking until the mixture has a fragrant, toasty aroma, 10 to 15 minutes more. Remove the granola from the oven and season with salt to taste.

Cool the granola on the baking sheets, breaking up any unwieldy clumps with the spatula. When completely cool, transfer the granola to a large mixing bowl and mix in the coconut, cherries, raisins, and chocolate. Store in an airtight container at room temperature for up to 1 month.

SMOKED SCOTTISH OATCAKES

**MAKES ABOUT
24 OATCAKES**

1½ cups (135 g) smoked thick-cut rolled oats (see page 56)

1 cup (125 g) all-purpose flour

⅓ cup (75 g) packed light brown sugar

½ teaspoon baking soda

½ teaspoon fine sea salt

½ cup (110 g) cold unsalted butter, diced

¼ cup (115 g) full-fat plain yogurt

Whole milk, as needed (optional)

Subtly sweet and salty and straddling the line between a cookie and a cracker (or a *biscuit,* as they'd say in the U.K.), oatcakes remain one of my favorite snacks ever since I first discovered them on train rides across Scotland. Their nubby texture and wholesome flavor work at any time of day, especially with a slather of almond butter and a pinch of flaky salt, or sliced tart apples and aged Cheddar. As a bonus, oatcakes are sturdy and portable, so they're great for picnics, camping trips, and lunch box treats. I tried recipes for years before landing on one from Molly Wizenberg's blog, *Orangette.* Made with lightly smoked oats, this version is even more alluring. Meet the new star of your cheese platter.

Preheat the oven to 350°F (175°C). Line two baking sheets with parchment paper.

In a large bowl, whisk together the smoked oats, flour, brown sugar, baking soda, and salt. Add the butter and use your fingers to press and squeeze the ingredients into a coarse meal. Stir in the yogurt until a soft dough forms. (If your yogurt is on the thick side, add a tablespoon or so of milk, just enough to bring the dough together.) The dough should be a little crumbly; don't worry if it's on the sticky side, the flour you use in the rolling process will smooth things out.

Turn the dough out onto a lightly floured work surface and roll or pat it (with a lightly floured rolling pin or your hands) to a ¼-inch (6 mm) thickness. Using a 2-inch (5 cm) round cookie cutter, stamp out oatcakes, then use a bench scraper to transfer the cakes to the prepared baking sheets. Gather, reroll, and cut more oatcakes from any scraps of dough.

Bake the oatcakes for about 15 minutes, until they are golden brown around the edges. Transfer the cakes to a wire rack to cool completely, then store in an airtight container at room temperature for up to 1 week.

RED QUINOA, EGG & AVOCADO SALAD

When I'm depleted from chasing deadlines and various other domestic duties, I crave this salad because (a) it's super tasty, and (b) it's packed with so many nourishing ingredients. Once you have smoked quinoa on hand, a few minutes of chopping will provide sustenance for several days of meals on the fly. After a bowl—and a few deep breaths—my superpowers are restored. The ingredients list should definitely serve as a guide—feel free to add black beans, charred corn, crumbled cheese, or any other favorite ingredients as desired. To make the salad more substantial, sometimes I spread a schmear of roasted red pepper hummus inside the bowl before filling it with quinoa.

Bring the water to a boil in a saucepan over medium-high heat and add the eggs. Turn the heat to low and simmer for 9 minutes. Use a slotted spoon to transfer the eggs to another container and rinse with cold water to cool.

Return the water to a boil over medium heat and add the quinoa and a pinch of salt. Turn the heat to low, cover the pan, and simmer for 15 minutes. Remove the pan from the heat and let the quinoa sit, covered, for 10 minutes, until the grains are tender and have absorbed all the liquid, then uncover the pan and set the quinoa aside to cool briefly.

Use a fork to fluff the quinoa, then transfer it to a large bowl. Add the olive oil, lemon zest and juice, and the vinegar. Toss to combine, then season generously with salt and pepper. Add the tomatoes, spinach, cilantro, and a few dashes hot sauce and toss again. Peel the eggs and garnish each serving with a half (or quarters) of the soft-boiled eggs, avocado, toasted seeds, and a sprinkling of salt and pepper.

SERVES 4 TO 6

3 cups (710 ml) water

3 eggs

2 cups (340 g) smoked red quinoa (see page 56)

Kosher salt

¼ cup (60 ml) extra-virgin olive oil, plus more as desired

Finely grated zest and juice of 1 lemon

1 teaspoon sherry vinegar

Freshly ground black pepper

1 pint (300 g) grape or cherry tomatoes, halved

A couple handfuls of baby spinach or arugula leaves

2 tablespoons chopped fresh cilantro, plus more for garnish

Vinegar-based hot sauce (such as Cholula)

1 ripe avocado, peeled and sliced

Toasted sesame or poppy seeds, for garnish (optional)

QUINOA & CARROT SALAD
with Meyer Lemon Vinaigrette

**This is the kind of perfectly simple, nourishing salad I want to eat
once a week (and it's easy to prep during a bulk smoking session).
The tastiest results come from using the freshest ingredients, like
locally grown carrots, sunny Meyer lemon juice, and your very best
olive oil. This salad is a delicious sidekick to smoked chicken (see
page 158) or beef tenderloin (see page 192), but it's also a satisfying
meal on its own. I frequently change up the mix, adding canned
chickpeas, toasted pepitas, crumbled queso fresco, or fresh herbs.**

Prepare a charcoal grill for two-zone cooking and build a medium fire, or heat
a gas grill to medium-high. When the coals are glowing red and covered with
a fine gray ash, add your smoke source (chips, chunks, or log). Carefully wipe
the preheated grill grates with a lightly oiled paper towel. Using a grill brush,
scrape the grill grates clean, then carefully wipe with a lightly oiled towel again.
If you're using a grill basket, allow it to preheat for 5 minutes before cooking.

While the grill heats, cook the quinoa on the stovetop. Bring the water to a
boil in a saucepan over medium-high heat and add the quinoa and a pinch of
salt. Turn the heat to low, cover the pan, and simmer for 15 minutes. Remove
the pan from the heat and let the quinoa sit, covered, for 10 minutes, until the
grains are tender and have absorbed all the liquid, then uncover the pan and
let the quinoa cool briefly.

Meanwhile, trim the carrots, leaving a small portion of the green stem intact
and reserving the nicest fronds. Place the carrots in a large bowl, drizzle with
enough olive oil to coat, season generously with salt and pepper, and toss to
combine. Remove the fronds from the stems, rinse and dry and then coarsely
chop until you have about ¼ cup (10 g); set aside.

When the fire begins to produce a steady stream of smoke, place the carrots
and green onions in the grill basket over direct heat and cover the grill. Open
the lid every minute or so to turn the carrots and onions and rotate the pan
around the heat as needed to prevent burning, until the vegetables are nicely
charred and just tender, about 5 minutes for the green onions and 20 minutes
for the carrots. Use tongs to transfer the vegetables as they finish cooking to
a cutting board to cool.

Slice the carrots as desired and add them to a large bowl with the quinoa, Meyer
lemon zest and juice, and a generous drizzle of olive oil. Trim the stems from the
green onions, chop, and add to the quinoa with the arugula and carrot fronds.
Toss to combine. Season with salt and pepper to taste, and serve warm or at
room temperature.

SERVES 4

3 cups (710 ml) water

2 cups (340 g) smoked
tricolor quinoa (see page 56)

Kosher salt

2 bunches young carrots
(preferably a mix of colors),
with greens

Extra-virgin olive oil, for
drizzling

Freshly ground black pepper

3 green onions

Finely grated zest and juice
of 1 Meyer lemon

Handful of arugula or
⅓ cup (15 g) chopped
fresh flat-leaf parsley

SMOKED FARRO
with Wild Mushrooms & Halloumi

SERVES 4

1½ cups (270 g) smoked farro (see page 56)

Kosher salt

1 pound (450 g) wild mushrooms (such as oyster, maitake, shiitake, cremini, or a mix)

Extra-virgin olive oil, for drizzling

Freshly ground black pepper

6 ounces (170 g) halloumi, cut into ¼-inch (6 mm) slices

2 tablespoons freshly squeezed lemon juice

1 bunch green onions, white and light green parts, thinly sliced

¼ cup (10 g) lightly chopped fresh flat-leaf parsley

This recipe is an example of how the heat of the grill and the aroma of smoldering hardwood dramatically transform ingredients. The chewy texture and earthy flavor of smoked farro melds beautifully with crispy grilled mushrooms. Topped with molten grilled halloumi (a firm brined cheese from Cyprus that's perfect for grilling or panfrying), this pilaf turns into a meal that needs nothing more than a cold glass of rosé. Leftovers are ideal for lunch; just allow the mixture to come to room temperature before serving.

Place the smoked farro in a saucepan and add enough cold water to cover by about 1 inch (2.5 cm). Soak the farro for 20 minutes, then drain in a colander. Return the farro to the pan and cover with 3 inches (7.5 cm) of fresh cold water. Add a few generous pinches of salt and bring to a boil over high heat. Turn the heat to low and simmer, covered, for about 20 minutes, until the farro is tender but still chewy. Drain the farro in a colander and allow it to dry out a bit while you grill the mushrooms and halloumi.

Prepare a charcoal grill for two-zone cooking and build a medium fire, or heat a gas grill to medium-high. Carefully wipe the preheated grill grates with a lightly oiled paper towel. Using a grill brush, scrape the grill grates clean, then wipe with a lightly oiled towel again and place a grill basket over direct heat, if using.

Meanwhile, trim the wild mushrooms and cut them into thick slices (or halve the cremini). Place the mushrooms in a large mixing bowl, drizzle with enough olive oil to lightly coat, season generously with salt and pepper, and toss to combine. Transfer the farro to a separate large mixing bowl.

Place the mushrooms in the grill basket (or directly on the grates) and grill, flipping them and rotating the basket around the heat as needed for even cooking, until they're nicely browned and crisp around the edges, 7 to 9 minutes. Add the mushrooms and their juices to the farro and return the grill basket to the heat.

Place the halloumi slices in the same bowl you used for the mushrooms, drizzle with enough olive oil to lightly coat, and toss to combine. Place the halloumi in the grill basket and cook until browned and crisp, about 2 minutes per side, then add the halloumi to the farro and mushrooms. Add the lemon juice, green onions, and a generous drizzle of olive oil, tossing gently with a rubber spatula to combine. Add the parsley and a generous grinding of pepper and fold gently. Add more salt and pepper to taste. Serve immediately, or store in a sealed container in the refrigerator for up to 4 days. For the best texture and flavor, remove the dish from the refrigerator 30 minutes before serving.

SMOKED BARLEY
with Blistered Tomatoes & Burrata

SERVES 4 TO 6

2 cups (360 g) smoked pearled barley (see page 56)

2 pints (600 g) cherry or grape tomatoes (preferably a mix of colors and varieties)

½ cup (120 ml) extra-virgin olive oil, plus more for drizzling and serving

Salt and freshly ground black pepper

¼ cup (60 ml) elderberry vinegar or another deeply flavored red wine vinegar, plus more as needed

2 spring onions or 4 green onions, trimmed and thinly sliced

Red pepper flakes or crumbled chile pequin, to taste

Handful of fresh Thai basil leaves, torn

3 rounds of burrata (about 12 ounces/340 g)

Flaky salt

A couple of bombshell ingredients—and careful seasoning—make this deceptively simple salad pretty extraordinary. With its quivering heart of cream, burrata brings a luxurious texture to the chewy smoked grains. A generous amount of olive oil (use your best) and a spunky vinegar (I've used fruity elderberry, pomegranate, and best-quality red wine vinegars to great affect) pull all the other ingredients together. Feel free to follow your whims with the aromatics: you could certainly add shaved fennel and/or celery, or chopped olives to the mix, or use a different cheese, such as shaved ricotta salata or coarsely chopped Parmesan or Pecorino Romano.

Prepare a charcoal grill for two-zone cooking and build a medium-high fire, or heat a gas grill to high.

When the coals are glowing red and covered with a fine gray ash, add your smoke source (chips, chunks, or log). Return the cooking grate to its position, allow it to preheat, and then carefully wipe the grates with a lightly oiled paper towel. Using a grill brush, scrape the grill grates clean, then carefully wipe with a lightly oiled towel again.

While the grill heats, cook the barley on the stovetop. Place the smoked barley in a large saucepan and add enough cold water to cover by 4 inches (10 cm). Bring the water to a boil over high heat. Turn the heat to low and simmer until tender, about 25 minutes. Drain the barley in a colander and rinse briefly under cold water to cool. Drain again, shaking out the excess water.

Place a grill basket over direct heat to preheat for 5 minutes. While the basket heats, place the tomatoes in a mixing bowl, drizzle with enough olive oil to lightly coat, season with salt and pepper, and toss to combine. Place the tomatoes in the grill basket and grill until blistered and softened (shaking the basket for even cooking), 3 to 4 minutes. Immediately transfer the tomatoes to a large bowl (to retain their juices).

Add the barley to the bowl with the tomatoes, along with ½ cup olive oil and vinegar. Season generously with salt and pepper and toss to combine. Add the onions, red pepper flakes, and basil and toss again. Taste and adjust the seasonings, adding more vinegar or pepper as desired.

Nestle the rounds of burrata into the barley, drizzle the cheese with olive oil, and sprinkle with flaky salt and another grinding of pepper. Serve at room temperature.

BLACK RICE BOWL
with Roots & Radishes

Like the best bowls, this one is full of surprises and beautiful to behold. You can prepare the starring players (rice, roasted vegetables, dressing) in advance, so it's easy to assemble individual servings or a healthful meal on the fly. Black rice (also called Forbidden rice) turns purple when it's cooked in a pot of boiling water (like pasta) until the grains are perfectly plump and chewy. The hearty root vegetables, spicy radishes, and kale benefit from the umami depth of gingery miso dressing. Finally, golden raisins provide a burst of sweetness, and red-tinged radish sprouts give a peppery finish (you can also use sunflower or any other variety of microgreens). There's plenty going on here, but rice bowls are a more-is-more affair, so consider other toppings, like pickled vegetables, smoked nuts, sesame seeds, fresh herbs (cilantro, basil, mint), or Korean red pepper flakes.

Preheat the oven to 400°F (200°C).

To make the rice bowl, bring a large pot of generously salted water to a boil over medium-high heat, add the rice, and cook for 25 to 30 minutes, until the rice is tender and chewy. Drain in a fine-mesh sieve and set aside. (Store the rice in a sealed container in the refrigerator for up to 1 week.)

Place the root vegetables and shallots in a large bowl, drizzle with enough olive oil to coat, season generously with salt and pepper, and toss to combine. Spread out the vegetables onto a rimmed baking sheet and roast them for 45 to 50 minutes, using a spatula to flip them every 15 minutes, until browned and tender. Set the roasted vegetables aside to cool.

Meanwhile, to make the dressing, place the ginger and garlic in the bowl of a food processor and pulse into a coarse puree. Add the water, vinegar, miso, soy sauce, peanut oil, sesame oil, and cayenne and blend until smooth. (Store the dressing in a sealed container in the refrigerator for up to 1 week.)

Toss the kale with 3 tablespoons of the dressing in a large mixing bowl. Using your fingers, gently massage the kale until it turns deep green and softens, 1 to 2 minutes total, and then sprinkle lightly with salt to taste.

To serve, divide the rice among bowls (the rice and remaining ingredients can be warm, room temperature, or cold, as desired) and top with the roasted vegetables, kale, radishes, raisins, green onions, sprouts, and desired toppings. Serve with the remaining dressing on the side.

SERVES 4 TO 6

Rice Bowl

2 cups (370 g) smoked black rice (see page 56)

4 cups (540 g) diced root vegetables (carrots, parsnips, turnips, beets, or sweet potatoes)

2 shallots or 1 red onion, diced

Extra-virgin olive oil, for drizzling

Kosher salt and freshly ground black pepper

1 bunch lacinato kale, stemmed and thinly sliced

6 to 8 assorted radishes, trimmed and thinly sliced

¼ cup (30 g) golden raisins or currants

4 green onions, white and light green parts, thinly sliced, for garnish

A generous pinch of radish sprouts or microgreens, for garnish

Miso-Ginger Dressing

1-inch (2.5 cm) piece fresh ginger, peeled and thinly sliced

1 clove garlic, thinly sliced

¼ cup (60 ml) water

2 tablespoons seasoned rice vinegar

2 tablespoons red miso

1 tablespoon low-sodium soy sauce

¼ cup (60 ml) peanut or grapeseed oil

1 tablespoon dark sesame oil

Pinch of cayenne

CHAPTER FOUR ——————

NUTS & SEEDS

Caked in salty seasonings, canned "smoked almonds" were ubiquitous in my childhood, and a mandatory gift for my father on every Dad-centric holiday. I still have a soft spot for them, even though their "smoked" flavor comes mostly from artificial ingredients, but they're not nearly as delicious as nuts that you smoke yourself.

If there's an ingredient that disappears most quickly from my larder, it's smoked nuts and seeds, in part because I rely on them for fast protein. Smoked nuts like cashews and pecans emerge at happy hour, garnish green salads for working lunches, and get tucked in my computer bag for road trips and school events.

With their natural fat content, nuts and seeds absorb the appealing qualities of wood smoke almost as well as meat. In fact, the process infuses them with a rich, bacony note that gives vegetable dishes more muscle. (Those oils also cause them to go rancid over time, so store them in the refrigerator to make them last longer.)

You can smoke either raw or sprouted nuts (my choice for nut butters) or varieties that have been roasted and salted (I use them for spiced nut mixes). To ensure even smoking, be sure to stir nuts and seeds a time or two during the process, and watch them closely toward the end of the smoking time so they don't become too dark and take on an acrid flavor.

SMOKED NUTS & SEEDS

Prepare a charcoal grill for two-zone cooking and build a medium fire, or heat a gas grill to medium-high. When the coals are glowing red and covered with a fine gray ash, use tongs to remove the cooking grate and place a drip pan with 1 inch (2.5 cm) of warm water on the side with no coals, and add your smoke source (chips, chunks, or log). Return the cooking grate to its position, and then carefully wipe the grates with a lightly oiled paper towel. Using a grill brush, scrape the grill grates clean, then carefully wipe with a lightly oiled towel again.

Place the nuts or seeds in a disposable aluminum pan or atop two sheets of heavy-duty aluminum foil (crimp the edges of foil upward to create a rim and prevent the nuts or seeds from sliding off). When the fire begins to produce a steady stream of smoke, place the nuts or seeds over indirect heat, close the grill, vent the grill for smoking, and smoke for 20 to 30 minutes, until they're slightly darkened and fragrant. To ensure even results, stir the ingredients and rotate the individual containers (if you're smoking more than one item) around the heat after 15 minutes, and keep an eye on their color after 20 minutes so they don't become too dark.

USE THIS METHOD TO SMOKE:

NUTS

Almonds

Cashews

Hazelnuts

Macadamia

Marcona almonds

Peanuts

Pecans

Walnuts

SEEDS

Chia

Flax

Hemp

Millet

Pepitas

Sesame

Sunflower

CURRY-CHILE PEANUTS

I love to serve these addictive, sweet-and-spicy peanuts with cocktails, and they always disappear quickly. As you'll see, the smoking process is done à la minute (rather than starting with already smoked nuts) so all of the aromatics are flavored by the wafting smoke. It's a fun and fragrant snack to prepare when guests are over because the aroma perks everyone's appetite (the only challenge is waiting for the nuts to cool before digging in). If you don't want to scrub a cast-iron grill afterward, you can begin with smoked peanuts (see page 72) and prepare them the same way on your stove. I leave the chiles whole, because the heat is less intense (and they look pretty in the bowl). To kick up the heat, coarsely chop the chiles after you toast them so you can eat them along with the nuts.

Prepare a charcoal grill for two-zone cooking and build a medium fire, or heat a gas grill to medium-high.

When the coals are glowing red and covered with a fine gray ash, add your smoke source (chips, chunks, or log). Carefully wipe the preheated grill grates with a lightly oiled paper towel. Using a grill brush, scrape the grill grates clean, then carefully wipe with a lightly oiled towel again.

Place the oil and chiles in a large skillet (preferably cast iron) over direct heat and cook, stirring constantly, until the chiles begin to sizzle and smell toasty and aromatic. Remove the skillet from the heat and add the honey, Spicy Curry Salt, pepper, and peanuts and stir until the nuts are evenly coated.

Return the skillet to the grill over indirect heat, close the grill, vent the grill for smoking, and smoke the mixture for 10 to 20 minutes, stirring every few minutes, until the nuts are toasted and richly fragrant. Remove the skillet from the grill, transfer the nuts to a bowl, and continue to stir the nuts every few minutes so they don't clump as they cool. Allow them to cool completely, and then serve immediately or store in a sealed container at room temperature for up to 1 week.

MAKES ABOUT 4 CUPS (450 G)

2 tablespoons olive oil

4 dried arbol chiles, stemmed and seeded

2 tablespoons honey

1 teaspoon Spicy Curry Salt (page 26)

½ teaspoon freshly ground black pepper

1 pound (450 g) roasted salted peanuts

BIRDSEED MUFFINS

MAKES 12 MUFFINS

Topping

2 tablespoons smoked sesame seeds (see page 72)

2 tablespoons smoked flaxseeds (see page 72)

2 tablespoons smoked millet (see page 72)

2 tablespoons poppy seeds

Muffins

¼ cup plus 2 tablespoons (55 g) smoked hulled raw sunflower seeds (see page 72)

1½ cups (190 g) all-purpose flour

½ cup (60 g) whole-wheat flour

2 tablespoons smoked wheat bran or wheat germ (see page 56)

1¼ teaspoons baking powder

½ teaspoon baking soda

¼ teaspoon kosher salt

½ cup (45 g) smoked thick-cut rolled oats (see page 56)

¼ cup (45 g) smoked millet (see page 72)

¼ cup (45 g) smoked sesame seeds (see page 72)

1 tablespoon smoked flaxseeds (see page 72)

1 tablespoon poppy seeds

Most muffins are supersweet, cake-like confections that are heavy on oil and sugar and lacking in wholesome ingredients. This is not that kind of muffin. If healthful, truly flavorful muffins have a redemption, it's this moist, not-too-sweet incarnation, adapted from Nancy Silverton's *Pastries from the La Brea Bakery*. Packed with pebbly, crunchy seeds and other tasty, nourishing ingredients, they're delicious warm from the oven with a pat of Irish butter, served with soups or salads, and packed in lunch boxes.

In this version, I smoke the seeded, whole-grain base as well as the seed topping. The subtle smoke flavor tilts these further into the savory realm, enhancing the earthiness of the whole grains and the distinct personality of each seed. I don't smoke poppy seeds because I don't want to obscure their delicate flavor (and they toast during the baking process).

This recipe typically sends me to the bulk section of Whole Foods or my local food co-op. To make the process more time efficient, I usually smoke a couple of individual containers of the premeasured ingredients (for both the muffins and the topping) all at once, and then I store them in the freezer so they're ready to go whenever I'm ready to bake.

To make the topping, in a small bowl, toss together the seeds until combined. Set aside.

To make the muffins, preheat the oven to 350°F (175°C). Spray a 12-cup muffin pan with nonstick spray, or line it with paper muffin liners.

Place the smoked sunflower seeds, the flours, smoked wheat bran, baking powder, baking soda, and salt in the bowl of a food processor and process until the sunflower seeds have the same consistency as the flours. Add the smoked oats, millet, sesame seeds, flaxseeds, and poppy seeds and pulse a few times, just to combine.

In the bowl of a stand mixer fitted with the paddle attachment, cream the butter on low speed until softened, 2 to 3 minutes. Add the brown sugar and beat on medium speed until light and fluffy, 2 to 3 minutes. Add the eggs, one at a time, beating well after each addition. Add the honey and beat on medium-low speed until well blended. Slowly pour in the buttermilk and mix until incorporated. Add the flour mixture in three additions, mixing on low just until the dry ingredients disappear into the batter (do not overmix).

Sprinkle ½ teaspoon of the topping in the bottom of each muffin cup. Scoop the batter into the muffin cups, filling them to the rim. Sprinkle 1 teaspoon of the topping over each muffin.

Bake for 20 to 25 minutes, until the muffins are golden and a toothpick inserted in the center comes out clean. Let the muffins cool in the pan for 5 minutes, then turn out onto a wire rack to cool slightly. Serve warm, or wrap in foil and store at room temperature for 3 days.

½ cup (110 g) cold unsalted butter, cut into 1-inch (2.5 cm) cubes

½ cup (100 g) packed light brown sugar

2 eggs

¼ cup (60 ml) honey

1¼ cups (300 ml) buttermilk

MESQUITE-SMOKED PECAN ROLLS

Starter

Pinch of active dry yeast

1 cup (125 g) all-purpose flour

1 cup plus 1 tablespoon
(255 ml) water

Dough

2 cups (250 g) all-purpose
flour, plus more for dusting

1 teaspoon active dry yeast

1½ teaspoons fine sea salt

1 tablespoon plus 1 teaspoon
butter, at room temperature

⅔ cup (90 g) mesquite-
smoked pecans (see page 72)

Towering pecan trees provide a green canopy throughout our neighborhood in Austin and the Texas Hill Country. Each fall, the ripe nuts fall from the trees and our dog walks are interrupted by Dilley, our chocolate Lab, sniffing them out for snacks. My husband, David, developed these rolls as a way to incorporate local Texas ingredients into his bread. Usually reserved for smoking beef, mesquite's stronger, distinctive aroma pairs beautifully with rich nuts. Investing the time to begin the dough with a starter (also called a sponge) the night or morning before baking will create rolls with a deeper flavor—the perfect vehicle for the smoky nuts. These rolls are perfect on a cheese platter, for picnic-sized Gruyère and butter sandwiches, and with creamy vegetable soups or braised meats.

To make the starter, in a bowl, blend the yeast into the flour with your fingers. Make a well in the center of the mixture and add the water. Blend the mixture together with your fingers until the water is fully incorporated and you can feel that there are no lumps (it should have the consistency of a thick pancake batter). Cover the bowl with plastic wrap and let the mixture ferment at room temperature for at least 12 hours and up to 18 hours.

To make the dough, use a rubber spatula to transfer all of the starter to the bowl of a stand mixer fitted with the dough hook. In a separate bowl, whisk together the flour, yeast, and salt and add it to the starter. Add the butter and mix on low speed for 7 to 8 minutes, until the dough is smooth and begins to pull away from the sides of the bowl. Remove the dough hook and allow the dough to rest for 15 minutes.

Turn the dough out onto a lightly floured surface and press it out gently into a ½-inch-thick (1.3 cm) rectangle. Grab the top edge and stretch it toward you over the top of the dough about two-thirds of the way and press it gently into the dough. Stretch the bottom edge up and away from you, over the top of the first fold about two-thirds of the way and press it gently into the dough. Rotate the dough 90 degrees and repeat the two folds, stretching first the top edge toward you and then the bottom edge away from you.

Turn the dough over and form it into a ball by placing your hands on the side opposite you, palms facing you and gently pulling the dough toward you, letting it grip the table and stretch the surface. At the same time as you are

continued

pulling the dough toward you, move both hands to the left, causing the dough to turn and start to tighten into a ball. Release and move your hands to the back of the dough again and repeat the pulling toward yourself and shifting your hands to the left to further tighten and round the dough. Repeat until you have a smooth ball of dough. If the surface starts to tear, pull more gently or stop and return the dough to the bowl of the standing mixer. Allow the dough to rest for 15 minutes more.

Reinsert the dough hook, add the smoked pecans, and mix at the lowest speed just until the nuts are evenly distributed. Remove the hook, cover the bowl with plastic wrap, and allow the dough to rise in a warm, draft-free area until it has doubled in size, 1 to 1½ hours.

Turn the dough out on a lightly floured surface and repeat the stretching and folding process. Stretch the dough into a smooth ball following the method given, then return the ball to the bowl with the smooth side up and cover with plastic. Allow the dough to rest for 30 minutes more.

Turn the dough out onto a lightly floured surface and divide it into 12 equal pieces. (Cover the dough with a tea towel while you shape each piece.) Line a baking sheet with parchment paper. Take a piece of dough and press it into a rustic circle about 3 inches (7.5 cm) in diameter. Fold each of the corners into the center to start a round shape. Turn the piece over and make a cage with your hand over the dough piece, the palm of your hand resting lightly on the top and your fingers extending down to the table. Rotate your hand counterclockwise, making the dough piece turn and the surface tighten. The dough should grip the table slightly but not stick, so as to stretch the gluten and make a tight ball. If it slides around without gripping, brush some flour away; if it sticks too much, add a small amount of flour. Place the tightened roll on the prepared baking sheet and repeat with all of the dough pieces, evenly spacing them on the baking sheet. Cover the rolls with a clean towel and let rise until doubled in size, about 1 hour.

Preheat the oven to 450°F (230°C) and position an oven rack in the middle and another on the rack directly below. Place a heavy skillet or metal pan on the bottom rack to preheat along with the oven.

When the rolls have risen, snip the top of each roll with a pair of scissors and place the baking sheet on the center rack of the oven. Quickly add ½ cup (120 ml) water to the preheated pan to create some steam and then close the oven door. Bake the rolls for 15 to 18 minutes, until they're evenly browned on top, then transfer them to a wire rack to cool completely. Serve immediately, or store in a paper bag (or wrapped in aluminum foil) up to 3 days.

SMOKED ALMOND LOAF
with Raspberry & Coconut

MAKES 1 LOAF

1¼ cups (300 ml) whole milk

2 eggs

1 teaspoon pure vanilla extract

2½ cups (315 g) all-purpose flour

2 teaspoons baking powder

1 teaspoon ground cardamom

½ teaspoon kosher salt

1 cup (200 g) sugar

¾ cup (75 g) smoked sliced almonds (see page 72)

¾ cup (95 g) smoked dried sweetened coconut flakes (see page 18)

6 tablespoons (85 g) unsalted butter, melted, plus butter for serving

¼ cup (160 g) raspberry jam

Infused with the toasty goodness and subtle crunch of smoked almonds and coconut, this moist, fragrant quick bread is delicious on its own or toasted in thick slabs and slathered with butter. A horizon line of raspberry jam filling makes each slice beautiful and provides a pop of sweet, fruity flavor. For added perfume, add finely grated lemon or lime zest to the batter.

Preheat the oven to 350°F (175°C).

In a small bowl, whisk together the milk, eggs, and vanilla. In a separate bowl, sift together the flour, baking powder, cardamom, and salt. Add the sugar, ½ cup (50 g) of the smoked almonds, and the smoked coconut and stir to combine. Make a well in the center of the dry ingredients and pour in the milk mixture. Use a rubber spatula to fold the batter until only a few dry streaks remain. Add the butter and stir just until the batter has a smooth, even texture (do not overmix).

Grease a 9 by 5-inch (23 by 13 cm) loaf pan with vegetable oil or nonstick cooking spray. Pour half of the batter into the pan and use a rubber spatula to gently smooth the top. Use a spoon to spread the raspberry jam down the center of the batter, leaving a 1½- to 2-inch (4 to 5 cm) border around the perimeter. Top with the remaining batter, gently smooth the top, and then sprinkle with the remaining ¼ cup (25 g) smoked almonds.

Bake until a toothpick inserted into the center comes out clean, 1 to 1¼ hours. Let the bread cool in the pan for 5 minutes, then turn out onto a wire rack to cool completely. Serve the bread in thick slices (toasted, if desired) with butter or a drizzle of salted honey.

SPICY SMOKED NUTS
with Rosemary

Texans refer to rosemary as "bulletproof" because it flourishes almost anywhere, even in intense heat and rocky soil, which means I always have plenty on hand (after walking to the backyard with garden shears) to enhance cocktails, roast chickens, or these addictive nuts (a happy hour favorite on our back porch). Warm spices and a touch of sweetness round out the smoky notes of the pecans and almonds (feel free to swap in cashews, Marcona almonds, or hazelnuts, as desired).

Preheat the oven to 325°F (165°C) and line a rimmed baking sheet with parchment paper.

Place the smoked nuts in a mixing bowl and add the rosemary, salt, brown sugar, cinnamon, cumin, cayenne, a few grinds of black pepper, and the egg white. Toss the mixture until the nuts are thoroughly coated. Pour the nuts on the prepared baking sheet and spread them into a single layer.

Roast the nuts for 12 to 15 minutes, stirring with a metal spatula after about 6 minutes, until they're lightly browned and fragrant (watch them toward the end of cooking to ensure they don't get too dark). Transfer the baking sheet to a wire rack and allow the nuts to cool completely. Serve immediately, or store the nuts in a sealed container at room temperature for up to 2 weeks.

MAKES ABOUT 4 CUPS (440 G)

2 cups (220 g) smoked pecan halves (see page 72)

2 cups (220 g) smoked whole almonds (see page 72)

1 generous tablespoon chopped fresh rosemary

1½ teaspoons kosher salt

1 generous teaspoon dark brown sugar

½ teaspoon ground cinnamon

½ teaspoon ground cumin

¼ teaspoon cayenne

Freshly ground black pepper

1 egg white

LINGUINE & SMOKED WALNUT PESTO
with Yellow Tomatoes

SERVES 6 TO 8

¾ cup (175 ml) olive oil, plus more for drizzling

1 large shallot, chopped (about ¼ cup/40 g)

½ teaspoon red pepper flakes or crumbled chile pequin

Kosher salt

¼ cup (30 g) golden raisins

1 clove garlic, lightly crushed and peeled

½ cup (60 g) smoked walnuts (see page 72)

3 ounces (85 g) spinach leaves

1 bunch basil (leaves and tender stems)

1 tablespoon freshly squeezed lemon juice, plus more as needed

⅓ cup (35 g) freshly grated Parmesan, plus more for serving

1 pint (300 g) yellow pear tomatoes (or another cherry or grape tomato)

Freshly ground black pepper

1 pound (450 g) whole-wheat linguine

With its sultry flavors and gorgeous burst of sweet, charred tomatoes, this lusty pasta might inspire a marriage proposal in certain regions of Italy. Swapping in smoked walnuts deepens the earthiness of the classic Genovese pesto. One extra step: Sautéing shallot, red pepper flakes, and golden raisins provides a subtle undercurrent of sweetness and heat that perfectly balances the other robust flavors.

Prepare a charcoal grill for two-zone cooking and build a medium-high fire, or heat a gas grill to high. When the coals are glowing red and covered with a fine gray ash, add your smoke source (chips, chunks, or log). Carefully wipe the preheated grill grates with a lightly oiled paper towel. Using a grill brush, scrape the grill grates clean, then carefully wipe with a lightly oiled towel again and place a grill basket over direct heat.

Meanwhile, bring a large pot of generously salted water to a boil over high heat on the stovetop.

In a small skillet, heat 2 tablespoons of the olive oil over medium heat. Add the shallot, red pepper flakes, and a pinch of salt and cook, stirring frequently until the shallot is softened and golden, 4 to 5 minutes. Add the raisins, stirring to coat them in warm oil, then remove the pan from the heat.

Place the garlic and ½ teaspoon salt in a food processor and pulse into a coarse paste. Add the warm shallot-raisin mixture and pulse until combined. Add the smoked walnuts, spinach, basil, and lemon juice and process until combined. With the processor running, slowly drizzle in the remaining ½ cup plus 2 tablespoons (150 ml) olive oil, then add the Parmesan and pulse until just combined (do not overmix the cheese). Transfer the pesto to a large mixing bowl.

Place the tomatoes in a bowl, drizzle with enough olive oil to lightly coat, season with salt and pepper, and toss to combine. Pour the tomatoes into the preheated grill basket and cook, stirring as needed, until the tomatoes are juicy and blistered, 2 to 3 minutes. Remove the basket from the heat.

Add the linguine to the boiling water and cook according to the package instructions to al dente. Use tongs to transfer the pasta directly from the pot to the bowl of pesto (the cooking water that clings to the pasta will help loosen the pesto). Toss the pasta until evenly coated, then add the tomatoes and toss again. Taste and add additional salt, pepper, and lemon juice as needed. Serve the pasta in bowls, garnished with Parmesan.

PIMENTO CHEESE
with Smoked Pecans

**MAKES ABOUT 4 CUPS
(440 G)**

1½ pounds (680 g) extra-sharp Cheddar cheese, grated

4 ounces (115 g) cream cheese, at room temperature

¾ cup (165 g) mayonnaise (preferably Duke's)

2 green onions, white and light green parts, minced

½ teaspoon cayenne

½ teaspoon freshly ground black pepper, plus more for garnish

One 7-ounce (200 g) jar whole peeled pimientos or piquillo peppers, drained and chopped

⅓ cup (45 g) smoked pecans (see page 72), lightly chopped

Crackers (such as sesame, Triscuits, or Croccantini), for serving

My husband and I got married in Pawleys Island, South Carolina, and it's not an exaggeration to say that the location was partly chosen so our Low Country favorites—like shrimp and grits and pimento cheese—would be on the menu. Use a food processor or a hand grater to grate the cheese for this recipe (preshredded cheese won't hold together as well). You can serve the pimento cheese immediately (I love it on crunchy crackers sturdy enough to hold up to a slather, but it's also great on toasted bread or bagels) or refrigerate it for a couple of hours to allow the smoky pecans to permeate the luscious mixture.

In a large mixing bowl, combine the Cheddar, cream cheese, mayonnaise, green onions, cayenne, and black pepper. Add the pimientos and use a rubber spatula to mix the ingredients until the cheese is spreadable. Fold in the pecans until evenly combined.

Transfer the pimento cheese to a serving bowl or ramekin, top it with a final grind of black pepper and serve cold or at room temperature with the crackers. Store leftovers in a sealed container in the refrigerator for up to 1 week.

SOBA NOODLE SALAD
with Almond Butter Dressing

This is my kind of weeknight meal: noodles tossed in a tasty, easy to prepare sauce and joined with a bunch of fresh vegetables, herbs, and spicy Asian condiments. If you use the spicier Harissa Cashew Butter here, adjust the Sriracha accordingly to reach your desired level of heat. Whisked into a gingery vinaigrette, smoked nut butter gives this dressing some muscle and makes the final mix more satisfying. These noodles are at their best immediately, at room temperature, though I'm always happy to eat the cold leftovers the following day. Green beans (blanched or grilled) and/or grilled corn kernels would be delicious additions to this salad.

To make the dressing, place the garlic and ginger in the bowl of a food processor and pulse into a coarse puree. Add the almond butter, tamari, rice vinegar, honey, sesame oil, and Sriracha and process until smooth. Taste and adjust the seasonings as desired. Stored in an airtight container, the dressing will keep in the refrigerator for up to 3 days (the dressing will thicken up after it's refrigerated, so for the best texture, remove it from the refrigerator 30 minutes before serving).

Bring a large pot of generously salted water to a boil over high heat. Add the noodles and cook according to the package instructions until they're tender but still firm. Drain the noodles in a colander and rinse with cold water.

Peel the carrots and then use the vegetable peeler to shave the carrots into ribbons. Use a fork to score the unpeeled cucumbers lengthwise (this releases their fragrance and helps them absorb the dressing) and julienne or thinly slice them into rounds, as desired. Add the noodles, carrots, bell pepper, and cucumbers to the dressing and toss to combine. Add the basil and cilantro and toss again. Divide the salad among bowls or transfer to a platter. Garnish with the chopped nuts, sesame seeds, and green onions and serve with lime wedges on the side. Store leftovers in a sealed container in the refrigerator for up to 2 days (loosen the noodles with an additional drizzle of oil or rice vinegar before serving, if desired).

VARIATION

For a heartier dish to serve in cooler seasons, swap in 1½ pounds (680 g) of roasted vegetables (such as broccolini, wild mushrooms, kale, cauliflower, and carrots) for the fresh vegetables. Just toss the vegetables with enough olive oil to lightly coat, season with salt and pepper, and roast on a baking sheet for about 30 minutes, until crisp and golden brown.

SERVES 4

Dressing

1 clove garlic, lightly crushed and peeled

½-inch (1.3 cm) piece fresh ginger, peeled and lightly chopped

¼ cup (50 g) Smoked Marcona Almond Butter (page 86) or Spicy Harissa Cashew Butter (page 86)

2 tablespoons tamari

2 tablespoons seasoned rice vinegar

1 tablespoon honey

1 tablespoon toasted sesame oil

1 to 2 teaspoons Sriracha, as desired for heat

12 ounces (340 g) soba noodles

2 carrots

2 Persian cucumbers

1 red bell pepper, seeded and julienned

½ cup (20 g) Thai basil leaves, torn

½ cup (20 g) fresh cilantro (leaves and tender stems), lightly chopped

Smoked almonds, cashews, or peanuts (see page 72), lightly chopped, for garnish

Toasted black and white sesame seeds, for garnish

Thinly sliced green onions, white and light green parts, for garnish

Lime wedges, for serving

THREE LIFE-CHANGING NUT BUTTERS

Making nut butter takes patience—it can take 10 to 12 minutes to transform nuts from a coarse meal into a smooth silky butter. Stop to scrape down the sides of your machine as needed, and taste the final results and adjust the seasonings as desired.

Smoked Marcona Almond Butter

MAKES ABOUT 1¼ CUPS (310 G)

3 tablespoons canola oil

2 tablespoons fresh chopped rosemary

2 cups (280 g) smoked Marcona almonds (roasted and salted; see page 72)

Fine sea salt

Whisk this richly flavored butter into vinaigrettes (for kale or spinach salad) or serve it with pear, apple, Asian pear, celery, and fennel.

In a small skillet, heat 2 tablespoons of the oil over medium heat. When the oil begins to shimmer, add the rosemary and cook, stirring occasionally, until the leaves are fragrant and sizzling, about 2 minutes. Remove the pan from the heat.

Place the almonds in the bowl of a food processor or high-speed blender and process until the nuts begin to form oily clumps, about 6 minutes. Drizzle in the rosemary oil, season with salt to taste, and process until the butter is smooth and creamy, 5 to 7 minutes more. Store in an airtight container in the refrigerator for up to 3 weeks.

Spicy Harissa Cashew Butter

MAKES 2 CUPS (310 G)

2 cups (260 g) smoked roasted and salted cashews (see page 72)

2 teaspoons harissa spice blend, or 1 tablespoon harissa paste

Pinch of cayenne (optional)

Fine sea salt

This slather is terrific on flatbread, with vegetable crudités, or on crackers. You can also thin it with olive oil and brush it onto grilled chicken, lamb, or pork kebabs just before they come off the grill.

Place the cashews in the bowl of a food processor or high-speed blender and process until the nuts begin to form oily clumps, about 6 minutes. Add the harissa and cayenne, season with salt to taste, and process until the butter is smooth and creamy, 5 to 7 minutes more. Store in an airtight container in the refrigerator for up to 3 weeks.

Seedy Sunflower Butter

With a delightful pop of tiny seeds (bonus: they also add essential amino acids, protein, and fiber), this smoky butter is delicious on toast, quick breads, waffles, and pancakes. I don't typically have chia and hempseeds on hand, so I hit the bulk aisle of my local natural foods market and buy just enough for this recipe (feel free to swap in an equal amount of flaxseeds or pumpkin seeds).

Place the sunflower seeds in the bowl of a food processor or high-speed blender and process until a butter forms, scraping down the sides as needed, 15 to 20 minutes. Add the chia seeds, hempseeds, and salt and pulse until combined. Taste and adjust the flavor as needed, adding more salt, if desired. Store in an airtight container at room temperature for up to 2 weeks or in the refrigerator for up to 1 month.

VARIATIONS

Use the following riffs on the classic PB&J and other creations to step up your next sandwich.

Smoked Marcona
   Almond Butter +
   apricot jam + toasted
   rosemary bread

Spicy Harissa Cashew
   Butter + ciabatta +
   sliced lamb + pickled
   red onions

Seedy Sunflower
   Butter + fig preserves
   + walnut bread

Seedy Sunflower
   Butter + whole-grain
   English muffin + sliced
   pear

Seedy Sunflower
   Butter + multigrain
   bread + ripe peaches
   or nectarines + honey

MAKES ABOUT 1⅔ CUPS (415 G)

1 pound (450 g) smoked hulled raw sunflower seeds (see page 72)

1 tablespoon chia seeds

1 tablespoon shelled hempseeds

½ teaspoon pink Himalayan sea salt, or to taste

CHAPTER FIVE

DRIED PEAS, BEANS & LEGUMES

The first time I simmered a pot of smoked chickpeas, I was amazed at how well the smoky fragrance of the dried beans carried itself through the cooking process. As you're about to discover, smoked beans, peas, and other legumes provide a foundation for deeply flavored soups and chili, brilliant antipasti (round out the plate with cheese, charcuterie, smoked olives, and toasted nuts), and fantastic salads. The smoky flavors also offer a satisfying complexity for vegetarian meals—no ham hock required.

I actually smoke both dried and cooked peas, beans, and legumes, depending on the final results I'm after. Smoking dried beans yields a delicate smoky flavor after they're cooked. By contrast, smoking cooked (or even canned) beans and the like produces a more pronounced smoky flavor in a shorter time because the density and moister texture of the cooked beans helps them absorb the aromas in the cooking chamber. In general, I prefer the first method for beans destined for soup or the base of something else (like bean dip), and the second method when I plan to serve them simply dressed, in a salad or as a side dish, so the earthy flavors are front and center.

The fragrance of cooked smoked beans intensifies overnight, especially when they are marinated in oil or juices—meaning the subtle hint of smoke you taste when you first prepare a French lentil salad blooms and becomes more pronounced the following day (to my delight).

As with grains and nuts, the color of the dried (and precooked) peas and beans darkens slightly with smoking, so stir them a few times during the process to ensure even results.

SMOKED PEAS, BEANS & LEGUMES

Prepare a charcoal grill for two-zone cooking and build a medium-high fire, or heat a gas grill to high.

When the coals are glowing red and covered with a fine gray ash, use tongs to remove the cooking grate and place a drip pan with 1 inch (2.5 cm) of warm water on the side with no coals, and add your smoke source (chips, chunks, or log). Return the cooking grate to its position, allow it to preheat, and then carefully wipe the preheated grill grates with a lightly oiled paper towel. Using a grill brush, scrape the grill grates clean, then carefully wipe with a lightly oiled towel again.

To smoke dried peas, beans, or legumes, place them in a disposable aluminum pan or atop two sheets of heavy-duty aluminum foil (crimp the edges of foil upward to create a rim and prevent them from sliding off). When the fire begins to produce a steady stream of smoke, place the pan over indirect heat, close the grill, vent the grill for smoking, and smoke for 25 to 40 minutes, until the peas, beans, or legumes are deeply fragrant and have darkened slightly. For even results, stir the ingredients and rotate the individual containers (if you're smoking more than one item) around the heat after 15 to 20 minutes, and keep an eye on their color after 30 minutes to ensure they don't become too dark.

To smoke cooked peas, beans, or legumes, toss them with enough olive oil to generously coat and place in a disposable aluminum pan. When the fire begins to produce a steady stream of smoke, place the pan over indirect heat, close the grill, vent the grill for smoking, and smoke for 15 to 25 minutes, until the peas, beans, or legumes are deeply fragrant and have darkened slightly. For even results, stir the ingredients and rotate the individual containers (if you're smoking more than one item) around the heat every 5 minutes, and keep an eye on their color toward the end of the process to ensure they don't become too dark.

MASTER RECIPE

USE THIS METHOD TO SMOKE:

Black beans

Black-eyed peas

Chickpeas

Lentils (all varieties)

Pinto beans

White beans (cannellini, great northern, or navy)

Yellow or green split peas

LUCK & MONEY

At my home in Austin, New Year's Day means a polar bear plunge in Barton Springs and brunch with friends. To bolster our courage, we serve spicy Bloody Marys or Buck Snorts (page 47) and this warming dish, known as Luck & Money. Eating peas and greens on New Year's Day is a Southern tradition that promises to bring good luck (from the peas) and fortune (courtesy of the greens) for the coming year. But don't save this nourishing combination for one day a year; it's delicious anytime, especially with cornbread to soak up the flavorful cooking liquid (or potlikker). My local supermarket has a freezer case of frozen fresh black-eyed peas that I prefer for this dish (because they have a fresher flavor and texture than dried ones). I thaw them and smoke the peas just as I would smoke the dried variety. But you can also use any variety of dried beans, including butter beans, creamers, or flageolets. To add another layer of smoke, feel free to add bacon or lightly char the greens on the grill before adding them to the pot (this works particularly well with leafy kale).

Rinse the peas, discarding any pebbles, place them in a large pot, and add enough cold water to cover by 3 inches (7.5 cm). Add the bay leaves and bring the peas to a boil over medium-high heat, then turn the heat to low and simmer until the peas are just tender (but not mushy), about 25 minutes, skimming off any scum that rises to the surface. Drain the peas in a colander, discard the bay leaves, and let the peas cool.

In another large pot, warm the canola oil over medium heat. Add the onion and garlic and cook, stirring occasionally, until softened and fragrant, 4 to 5 minutes. Add the greens and use two wooden spoons to stir and toss until the greens are combined with the onion, garlic, and oil. Add the red pepper flakes, season lightly with salt and pepper, and cook, stirring frequently, until fragrant, about 2 to 3 minutes more. Add the wine and mustard, turn the heat to low, and simmer, stirring every now and then, until the greens are tender, 30 to 40 minutes.

Stir in the cooked peas, the vinegar, and the hot sauce. Bring the mixture to a simmer over medium-high heat, and then the lower the heat and simmer gently for 10 minutes to allow the flavors to meld. Serve in shallow bowls and pass the hot sauce. Refrigerate leftovers in a sealed container for up to 5 days.

SERVES 6 TO 8

2 cups (330 g) smoked black-eyed or field peas (dried or thawed frozen beans) or your favorite variety of dried peas (see page 90)

3 fresh bay leaves, torn

¼ cup (60 ml) canola oil

1 yellow onion, minced

3 cloves garlic, minced

2 pounds (900 g) greens (such as collards, mustard greens, or kale), stemmed and chopped

1 teaspoon Korean red pepper flakes (gochugaru), crumbled chile pequin, or red pepper flakes

Kosher salt and freshly ground black pepper

½ cup (120 ml) dry white wine

2 to 3 tablespoons Creole mustard or other spicy whole-grain mustard, as desired for heat

¼ cup (60 ml) apple cider vinegar

2 tablespoons hot sauce (such as Cholula)

SMOKED BEAN DIP
with Pickled Jalapeños

**MAKES ABOUT 4 CUPS;
SERVES 6 TO 8**

1 pound (450 g) smoked dried pinto beans (see page 90)

1 white onion, chopped

3 cloves garlic, thinly sliced

2 or 3 fresh bay leaves

1 turkey neck, 3 or 4 chicken necks, 3 slices thick-cut bacon, a ham hock, or 2 smoked chicken wings (optional)

1 large pickled jalapeño chile, stemmed and sliced, plus more for garnish

1 teaspoon jalapeño brine, plus more as desired

1 teaspoon hot sauce (such as Crystal), plus more as desired

1 teaspoon pure ground chile powder (such as New Mexico or ancho)

½ teaspoon ground cumin

¼ teaspoon onion powder

¼ teaspoon garlic powder

¼ teaspoon cayenne

Corn chips, for serving

Inspired by the canned variety sold by Frito-Lay (a guilty pleasure, I confess), this homemade version of an iconic Tex-Mex bean dip is way more delicious (without the dubious ingredients). I'd always soaked dried beans before cooking them until a couple friends (and accomplished bean cookers) convinced me to skip this step. Now I simply rinse beans and cook them on the stovetop at a very low simmer, the result is a deeper "bean" flavor and perfectly tender, creamy texture. Adding meat to the bean cooking liquid isn't essential here, but it creates a richer stock and the added fat creates a luscious texture. I like to simmer pintos with a fresh turkey neck, but you could also use chicken necks, bacon, a ham hock, or a smoked wing or two. Stock up on corn chips and cold beer regardless—even a vegetarian version of this dip will please a crowd with its smoky bean-and-briny-jalapeño essence. You won't need all the beans for this dip. Serve the brothy, smoky leftovers in flour tortillas or alongside crispy fried eggs.

Place the dried beans in a large pot and rinse them a couple times with cold water. Drain the beans in in a colander and then return them to the pot with the onion, garlic, bay leaves (to taste), and turkey neck in a large pot and add enough cold water to cover by 5 to 6 inches (13 to 15 cm). Bring the beans to a boil over medium-high heat, then turn the heat to low and simmer until the beans are creamy and tender, about 1 hour, skimming off any scum that rises to the surface. If time allows, let the beans cool in their broth (this slow cooling process creates an especially creamy texture). Drain the beans in a colander, reserving ¼ cup (60 ml) of the cooking liquid (discard any meat and bay leaves).

Ladle 3 cups (500 g) of the cooked beans and the ¼ cup (60 ml) reserved cooking liquid into a food processor. Add the jalapeño slices and brine, the hot sauce, chile powder, cumin, onion powder, garlic powder, and cayenne and blend until smooth, 3 to 4 minutes. Taste and adjust the seasonings, adding more jalapeño brine or hot sauce as desired. Serve the dip either warm or chilled—it's good either way—with the chips and beer.

SMOKED FRENCH LENTIL SALAD

SERVES 6 TO 8

1 pound (450 g) smoked French green or black beluga lentils (see page 90)

1 yellow onion, halved and stuck with 2 cloves (1 per half)

2 cloves garlic, lightly crushed and peeled

2 or 3 fresh bay leaves, torn

¼ cup (60 ml) red wine vinegar

¼ cup (60 ml) extra-virgin olive oil

Kosher salt and freshly ground black pepper

I've been making various versions of this perfectly simple salad since Patricia Wells's *Bistro Cooking* was published in 1989. Pay close attention to seasoning (add more salt and vinegar as needed) and use your very best olive oil to elevate this handful of ingredients into a truly crave-worthy meal. I typically serve this salad in the style of a Parisian crudités plate, with roasted beets, a grated carrot salad, and toasted bread slathered with goat cheese, an additional drizzle of oil, and a scattering of fresh herbs.

Rinse the lentils and discard any pebbles. Place the lentils, onion, garlic, and bay leaves (to taste) in a saucepan and add enough cold water to cover by 2 inches (5 cm). Cover the pan and bring the lentils to a boil over medium heat, then turn the heat to low and simmer until the lentils are tender, 25 to 35 minutes, skimming off any scum that rises to the surface. Remove the pan from the heat.

Discard the onion, garlic, and bay leaves and drain any excess liquid. Whisk the vinegar, oil, and a generous pinch of salt together in a small bowl. Pour the dressing over the warm lentils and toss to evenly coat.

Season with pepper and additional salt, as needed, and serve warm or at room temperature.

SMOKED YELLOW PEA SOUP
with Harissa Oil & Olives

I love the hearty, soothing texture of yellow split peas. For years, I foolishly relegated them to Swedish pea soup (cooked with ham and traditionally served on Thursdays), until I finally realized that their neutral flavor works well with just about anything you're craving. They're delicious teamed up with ginger, turmeric, coriander, curry, and coconut milk, for instance, but my current favorite is this Mediterranean-inspired combination punched up with olives and cilantro. For a richer, smokier soup, replace the water with Smoked Chicken Stock (page 161).

In a 4-quart (3.8 L) heavy pot, heat the oil over medium-high heat until it shimmers. Add the onions, carrot, celery, garlic, rosemary, red pepper flakes, and a pinch of salt and cook, stirring occasionally, until the vegetables have softened, about 5 minutes. Add the cumin, coriander, pepper, and bay leaves and stir to combine. Add the split peas, thyme sprigs, and water and bring the mixture to a boil. Turn the heat to low and simmer until the peas are tender and the soup has thickened, 30 to 35 minutes. Discard the bay leaves.

Use an immersion blender to puree a portion of the soup, leaving some texture (or use a regular blender to puree half of the soup), and stir in the lemon juice. Taste and adjust the seasonings, adding more salt and pepper as desired. (For a thinner consistency, add more water as desired.) Ladle the soup into bowls and garnish with a drizzle of Harissa Oil, a spoonful of chopped olives, and a sprinkling of cilantro.

Harissa Oil

A drizzle of this spicy, brick-red oil is delicious over bean soups or eggs poached in tomato sauce. To make it, place 2 to 3 tablespoons (as desired for heat and intensity) harissa spice blend or harissa paste (sold in tubes or a jar) in a small bowl and whisk in about twice the amount of extra-virgin olive oil (to create the intensity and consistency that you desire). Use a spoon to drizzle the oil over the soup, bean or grain salads, or grilled chicken. Store leftovers in a sealed container in the refrigerator for up to 2 weeks.

SERVES 6 TO 8

3 tablespoons extra-virgin olive oil, plus more for garnish

1½ yellow onions, chopped

1 large carrot, peeled and chopped

2 celery stalks, finely chopped

2 cloves garlic, crushed and thinly sliced

2 tablespoons finely chopped fresh rosemary

Pinch of crushed red pepper flakes or crumbled chile pequin

Kosher salt

2 teaspoons ground cumin

1 teaspoon ground coriander

½ teaspoon freshly ground black pepper, plus more as desired

2 fresh bay leaves

1 pound (450 g) smoked yellow split peas (see page 90)

2 sprigs thyme

6 cups (1.4 L) water, plus more as needed

Juice of ½ lemon, plus more as desired

Harissa Oil (recipe at left), for garnish

½ cup (70 g) pitted oil-cured black olives, chopped, for garnish

½ cup (25 g) chopped fresh cilantro (leaves and tender stems), for garnish

SMOKED BLACK BEANS FIVE WAYS

MAKES ABOUT 7 CUPS; SERVES 6 TO 8

1 pound (450 g) smoked dried black beans (see page 90)

2 white or yellow onions, chopped

4 cloves garlic, peeled and crushed

2 fresh bay leaves, torn

Kosher salt and freshly ground black pepper

1 to 2 teaspoons red wine vinegar (as desired for acidity), for seasoning

I've been following this basic method for cooking black beans since I moved to Chicago just after college (where I spent *a lot* of time sending out resumes and exploring neighborhood Mexican markets). The short list of ingredients allows the satisfying, earthy flavor of the smoked back beans to shine. And while I could eat these beans several nights a week, it's also fun to mix up the supporting players with ingredients like chorizo, roasted peppers, juicy ripe tomatoes, or thick Mexican crema. Once they're simmered, you can serve the brothy whole beans with their cooking liquid; drained and tossed with grains, vegetables, and herbs; or pureed into a creamy, smoky base for tostadas or breakfast tacos. Whether you keep them simple or embrace one of the following variations (I hope you'll try them all), you'll end up with a fragrant pot of beans that will provide sustenance throughout the week.

Rinse the beans and discard any pebbles. Place the beans, onions, garlic, and bay leaves in a large pot and add enough cold water to cover by 4 inches (10 cm). Bring the beans to a boil over medium-high heat, then turn the heat to low and simmer gently until the beans are very tender, about 2 hours, skimming off any scum that rises to the surface. If time allows, let the beans cool in their broth. Otherwise discard the bay leaves, taste and adjust the seasonings, adding salt, pepper, and vinegar to taste, and serve as desired.

VARIATIONS

Green Chiles con Crema: Puree 2 cups (330 g) of the cooked beans (and their cooking liquid) with 2 roasted poblano chiles (stemmed, seeded, and peeled) and 2 charred jalapeño or serrano chiles (stemmed and seeded). Serve the beans topped with a drizzle of Mexican crema and grated Cotija cheese.

Pancho Fresca: Use an immersion blender or food processor to process 3 cups (500 g) of the cooked beans (and their cooking liquid) with 3 ripe chopped Roma tomatoes (and their juice), 1 bunch cilantro (leaves and tender stems), 1 white or yellow onion (chopped), and 1 serrano chile (stemmed, seeded, and chopped) until combined but not completely smooth. Return the mixture to the pot, add 1 tablespoon sherry vinegar, and stir to combine. Serve the warm beans as a taco filling or over steamed long-grain rice or quinoa.

Sunday Beans with Chorizo: Cook the beans as directed above. While the beans are simmering, sauté 8 ounces (225 g) Mexican chorizo and ½ chopped red onion over medium-high heat until browned, 6 to 7 minutes. Add the chorizo and 2 tablespoons chopped fresh oregano to the beans during the last 30 minutes of cooking. Taste and adjust the seasonings as desired, and then serve the beans in flour tortillas, topped with fried eggs, or alongside huevos rancheros.

Nuevo Laredo: Before cooking the beans, in a large pot, sauté the onions and garlic with 4 ounces (115 g) diced Cowgirl Bacon (page 182) until the bacon is browned but still juicy, 5 to 6 minutes. Add the beans, bay leaves, 1 large carrot (peeled and halved), 2 chipotle chiles in adobo (chopped), and enough cold water to cover by 4 inches (10 cm), then cook as directed. Serve the beans with a dollop of Mexican crema and a sprinkling of chopped fresh marjoram or oregano.

Recommended by Enrique: Before cooking the beans, sauté the onions and garlic with 1 green bell pepper (seeded and chopped) and 1 red bell pepper (seeded and chopped) until the vegetables have softened, 5 to 7 minutes. Stir in a heaping tablespoon of tomato paste, 2 teaspoons ground cumin, and 1 teaspoon freshly ground black pepper and cook, stirring frequently, for 1 minute. Add ¼ cup (60 ml) dry white wine or beer and cook until the liquid is reduced by half, 5 to 6 minutes. Add the beans and enough cold water to cover the beans by 4 inches (10 cm), then cook as directed. Serve with steamed rice or alongside crispy grilled pork chops.

SMOKY LENTIL TACOS
with Red Cabbage Slaw

SERVES 4 TO 6

1 pound (450 g) smoked brown lentils (see page 90)

2 fresh bay leaves, torn

1 teaspoon red wine or apple cider vinegar

1 tablespoon pure ground chile powder (such as New Mexico or ancho)

2 teaspoons ground cumin

1 teaspoon ground coriander

½ teaspoon dried Mexican oregano

Kosher salt

2 tablespoons extra-virgin olive oil

1 white or yellow onion, finely chopped

2 cloves garlic, minced

Freshly ground black pepper

3 tablespoons tomato paste

¼ cup (60 ml) hot sauce (such as Cholula), plus more as needed

Red Cabbage Slaw

½ head red cabbage, cored and very thinly sliced (about 4 cups/280 g)

Freshly squeezed juice of 1 lime, plus more as needed

½ cup (110 g) mayonnaise (preferably Duke's), plus more as needed

½ cup (10 g) chopped fresh cilantro (leaves and stems)

Corn tortillas, for serving

Sliced avocados, for serving

Grated Cotija cheese, for serving

My friend Amy Brotman is a vegetarian and the kind of very organized cook (with a freezer brimming with labeled jars of beans, soups, and sauces) that I aspire to be. When she pulled out "lentil taco meat" for an impromptu weeknight dinner, I knew I'd need the recipe. The seasonings and tomato paste create saucy, satisfying lentils with a convincingly "meaty" flavor and texture that would be welcome at any taco night. This filling is especially good with brown Spanish pardina lentils (available in bulk or online) and the most flavorful corn tortillas you can find.

Rinse the lentils and place them in a saucepan with the bay leaves, vinegar, and enough cold water to cover by 3 inches (7.5 cm). Bring to a boil over medium-high heat, then turn the heat to medium-low and simmer until the lentils are just tender, 23 to 25 minutes. Discard the bay leaves and drain the lentils in a colander. Set aside to cool.

In a small bowl, combine the chile powder, cumin, coriander, oregano, and ½ teaspoon salt and set aside.

In a large, deep skillet, heat the olive oil over medium-high heat. Add the onion, garlic, several grinds of pepper, and a pinch of salt and cook, stirring occasionally, until the mixture is fragrant and the onion is lightly browned, 4 to 5 minutes. Stir in the spices and cook for 1 to 2 minutes more, until the onion is well coated with the seasonings.

Add the lentils, tomato paste, 2 tablespoons hot sauce, and a splash of water and lower the heat to medium. Cook the lentils, stirring frequently, until they begin to thicken and meld with the tomato sauce, about 5 minutes (add additional water if the mixture becomes too dry). When the lentils begin to hold together, use a fork to mash a portion of them into a "meaty" texture. Taste and adjust the seasonings, adding additional salt or hot sauce as desired. Turn off the heat and cover the skillet while you prepare the slaw.

To make the slaw, place the cabbage in a bowl, add the lime juice and a generous pinch of salt, and toss to combine. Add the mayonnaise, the remaining 2 tablespoons hot sauce, and cilantro and toss, adding more mayo as desired for a creamy consistency. Taste and add additional salt, pepper, lime juice, or hot sauce as desired.

Serve the warm lentils in the tortillas topped with the slaw, avocado slices, and a sprinkling of cheese. Store any leftover lentils in a sealed container in the refrigerator for up to 1 week (or freeze them, as Amy does, for up to 3 months).

SMOKED CHICKPEA SALAD
with Pickled Cauliflower

1 pound (450 g) smoked dried chickpeas (see page 90)

½ cup (120 ml) extra-virgin olive oil

¼ cup (60 ml) red wine vinegar, plus more as needed

2 shallots, or 1 bunch green onions, white and light green parts, thinly sliced

Kosher salt and freshly ground black pepper

1 cup Lunchette Pickled Cauliflower (recipe follows)

1 seedless cucumber, peeled and chopped

¼ cup (10 g) chopped fresh dill

¼ cup (10 g) chopped fresh flat-leaf parsley

The earthy flavor of smoked chickpeas pairs especially well with bright, vivid flavors like those of pickled vegetables, cucumber, and fresh dill. This beautiful cauliflower pickle recipe comes from my friends Naomi and Joel Crawford, owners of Pizza Politana and Lunchette in Petaluma, California. The pickle recipe makes four quart jars that you'll be happy to have on hand for snacking and future meals, but you can cut it in half if you prefer.

Rinse the chickpeas and discard any pebbles. Place the chickpeas in a large pot and add enough water to cover with cold water by 4 inches (10 cm). Bring the chickpeas to a boil over medium-high heat, then turn the heat to low and simmer until the chickpeas are tender, about 45 minutes, skimming off any scum that rises to the surface. Drain the chickpeas in a colander and transfer them to a large mixing bowl. Add the olive oil, vinegar, and shallots, season with salt and pepper, and toss to combine.

Set the chickpeas aside to cool for about 10 minutes, then add the Pickled Cauliflower, cucumber, dill, and parsley and toss to combine. Taste and adjust the seasonings, adding more salt, pepper, or vinegar as desired. Serve immediately, or store in a sealed container in the refrigerator for up to 5 days.

2 or 3 heads cauliflower, cored and cut into florets

Kosher salt

4 cups (950 ml) white wine vinegar

¾ cup plus 2 tablespoons (175 g) sugar

1½ tablespoons Madras curry powder

1 tablespoon ground turmeric

4 pods green cardamom

4 bay leaves

4 teaspoons red pepper flakes, or 2 dried arbol chiles

Lunchette Pickled Cauliflower

In a large bowl, toss the cauliflower with a generous amount of salt (I use about 3 tablespoons) and let it sit for at least 30 minutes, or up to 1 hour. Rinse and drain the florets.

In a pot, combine the vinegar, 2 cups (475 ml) water, sugar, 2 tablespoons plus ½ teaspoons salt, curry powder, and turmeric and bring to a boil over high heat. Once the brine starts to boil, immediately turn off the heat.

Fill each of four 1-quart jars with cauliflower, then add 1 teaspoon cardamom, 1 bay leaf, and 1 teaspoon red pepper flakes (packing the vegetables tightly). Carefully divide the brine among the jars. Let the mixture cool 15 to 20 minutes, then seal with a tight-fitting lid. Let the jars stand at room temperature for 2 to 3 days before using, flipping and gently agitating each jar two times per day to distribute the spices (the longer the flavors have to develop, the deeper they will be). After that, store the sealed jars in the refrigerator for up to 6 months. Once opened, they'll keep in the refrigerator for up to 4 months.

SMOKED CHICKPEAS
with Spinach & Saffron Yogurt

Smoked Chickpeas

1 pound (450 g) smoked dried chickpeas (see page 90)

1½ teaspoons baking soda

Kosher salt and freshly ground black pepper

Saffron Yogurt

1 tablespoon hot water

A generous pinch of saffron (about ¾ teaspoon)

1 cup (245 g) full-fat Greek yogurt

Finely grated zest of 1 large lemon (preferably organic)

Kosher salt

½ cup (120 ml) olive oil, plus more for serving

2 large bunches spinach (about 2½ pounds/1.1 kg), stemmed and washed

1 large slab artisan bread, cut into 1-inch (2.5 cm) cubes

3 cloves garlic, thinly sliced

3 tablespoons fresh oregano, lightly chopped

1 teaspoon Spanish smoked paprika

1 small dried red chile (such as arbol), crumbled

½ cup (120 g) tomato sauce, or 2 tablespoons tomato paste

1½ tablespoons good-quality red wine vinegar

Grilled bread, for serving

In cooler seasons, I love preparing deep green spinach from Oak Hill Farms in Poteet, Texas. It's the best spinach available all year, so I incorporate it in my family's meals as often as possible. This braise, thickened with a bread sauce, is Spanish comfort food. Don't use baby spinach leaves in this recipe; you want to use flavorful bunches of the kind you have to clean yourself, preferably from a local grower. This is a flexible dish, so if you have a little less spinach or want to include a pinch of this or that, feel free. The smoked chickpeas retain their subtle flavor after they're simmered (and a garnish of Spanish smoked paprika echoes the sultry flavor). Serve the warm chickpeas in shallow bowls, topped with a dollop of saffron yogurt and grilled slices of bread (rubbed with a cut clove of garlic, drizzled with olive oil, and sprinkled with flaky salt).

Rinse the chickpeas and discard any pebbles. Place the chickpeas and baking soda in a large heavy saucepan and add enough cold water to cover by 4 inches (10 cm). Bring the chickpeas to a boil over medium-high heat, then turn the heat to low and simmer until the chickpeas are tender, 1½ to 2 hours, skimming off any scum that rises to the surface. Remove the pan from the heat and use a ladle to remove water until it's level with the chickpeas. Season with salt and pepper and set aside.

In the meantime, to make the saffron yogurt, combine the hot water and saffron in a small bowl and allow it to steep for a few minutes. Place the yogurt and lemon zest in a bowl and stir in the saffron and a sprinkling of salt. Cover and store in the refrigerator until ready to serve.

In a large saucepan, heat ¼ cup (60 ml) of the olive oil over medium heat. Add the spinach (in batches if necessary) and a large pinch of salt and cook, stirring occasionally, until just wilted, 4 to 5 minutes. Use tongs to transfer the leaves to a colander to drain.

Add the remaining ¼ cup (60 ml) oil to the saucepan and heat over medium heat. Add the bread cubes and toast, turning often, until golden all over, about 4 minutes. Add the garlic, oregano, paprika, and chile and cook for 1 minute, until the garlic is golden brown and has a nutty aroma. Transfer the bread mixture to a food processor, and pulse into a coarse paste.

Return the chickpeas to medium heat and stir in the bread mixture and the tomato sauce and vinegar. Cook, stirring occasionally, until the chickpeas are hot and have absorbed the flavors of the bread, 3 to 4 minutes. Season generously with salt and pepper. If the consistency is a little thick, add some water. Stir in the spinach and cook until heated through, about 2 minutes.

Ladle the chickpeas into shallow bowls and top with a dollop of saffron yogurt. Serve with grilled bread on the side. Refrigerate any leftover yogurt and chickpeas in separate sealed containers for up to 5 days.

SMOKED CANNELLINI BEANS
with Tuna

SERVES 6 TO 8

Beans

1 pound (450 g) smoked dried Marcella or cannellini beans (see page 90)

2 sprigs sage

3 or 4 fresh bay leaves

4 cloves garlic, peeled and crushed

1 Parmesan rind

Salt and freshly ground black pepper

Green Herb Oil

1 clove garlic, lightly crushed and peeled

½ teaspoon kosher salt

½ teaspoon red pepper flakes or crumbled chile pequin

2 cups (80 g) combination of chopped fresh basil, thyme, oregano, dill, or flat-leaf parsley

½ cup (120 ml) extra-virgin olive oil

Tuna

Two 5-ounce (140 g) cans high-quality tuna packed in olive oil, drained

1 shallot, thinly sliced

Finely grated zest and juice of 1 large lemon

Kosher salt and freshly ground black pepper

Grilled bread, for serving

Lemon wedges, for serving

The time-honored Italian pairing of white beans and tuna is a perennial favorite at our house. You can use any cannellini or white beans for this dish, but my favorite variety is the Marcella beans that I order online from Rancho Gordo, an heirloom bean grower in California. I toss the warm beans with a green herb oil and top them with the best-quality tuna packed in olive oil. You can also serve the beans with grilled tuna or another fish steak, shaved bottarga, or simmer them with an entire head of escarole (trimmed and chopped) added during the last 30 minutes of cooking.

I can't resist adding a Parmesan rind to any pot of white beans. I love how the cheese imparts a rich flavor. Even though you drain the beans for this recipe, save the flavorful cooking liquid and freeze it to make white bean soup or minestrone.

To prepare the beans, rinse the beans and discard any pebbles. Place the beans, sage, bay leaves (to taste), garlic, and Parmesan rind in a large saucepan and add enough cold water to cover by 4 inches (10 cm). Bring the beans to a boil over medium-high heat, then turn the heat to low and simmer very gently until the beans are tender, about 1 hour 15 minutes, skimming off any scum that rises to the surface. Remove the pan from the heat, and if time allows, let the beans cool in the cooking liquid.

Meanwhile, to make the green herb oil, combine the garlic, salt, and pepper flakes in the bowl of a food processor and pulse into a coarse paste. Add the herbs and pulse until combined. With the processor running, slowly drizzle in the olive oil until the mixture pulls together into an even puree, stopping to scrape down the sides of the bowl with a rubber spatula as needed.

Drain the beans in a colander and transfer to a large mixing bowl, discarding the sage, bay leaves, garlic, and Parmesan rind. Pour the green herb oil over the top and gently toss the mixture until combined. Season with salt and pepper, then transfer to a large serving platter.

In the same mixing bowl, combine the tuna, shallot, and lemon zest and juice and use a fork to gently combine (leaving the tuna in larger chunks, if possible). Season the tuna mixture with salt and pepper, then use a rubber spatula to place the mixture on the top of the beans. Serve immediately, with grilled bread and lemon wedges on the side. Store leftovers in a sealed container in the refrigerator for up to 4 days.

CHAPTER SIX ─────────────────

TOFU, VEGETABLES & LEAFY GREENS

This chapter harnesses the seductive possibilities of grilling with the influence of wood smoke to create outside-of-the-box meals that are easy enough to pull together on a weeknight. The thinking here is to infuse a starring vegetable (e.g., stunning farmers' market carrots, lacinato kale, ripe tomatoes, wild mushrooms) with wood smoke and then partner them with supporting players that round out the meal. The smoke-infused lead carries so much flavor that you typically don't need more than a few other ingredients (say a dressing, a tangle of noodles, a squeeze of citrus) to create an elevated version of a familiar dish. For instance, grill-smoked greens create a stellar slab pie, smoked carrots reinvent hummus, and smoked potatoes take a picnic staple to a new zip code.

GRILLED TOFU NOODLE SALAD

SERVES 4 TO 6

2 tablespoons toasted
sesame oil

2 tablespoons extra-virgin
olive oil

Two 12-ounce (340 g)
packages firm or extra-firm
tofu, cut crosswise into
6 equal slices

1 teaspoon Spicy Curry Salt
(page 26)

Finely grated zest of 1 lime

¼ cup (60 ml) freshly
squeezed lime juice

3 tablespoons seasoned
rice vinegar

2 tablespoons tamari

1 to 2 tablespoons sambal
oelek, as desired for heat

2 teaspoons honey

1 teaspoon finely grated
fresh ginger

1 clove garlic,
peeled and minced

Kosher salt

8 ounces (225 g) fresh udon
noodles, or 4 ounces (115 g)
dried udon or soba noodles

4 cups (600 g) assorted
vegetable pieces (such
as blanched broccoli
florets, carrot ribbons or
matchsticks, thinly sliced napa
or red cabbage, or sliced bell
peppers)

3 green onions, white and
light green parts, thinly sliced

⅓ cup (15 g) chopped fresh
cilantro (leaves and tender
stems)

If you're like me, Monday is a clean slate (the first day of the rest of your life . . .) that I like to kick off on a virtuous note. More often than not, that means a tangle of noodles paired with a heap of vegetables, fresh herbs, and spicy, spunky condiments. Enter this salad: You can cube the tofu if you prefer, but I like larger rectangles for grilling, because they're easier to wrangle and fun to eat. The tofu can be grilled a day or two in advance (something that's easy to do with the lingering heat from another dinner). You'll only need about half of the tofu for this salad, but I always grill extra so I have leftovers to make a grain or rice bowl or a salad more substantial in a flash.

Prepare a charcoal grill for two-zone cooking and build a medium-high fire, or heat a gas grill to high.

When the coals are glowing red and covered with a fine gray ash, use tongs to remove the cooking grate and place a drip pan with 1 inch (2.5 cm) of warm water on the side with no coals, then add your smoke source (chips, chunks, or log). Return the cooking grate to its position, allow it to preheat, and then carefully wipe the preheated grill grates with a lightly oiled paper towel. Using a grill brush, scrape the grill grates clean, then carefully wipe with a lightly oiled towel again.

In a small bowl, combine the sesame and olive oils. Using a brush or your fingers, coat the tofu with oil and sprinkle with the Spicy Curry Salt. When the fire begins to produce a steady stream of smoke, place the tofu slices over direct heat, close the grill, vent the grill for smoking, and cook for about 2 minutes, until nice char marks appear. Use a large spatula (and a firm, decisive thrust) to flip the tofu over, brush it with more of the oil mixture, close the lid, and cook for 2 minutes more, until lightly charred. Transfer the grilled tofu to a plate and set aside (reserve the oil mixture).

Bring a large pot of generously salted water to a boil over high heat.

Meanwhile, in a large bowl, whisk together the lime zest and juice, rice vinegar, tamari, 1 tablespoon of the sambal oelek, the honey, ginger, and garlic to make a dressing for the salad. Taste the dressing and add salt or additional sambal oelek as desired.

continued

⅓ cup (15 g) fresh Thai basil leaves, thinly sliced or torn

½ cup (55 g) Curry-Chile Peanuts (page 73) or other nut

1 tablespoon smoked sesame seeds (see page 72)

Add the noodles to the boiling water and cook according to the package instructions. Drain the noodles in a colander, rinse with cold water, and set aside to drain again for a few minutes.

Place the noodles, assorted vegetables, green onions, cilantro, basil, Curry-Chile Peanuts, and dressing in a large bowl and toss until well combined. Divide the salad among bowls (or serve it family-style on a large platter) and top with slices of the grilled tofu and a sprinkling of smoked sesame seeds.

SWISS CHARD SLAB PIE
with Smoked Peppercorn Crust

When I cooked in the South of France, I rarely returned from the market without armfuls of Swiss chard. I learned to cook chard the French way, incorporating both the crisp, tasty stems (they have a celery-like texture) and the tender leaves. I've remained a devoted chard fan, so when I happened on this packed-with-greens recipe from Kristin Donnelly's book *Modern Potluck,* it became an instant staple in my repertoire. In this version, the buttery crust is perfumed with the aroma of smoked black peppercorns, and the filling gets a Nicoise treatment with currants and pine nuts. I've toted this pie on camping trips, taken it to potlucks, and made it for weeknight dinners—happily anticipating the leftovers that are good hot or cold, anytime of day. Sprinkling the pie with flaky salt before baking gives it a delightful salty edge.

To make the dough, place the flour, salt, and ground peppercorns in a food processor and pulse to combine. Add the butter and pulse until the mixture is coarse, with some large pieces of butter remaining. Sprinkle the ice water on top and pulse just until the dough comes together. Transfer the dough to a work surface lightly dusted with flour, divide the dough in half, and pat each half into a 6-inch (15 cm) square. Wrap the squares in plastic wrap and refrigerate for about an hour.

Meanwhile, to make the filling, carefully wash the chard leaves and stems to remove any traces of grit, and then dry thoroughly. Use a knife to separate the chard stems from the leaves. Finely chop the stems and coarsely chop (or tear) the leaves. In a large Dutch oven or heavy pot, heat the olive oil over medium-high heat. Add the onion, garlic, red pepper flakes, and a pinch of salt and cook, stirring occasionally, until the onion is just softened, about 5 minutes. Stir in the coriander, ginger, and chard stems and cook, stirring occasionally, until just softened, about 6 minutes. Stir in the wine and currants and continue to cook until the liquid is reduced by half, about 8 minutes. Add the chard leaves in large handfuls, letting them wilt before adding more, and then cook until the greens are tender and the liquid has evaporated, about 5 minutes. Transfer the chard mixture to a colander to drain and cool completely. When the mixture is cool, place it in a large mixing bowl and add the pine nuts and sour cream. Season with salt and pepper to taste, then use a rubber spatula to gently combine.

continued

SERVES 8 TO 10

Dough

3 cups (375 g) all-purpose flour, plus more for dusting

1 teaspoon kosher salt

1 teaspoon smoked black peppercorns (see page 18), coarsely ground

1¼ cups (285 g) cold unsalted butter, cut into cubes

⅔ cup (160 ml) ice water

Filling

3 pounds (1.4 kg) red Swiss chard (see Tip)

½ cup (120 ml) extra-virgin olive oil

1 large red onion, finely chopped

4 cloves garlic, thinly sliced

Generous pinch of red pepper flakes

Kosher salt

1 tablespoon ground coriander

1 tablespoon ground ginger

½ cup (120 ml) dry white wine

3 tablespoons currants

3 tablespoons smoked pine nuts (see page 72)

¾ cup (180 g) sour cream or full-fat Greek yogurt

Freshly ground black pepper

1 egg beaten with 1 tablespoon water, for egg wash

Flaky salt, for garnish

Preheat the oven to 400°F (200°C) and line a large rimmed baking sheet with parchment paper. On a lightly floured work surface, roll out one piece of dough to a 12 by 16-inch (30 by 40 cm) rectangle. Use a bench scraper and a rolling pin to transfer the dough to the prepared baking sheet. Spread the chard filling over the dough evenly, leaving a 1-inch (2.5 cm) border around the edges. Roll out the remaining dough to the same size and drape it over the filling. Fold the rim over itself and pinch the edges to seal. Cut a few slits in the top of the pie with a sharp knife, brush the top and edges with the egg wash, and sprinkle with flaky salt.

Bake the pie for 50 to 55 minutes, until the crust is golden and cooked through. Let the pie cool for at least 15 minutes before cutting, and then serve it warm or at room temperature. Wrap any leftovers in foil and refrigerate for up to 4 days.

SMOKED ONION & CHEDDAR TART

SERVES 6 TO 8

Cornmeal Crust

2½ cups (315 g) all-purpose flour, plus more as needed

¾ cup (95 g) finely ground yellow cornmeal

2 teaspoons sugar

1½ teaspoons kosher salt

1½ teaspoons chopped fresh rosemary

1 cup (225 g) cold unsalted butter, cut into small pieces

⅓ cup (80 g) Mexican crema or sour cream

¼ cup (60 ml) ice water, plus more as needed

Smoked Onions

3 large sweet yellow onions (about 2½ pounds/1.1 kg), thinly sliced

2 sprigs rosemary or thyme

2 or 3 fresh bay leaves

Extra-virgin olive oil, for drizzling

Kosher salt and freshly ground black pepper

Sweet, smoky onions combined with a kick of red chile, rich English Cheddar, and a hearty cornmeal crust create a rustic, savory one-crust pie that you can serve as an appetizer, for dinner (with a frisée salad), or on the brunch table (it's delicious with Champagne). To make the assembly easier, make the crust and smoke the onions up to two days in advance. When those elements are in place, the tart comes together quickly.

To make the cornmeal crust, place the flour, cornmeal, sugar, salt, and rosemary in the bowl of a food processor and pulse to combine. Add the butter and pulse until the mixture is coarse and pebbly. Add the crema and ice water and pulse until just combined. Transfer the dough to a lightly floured surface and lightly knead it into a ball (the dough should be soft and pliable but not sticky). Divide the dough in half, wrap each piece in plastic wrap, and refrigerate for at least 30 minutes or up to 2 days. (You only use one half of the dough for this tart, so double-wrap the second half in plastic and freeze for up to 2 months.)

Prepare a charcoal grill for two-zone cooking and build a medium-high fire, or heat a gas grill to high.

When the coals are glowing red and covered with a fine gray ash, use tongs to remove the cooking grate and place a drip pan with 1 inch (2.5 cm) of warm water on the side with no coals, then add your smoke source (chips, chunks, or log). Return the cooking grate to its position, allow it to preheat, and then carefully wipe the preheated grill grates with a lightly oiled paper towel. Using a grill brush, scrape the grill grates clean, then carefully wipe with a lightly oiled towel again.

To smoke the onions, place the onions, herbs, and bay leaves in a disposable aluminum pan (large enough to hold the onions and about 1½ inches/4 cm deep). Drizzle with enough olive oil to lightly coat, season with salt and pepper, and toss to combine. When the fire begins to produce a steady stream of smoke, place the onions over indirect heat, close the grill, vent the grill for smoking, and smoke for 20 to 25 minutes, until the onions are fragrant and have darkened a shade or two (if some edges have crisped and browned, that's good). Remove the onions from the heat, discard the herb sprigs and bay leaves, and set aside to cool. At this point, you can prepare the tart or refrigerate the onions in a sealed container for up to 2 days.

Preheat the oven to 400°F (200°C) and line a rimmed baking sheet with parchment paper.

In a large skillet, heat the olive oil over medium-high heat on the stovetop. Add the smoked onion mixture, the rosemary, red pepper flakes, and pepper and cook, stirring occasionally, until the onions are very soft and golden, about 10 minutes. Add the wine and continue to cook, stirring every now and then, until the onions are deeply golden and have a soft, melty consistency, about 10 minutes. Remove the pan from the heat and season generously with pepper and more salt, as desired. Transfer the onions to a mixing bowl to cool (or place the bowl in the refrigerator or freezer for a few minutes to speed up the process).

In a small bowl, use a fork to lightly beat the eggs. Stir the eggs into the cooled onion mixture.

To assemble the tart, lightly flour a work surface and roll out one dough half into a ¼-inch (6 mm)-thick rustic round or rectangle (it doesn't need to be perfectly shaped). Use a bench scraper and rolling pin to help lift the dough and transfer it to the prepared baking sheet.

Using a rubber spatula, spread the onion mixture over the dough, leaving a 1-inch (2.5 cm) border around the edges. Top the onions with the cheese. Fold the crust up and over the onion filling, crimping the dough as you go to seal any cracks. Bake until the crust is golden brown and the filling has set, 35 to 40 minutes. Cool on the baking sheet for 5 minutes, then transfer the tart to a wire rack to cool for 15 minutes, or until completely cool. Serve the tart warm or at room temperature, sliced into wedges or squares. Wrap leftovers in aluminum foil and refrigerate for up to 4 days.

1 tablespoon extra-virgin olive oil

1 tablespoon crumbled smoked rosemary (see page 18), or chopped fresh rosemary

½ teaspoon red pepper flakes or crumbled chile pequin

Freshly ground black pepper

⅓ cup (80 ml) dry white wine

2 eggs

8 ounces (225 g) English Cheddar cheese, grated

SMOKY RANCH DIP
with Charred Kale

**MAKES ABOUT 3 CUPS
(660 G)**

1 bunch lacinato kale (about
10 ounces/280 g)

½ teaspoon kosher salt,
plus more as needed

1 cup (240 g) full-fat
Greek yogurt

1 cup (240 g) mayonnaise

¼ cup (60 ml) buttermilk,
plus more as needed

¼ cup (10 g) finely
chopped chives

1 tablespoon Creole mustard
or other spicy whole-grain
mustard

1½ teaspoons fish sauce

1 teaspoon Worcestershire
sauce

1 teaspoon white wine vinegar
or apple cider vinegar

1 teaspoon hot sauce (such as
Cholula), plus more as needed

½ teaspoon garlic powder

½ teaspoon onion powder

½ teaspoon freshly ground
black pepper, plus more
as needed

One of my favorite pastimes is teaching gardening classes at my children's school. Every now and then, I secretly enlist the kiddos to be taste testers. I considered it a major victory that a class of third graders enthusiastically scarfed up this luscious dip (with baby carrots and pita chips), even after I told them it was made with lacinato kale from their garden. Aside from being a great way to get kids their greens, this dip is delicious with crudités (such as wedges of radicchio, watermelon radishes, celery, and carrots), hard-cooked eggs, and grilled meat kebabs. The kale I buy at my local market is very clean, so I don't wash it because moisture inhibits the process (if you must wash it, dry the leaves carefully before grilling). The kale won't char evenly on the grill, and that's fine—you want a mix of doneness that ranges from blackened and crackly bits to deep green and tender. I use chives here, but feel free to use other "ranch-style" herbs like dill, tarragon, or parsley.

Prepare a charcoal grill for two-zone cooking and build a medium fire, or heat a gas grill to medium-high.

Carefully wipe the preheated grill grates with a lightly oiled paper towel. Using a grill brush, scrape the grill grates clean, then carefully wipe with a lightly oiled towel again.

Working in batches, place the kale leaves perpendicular to the grates so they won't fall through and cook over direct heat until lightly charred, 1 to 2 minutes on each side. Transfer the kale to a cutting board to cool slightly. Use a knife to trim the thick ribs from each leaf (discard ribs), then coarsely chop the leaves.

Place the kale and salt in the bowl of a food processor and process into a coarse puree. Add the yogurt, mayonnaise, buttermilk, chives, mustard, fish sauce, Worcestershire, vinegar, hot sauce, garlic powder, onion powder, and pepper and process until the ingredients are combined and mostly smooth (the kale should still have a bit of texture to it). Taste and adjust the seasonings, adding more salt, pepper, or hot sauce as desired. For a thinner consistency, add more buttermilk as needed. Serve immediately or refrigerate in a sealed container for up to 3 days.

SMOKED CARROT HUMMUS

After my friend Amy made a version of this recipe—a riff on hummus that relies more on carrots than chickpeas—I couldn't quit dreaming about it. When fresh, locally grown carrots are available (like the ones I get from Johnson's Backyard Garden, one of Austin's urban farms), this creamy puree is a slather of springtime. Deepened with a whiff of wood fire, this version is delicious as a base for an open-faced sandwich on multigrain or rye toast (topped with slices of egg and sprouts), as a snack with seedy crackers or pita chips, or scooped up with crispy vegetables like fennel, celery, lettuce wedges, and cauliflower.

Bring a large pot of generously salted water to a boil over high heat. Add the carrots, turn the heat to medium-high, and cook until *just* tender, about 6 minutes (depending on the size of your carrots, when in doubt use a paring knife to gauge doneness). Drain the carrots in a colander and set aside to cool briefly.

Prepare a charcoal grill for two-zone cooking and build a medium fire, or heat a gas grill to medium-high.

When the coals are glowing red and covered with a fine gray ash, use tongs to remove the cooking grate and place a drip pan with 1 inch (2.5 cm) of warm water on the side with no coals, and add your smoke source (chips, chunks, or log). Return the cooking grate to its position, allow it to preheat, and then carefully wipe the preheated grill grates with a lightly oiled paper towel. Using a grill brush, scrape the grill grates clean, then carefully wipe with a lightly oiled towel again.

When the fire begins to produce a steady stream of smoke, place the carrots over direct heat and cook (flipping and rotating around the heat as necessary for even cooking) until they're nicely charred on both sides, 5 to 6 minutes total. Remove the carrots from the heat and set aside to cool briefly.

Place the carrots, chickpeas, olive oil, tahini, lemon zest and juice, cumin, paprika, and hot sauce in the bowl of a food processor and process until smooth and creamy, 3 to 4 minutes. Use a rubber spatula to transfer the hummus to a bowl and serve immediately. Store leftovers in a sealed container in the refrigerator for up to 3 days.

MAKES ABOUT 3 CUPS (660 GRAMS)

9 ounces (255 g) carrots (about 5 carrots), peeled and halved

One 15-ounce (430 g) can chickpeas, drained and rinsed

¾ cup (175 ml) extra-virgin olive oil

3½ tablespoons tahini

Finely grated zest and juice of 1 lemon, plus more juice as desired

1 teaspoon ground cumin

½ teaspoon Spanish smoked paprika

Several dashes of hot sauce (such as Cholula)

SMOKED BEET BORSCHT
with Rye Croutons

SERVES 6 TO 8

1 pound (450 g) beets

2 tablespoons extra-virgin olive oil, plus more for drizzling

2 tablespoons unsalted butter

1 large yellow onion, thinly sliced

Kosher salt

1 tablespoon pomegranate molasses or light brown sugar

2 carrots, peeled and chopped

2 celery stalks, chopped

2 cloves garlic, thinly sliced

2 tablespoons lightly chopped fresh oregano

Freshly ground black pepper

6 cups (1.4 L) water

Once you fall, truly and deeply, for grilling, it's really hard to walk away from a beautiful fire that's capable of cooking something. That's why my favorite way to "smoke" beets is to coal-roast them in a bed of glowing embers. The method is a smart way to make the most of the heat (and your efforts) after you've grilled something else. Dense vegetables like beets, winter squash, and onions don't need a lot of attention, just turn them every 15 minutes so they cook through evenly. (I set the timer on my phone to remind myself.) Once the beets are smoked, you can refrigerate them in a foil packet (complete with their ashy coating), or use your hands to peel the blackened skin from the beets before you store them in the refrigerator for up to five days. The alluring undercurrent of smoke that you've created and the beet's earthy sweetness create a stunning borscht brimming with flavor. You don't have to use all the garnishes here, but the combination of crunchy rye croutons, a swirl of dill cream, celery leaves, and a drizzle of spicy Harissa Oil (you can also use Aleppo pepper moistened with oil) make for a beautiful presentation.

To coal-roast the beets, prepare a charcoal grill for two-zone cooking and build a medium fire, or heat a gas grill to medium-high. When the coals are glowing red and covered with a fine gray ash, add your smoke source (chips, chunks, or log).

When the fire begins to produce a steady stream of smoke, nestle the beets into the embers, close the grill, vent the grill for smoking, and smoke, turning every 15 minutes or so, until they're just tender when pierced with a knife, 45 to 50 minutes. Remove the beets from the heat and allow them to cool (at which point, you can wrap them aluminum foil and refrigerate them for up to 5 days). Using your hands, peel the blackened skin from the beets; use a knife or paper towel to remove any blackened bits but do not rinse. Dice the beets and set aside.

Heat the oil and butter in a Dutch oven over medium-high heat on the stovetop. Add the onion and a pinch of salt, followed by the pomegranate molasses, and cook, stirring frequently, until the onions have softened, about 8 minutes (add a splash of water, if needed, to prevent them from sticking and browning). Add the carrots, celery, garlic, oregano, and several grinds of pepper and cook, stirring occasionally, until the mixture is fragrant and coated with oil, about 5 minutes

continued

Rye Croutons

2 (1-inch/2.5 cm)-thick slabs day-old rye bread, cut into 1-inch (2.5 cm) cubes

½ cup (120 g) sour cream

1 tablespoon finely chopped fresh dill

1 tablespoon sherry vinegar, plus more as desired

Harissa Oil (page 95), for garnish

Celery leaves, for garnish

more. Add the water and the beets, bring the mixture to a boil, then turn the heat to medium-low and simmer, partially covered, until all of the vegetables are tender, about 25 minutes.

While the soup simmers, make the rye croutons. Preheat the oven to 400°F (200°C). Place the bread cubes on a rimmed baking sheet, drizzle them with enough olive oil to lightly coat, and lightly season with salt. Bake the croutons for 8 to 10 minutes, until lightly browned and crisp. Remove from the oven and set aside.

To make the dill cream, stir together the sour cream and dill in a small bowl, and cover and refrigerate until needed.

When the vegetables are tender, remove the pot from the heat and let the borscht cool for a few minutes. Transfer the soup to a blender (in batches if necessary) or use an immersion blender to puree until the mixture is very smooth. Stir in the vinegar, taste, and adjust the seasonings, adding more salt, pepper, or vinegar, as desired.

Serve the soup immediately, or refrigerate it in a sealed container up to 2 days. Serve warm or cold garnished with the rye croutons, dill cream, Harissa Oil, and celery leaves.

SMOKED TOMATO SOUP

A silky tomato soup is high on my list of restorative comfort foods (especially when served with a gooey grilled cheese sandwich). A combination of smoked plum and canned tomatoes ensures this version is both bright and deeply sweet. When you want a richer soup, puree the final mix with a nip of brandy or Cognac and a splash of heavy cream. Replace the chicken stock with water for a vegetarian variation.

Prepare a charcoal grill for two-zone cooking and build a medium-high fire, or heat a gas grill to high. When the coals are glowing red and covered with a fine gray ash, use tongs to remove the cooking grate and place a drip pan with 1 inch (2.5 cm) of warm water on the side with no coals, and add your smoke source (chips, chunks, or log). Return the cooking grate to its position, allow it to preheat, and then carefully wipe the preheated grill grates with a lightly oiled paper towel. Using a grill brush, scrape the grill grates clean, then carefully wipe with a lightly oiled towel again.

To smoke the tomatoes, place the plum tomatoes and rosemary in a disposable aluminum pan. Drizzle with enough olive oil to lightly coat, season with salt and pepper, and toss to combine. When the fire begins to produce a steady stream of smoke, place the tomatoes over indirect heat, close the grill, vent the grill for smoking, and smoke for 30 to 40 minutes, until the tomatoes are lightly blistered and begin to release their juices. Set aside.

Heat the olive oil in a large pot over medium-high heat. Add the leek, onion, carrot, celery, and a pinch of salt and cook, stirring occasionally, until softened, about 5 minutes. Add the garlic, bay leaves, thyme, and red pepper flakes and cook until fragrant, 2 to 3 minutes more. Add the wine and use a wooden spoon to scrape up any vegetables that have stuck to the bottom of the pot. Add the chicken stock and canned tomatoes, breaking the tomatoes apart. Stir in the dried chile. Bring the soup to a boil, then turn the heat to medium-low and simmer, stirring occasionally, for 10 minutes.

Add the smoked tomatoes and rosemary sprigs to the pot (include any juices that have accumulated in the pan) and simmer, partially covered, for 30 to 40 minutes, until the soup has thickened slightly. Remove the soup from the heat and let it cool for a few minutes. Discard the rosemary sprigs, chile, and bay leaves, then transfer the soup to a blender (or use an immersion blender) and puree until very smooth. Return the soup to the pot, season to taste with salt and pepper, and serve with slices of bread.

SERVES 4 TO 6

Smoked Tomatoes

4 pounds (1.8 kg) plum tomatoes

2 sprigs rosemary

Extra-virgin olive oil, for drizzling

Kosher salt and freshly ground black pepper

2 tablespoons olive oil

1 leek, white and light green parts, thinly sliced

1 medium yellow onion, chopped

1 large carrot, peeled and chopped

2 celery stalks, chopped

Kosher salt

3 cloves garlic, thinly sliced

2 or 3 fresh bay leaves (to taste), torn

1 tablespoon chopped fresh thyme

Pinch of red pepper flakes or crumbled chile pequin

¼ cup (60 ml) dry white wine

6 cups (1.4 L) Smoked Chicken Stock (page 161) or regular chicken stock

One 28-ounce (794 g) can whole peeled San Marzano tomatoes

1 dried chile (such as ancho or pasilla)

Freshly ground black pepper

Slices of baguette or another crusty bread, for serving

WILD MUSHROOM RAMEN

SERVES 4 GENEROUSLY

1 cup (95 g) dried mushrooms (preferably shiitake)

4 cups (1.4 L) hot water

2 pounds (900 g) mixed fresh wild mushrooms, such as king trumpet, shiitake, porcini, and maitake

Vegetable oil, for drizzling

One 2-inch (5 cm) piece fresh ginger, peeled and finely grated

1 bunch garlic chives, trimmed and sliced into 1-inch lengths

4 green onions, white and light green parts, thinly sliced

¼ cup (60 ml) mushroom shoyu or soy sauce, or regular soy sauce, plus more as needed

1 cup (240 g) white miso

1 tablespoon fermented Korean red chile paste (gochujang), plus more as desired for heat

2 cups (475 ml) unsweetened cashew or almond milk

4 eggs, at room temperature

1 pound (450 g) fresh or dried ramen noodles, or other noodles of your choice

Shichimi togarashi, for garnish

Sambal oelek, for garnish

Traditional ramen is made from a broth that's lovingly tended for hours on end. *Tare* is the seasoning, or flavor bomb, that transforms the basic broth into, say, a miso or tonkotsu ramen, and it can be varied in infinite ways. In this recipe, *tare* infuses a mushroom broth enriched with nut milk. Wood-fired wild mushrooms, pungent aromatics like *gochujang*, a custardy soft-boiled egg, and springy noodles create a vegetarian riff that will satisfy any ramen craving.

Prepare a charcoal grill for two-zone cooking and build a medium fire, or heat a gas grill to medium-high. When the coals are glowing red and covered with a fine gray ash, add your smoke source (chips, chunks, or log). Carefully wipe the preheated grill grates with a lightly oiled paper towel. Using a grill brush, scrape the grill grates clean, then carefully wipe with a lightly oiled towel again and place a grill basket over direct heat.

While the grill heats, combine the dried mushrooms and hot water in a small bowl and set aside. In a large bowl, toss the wild mushrooms with enough olive oil to coat. When the fire begins to produce a steady stream of smoke, place the wild mushrooms in the heated grill basket and cook until charred and crisp on both sides, 6 to 7 minutes. Transfer the mushrooms to a bowl.

Remove the rehydrated mushrooms from the water and thinly slice, reserving all of the water. In a Dutch oven, heat 1 tablespoon of oil over medium-high heat. Add the ginger, half of the garlic chives, and green onions and cook, stirring frequently, until the mixture is fragrant, about 1 minute. Add the rehydrated mushrooms, shoyu, miso, the reserved mushroom water, and the gochujang, turn the heat to medium-low, and simmer for about 10 minutes, until the flavors have melded. Stir in the nut milk and cook until heated through.

Bring a pot of water to a boil over high heat. Add the eggs, turn the heat to low, and gently simmer for 6 minutes. Use a slotted spoon to remove the eggs and run them under cold water for about 30 seconds to stop the cooking process. When the eggs are cool enough to handle, peel them and set aside.

Using the same pot, return the water to a boil over high heat. Add the noodles and cook according to the package instructions. Drain the noodles and briefly rinse.

Divide the noodles among four bowls. Halve the eggs, add a ladle or two of the broth to each bowl, and top with equal portions of the grilled mushrooms, a halved egg sprinkled with togarashi, and the remaining garlic chives. Serve with additional shoyu, shichimi togarashi, or sambal oelek as desired.

CAVATAPPI
with No-Cook Smoked Tomato Sauce

To preserve the unadulterated perfection of ripe, sun-warmed tomatoes, this sauce relies on a smoking gun, which provides flavor-enhancing smoke without heat. It's the perfect summer meal that allows you to raid the garden and pull together dinner in the time it takes a pot of water to boil. For the best flavor, make this sauce with tomatoes that have never felt the chill of a refrigerator.

Combine the tomatoes, garlic, oregano, capers, and red pepper flakes in a large mixing bowl. Drizzle with the olive oil, generously season with salt and pepper, and toss to combine. Allow the mixture to stand at room temperature while you cook the pasta (or for up to several hours).

Bring a large pot of generously salted water to a boil over high heat.

Meanwhile, to smoke the tomatoes, add a pinch of wood chips to the burn chamber of a smoking gun, place the hose in the bowl with the end above the tomatoes, and cover the bowl with plastic wrap. Follow the manufacturer's instructions to ignite the wood chips and smoke for a few seconds, until the bowl is filled with a dense smoke. Remove the hose and reseal the plastic wrap. Let the smoke infuse for 3 minutes, then remove the plastic wrap. Taste, and if you want smokier results, repeat the process, stirring in between smoking to distribute the flavor.

Add the pasta to the boiling water and cook according to the package instructions to al dente (tender but still firm). Drain the pasta in a colander (do not rinse) and pour it into the mixing bowl, tossing all the ingredients together. Taste and adjust the seasonings, adding more salt or pepper as desired. Serve the pasta at room temperature in bowls and sprinkle with the grated cheese to your liking. Refrigerate any leftovers in a sealed container for up to 2 days.

SERVES 4 TO 6

3 pounds (1.4 kg) ripe, juicy tomatoes (preferably a variety of cherry, heirloom, and plum), cored and chopped

1 clove garlic, minced

2 tablespoons chopped fresh oregano

2 tablespoons capers

1 teaspoon red pepper flakes or crumbled chile pequin

⅓ cup (80 ml) best-quality extra-virgin olive oil

Kosher salt and freshly ground black pepper

1 pound (450 g) cavatappi, fusilli, or penne

½ to 1 cup (50 to 100 g) freshly grated Pecorino Romano or Parmesan

SMOKED POTATO SALAD
with Creole Mustard Dressing

SERVES 4 TO 6

2 pounds (900 g) Yukon gold or red potatoes (preferably organic), scrubbed but not peeled

¼ cup (10 g) finely chopped green onions, tender white and green parts

¼ cup (10 g) lightly chopped fresh flat-leaf parsley

¼ cup (60 ml) red wine vinegar

¼ cup (60 ml) extra-virgin olive oil

¼ cup (60 g) mayonnaise (preferably Duke's), plus more as desired

3 tablespoons Creole mustard or other spicy whole-grain mustard

Kosher salt and freshly ground black pepper

Hot sauce (such as Crystal), for finishing

Warning: With an undercurrent of smoke and a zippy dressing, this potato salad is likely to steal the show at your next barbecue. With their dense, moist texture, potatoes (particularly dense, waxy varieties like Yukon) lend themselves beautifully to the smoking process. A creamy dressing made with mayonnaise (I love Duke's mayonnaise because it has a luscious buttercream texture and no added sugar), plenty of red wine vinegar, and Creole mustard adds a "hey there" brightness that balances the main ingredient. Because this salad is brimming with personality, you can serve it alongside something relatively simple, like grilled pork chops or steak. However, if you love Cajun-inspired heat, this salad is right at home at a shrimp or crab boil.

Bring a large pot of generously salted water to a boil over high heat. Carefully add the potatoes, turn the heat to medium, and simmer for 18 to 20 minutes, until the potatoes are tender.

While the potatoes cook, prepare a charcoal grill for two-zone cooking and build a medium-high fire, or heat a gas grill to high. When the coals are glowing red and covered with a fine gray ash, use tongs to remove the cooking grate and place a drip pan with 1 inch (2.5 cm) of warm water on the side with no coals, and add your smoke source (chips, chunks, or log). Return the cooking grate to its position, allow it to preheat, and then carefully wipe the preheated grill grates with a lightly oiled paper towel. Using a grill brush, scrape the grill grates clean, then carefully wipe with a lightly oiled towel again.

When the fire begins to produce a steady stream of smoke, place the potatoes directly on the grates over indirect heat, close the grill, vent the grill for smoking, and smoke until they're puffed and golden brown, about 35 to 45 minutes.

Remove the potatoes from the grill, allow them to cool enough to handle, and then cut them into 1-inch (2.5 cm) chunks. Combine the green onions, parsley, vinegar, oil, mayonnaise, and mustard in a large bowl. Season with salt, pepper, and hot sauce to taste and whisk to combine. Fold in the potatoes with a rubber spatula, mixing gently so they hold their shape. Taste and adjust the seasonings, adding more salt, pepper, or hot sauce as desired. Serve immediately, or store in a sealed container in the refrigerator for up to 4 days. (For the best flavor, remove the salad from the refrigerator 30 minutes before serving.)

COAL-SMOKED EGGPLANT CURRY

I was fascinated to learn about an ancient Indian method of smoking food (and one that's still favored by street market vendors in Delhi) that involves placing a small dish of smoldering charcoal in the center of a curry, pouring a little oil over the embers, and then covering the dish for a minute or so to allow the smoky flavors to permeate. This modern-day translation follows the same lead by cooking the curry in the sauna of a smoke-infused grill. Serve the tender vegetables and their fragrant sauce with yogurt, fresh cucumbers, and steamed basmati rice or naan bread.

Prepare a charcoal grill for two-zone cooking and build a medium-high fire, or heat a gas grill to high.

When the coals are glowing red and covered with a fine gray ash, add your smoke source (chips, chunks, or log). Carefully wipe the preheated grill grates with a lightly oiled paper towel. Using a grill brush, scrape the grill grates clean, then carefully wipe with a lightly oiled towel again. Place a large cast-iron skillet or 15-inch (38 cm) paella pan over direct heat.

When the fire begins to produce a steady stream of smoke, pour the oil into the skillet. When the oil is hot and shimmering, add the onions and a pinch of salt and saute, stirring frequently, until the onions are soft and beginning to brown, about 8 minutes. Add the garlic, ginger, and chiles and saute for 2 to 3 minutes, stirring frequently, until fragrant. Add the eggplants and water and stir to combine. Move the skillet to indirect heat, close the grill, vent the grill for smoking, and smoke for about 12 minutes, stirring only once or twice, until the eggplant has collapsed. Add the tomatoes, chile powder, coriander, cumin, cardamom pods, and 1 teaspoon salt and cook, uncovered, until the tomatoes become jammy, 3 to 4 minutes. Remove the cardamom pods.

Stir in the chickpeas, close the grill, and allow the curry to smoke for 2 to 3 minutes, until deeply fragrant. Remove the curry from the grill, taste, and adjust the salt and/or chile powder as desired. Serve immediately with lemon wedges. Store any leftovers in a sealed container in the refrigerator for up to 3 days.

SERVES 4 TO 6

¼ cup (60 ml) vegetable oil

2 white onions, sliced

Kosher salt

5 cloves garlic, peeled and crushed

2 tablespoons finely grated fresh ginger

1 or 2 Thai bird's-eye chiles, as desired for heat

3 eggplants (2 pounds/900 g), sliced into 3 by 1-inch (7.5 by 2.5 cm) batons

6 tablespoons (90 ml) water

4 large ripe tomatoes, cored and cut into wedges

1¼ teaspoons pure ground chile powder (such as New Mexico or ancho)

1 teaspoon ground coriander

1 teaspoon ground cumin

2 cardamom pods, lightly crushed

Two 15-ounce (430 g) cans chickpeas, drained

Lemon wedges, for serving

CHAPTER SEVEN

FISH & SEAFOOD

Despite the fact that I make smoked fish pilgrimages a priority wherever I travel (from seafood markets on the Gulf to Russ and Daughters in New York City and a smokehouse in Duluth, Minnesota), I never used to consider making it myself—until recently. Smoking fish at home might sound intimidating, but it's no more complicated than firing up your grill. Once you add the aromatic wood to the fire, all you need to do is control the heat and let the smoke work its charm.

This chapter is devoted to preparing fresh catches in various ways, from grilling crabs and oysters on the half shell to devour immediately, to feasts to plan a party around, like an impressive side of smoked salmon (brunch, anyone?) or shellfish cooked paella-style with green rice. You'll be amazed at how a few minutes under the hood of a smoky grill will influence even quick-cooking items like scallops and shrimp and lead to spectacular meals easy enough to cook at your next beach house rental.

Keep in mind that most of these dishes come together quickly, so you'll be left with a good amount of fire and heat—a great opportunity to "cook ahead" by smoking dried ingredients (beans, seeds, nuts), grill-smoking tomatoes and chiles, or coal-roasting eggplant for a future meal.

WOOD-FIRED OYSTERS
with Ras el Hanout Butter

SERVES 4 TO 6

2 green onions, white and light green parts, minced

1 clove garlic, thinly sliced

1 serrano chile, stemmed, seeded, and finely chopped

1 teaspoon ras el hanout

½ teaspoon kosher salt

Several dashes of hot sauce (preferably Cholula)

½ cup (110 g) butter, at room temperature

24 fresh oysters, in the shell

Oysters grilled in the half shell are such a treat that they warrant their own occasion, like a happy hour with one or two of your besties, as in, "Hey, swing by after work with beer and I'll grill us some oysters." But hot, buttery bivalves are also a great thing to prepare as a snack or appetizer before you tackle the main event—say, a crawfish boil or steaks on the grill. The process (which is expedited with an oyster knife) is a fun thing to gather around and easy enough to do while you're chatting with guests and sipping an adult beverage. Even though the oysters cook quickly, I like to close the grill briefly during the process to make the most of the wafting, fragrant smoke. Grilled oysters are delicious with nothing more than a cube of cold butter (that melts while they sizzle) and a final squeeze of lemon and/or a splash of hot sauce, but this compound butter, infused with warm, transporting spices and my favorite smoky hot sauce, truly takes them to the next level.

Ras el hanout is basically the North African equivalent to India's garam masala. In Arabic, the phrase *ras el hanout* roughly translates to a "top shelf" blend of spices that often includes cumin, coriander, ginger, allspice, chile pepper, and turmeric, among others. Serve these oysters hot, right off the grill, with a cold, crisp lager (or maybe a nip of single-barrel bourbon) and either grilled slices of bread rubbed with garlic and drizzled with olive oil, or a crackly baguette for sopping up the juices.

Place the green onions, garlic, serrano, ras el hanout, salt, and hot sauce in the bowl of a food processor and pulse into a paste. Use a rubber spatula to transfer the paste to a mixing bowl, add the butter, and mix until combined. Using your hands, shape the butter into a log about 1½ inches (4 cm) in diameter, wrap it in plastic wrap, and refrigerate until firm, at least 1 hour, or up to 2 days.

Prepare a charcoal grill for two-zone cooking and build a medium fire, or heat a gas grill to medium-high.

When the coals are glowing red and covered with a fine gray ash, use tongs to remove the cooking grate and place a drip pan with 1 inch (2.5 cm) of warm water on the side with no coals, and add your smoke source (chips, chunks, or log). Return the cooking grate to its position, allow it to preheat, and then carefully wipe the preheated grill grates with a lightly oiled paper towel. Using a grill brush, scrape the grill grates clean, then carefully wipe with a lightly oiled towel again.

Using an oyster knife, shuck the oysters and discard the top shell. Disconnect the oyster from the bottom shell but keep the oyster in the shell. Top each oyster with a generous teaspoon of the butter. Place the oysters over direct heat (see the sidebar, below) and grill until the buttery juices bubble and the edges of the oysters begin to curl, about 2 minutes. Using tongs, transfer the oysters to a platter and serve immediately.

Two Ways to Smoke Oysters

Because oysters cook quickly, I've always cooked them over the direct heat of a medium fire. My friend Jody prefers to cook them more slowly, over indirect heat, until they darken slightly (like any smoked ingredient) and the edges of the oyster begin to curl. I've tried it both ways, repeatedly, and each is exceedingly good. Cooking them hot and fast delivers irresistible results (and waiting for them to sizzle provides an aromatic entertainment). If you have the time and patience to grill-smoke them for a more pronounced smokiness and slightly firmer, drier texture, try the indirect heat method, venting the grill for smoking (you don't need a drip pan for this quick process) and cooking them until the oysters are darkened, 6 to 8 minutes.

PEG LEG'S SMOKED TUNA DIP

SERVES 6 TO 8

Two 5-ounce (140 g) tuna steaks (about 2 inches/5 cm thick)

Extra-virgin olive oil, for drizzling

Kosher salt and freshly ground black pepper

2 tablespoons chopped fresh thyme

¼ cup (40 g) finely chopped yellow onion

4 green onions, white and light green parts, thinly sliced

1 small jalapeño or serrano chile, stemmed, seeded, and finely chopped

⅔ cup (70 g) mayonnaise (preferably Duke's)

⅓ cup (35 g) sour cream

2 tablespoons Creole mustard or other spicy whole-grain mustard

1 teaspoon Worcestershire sauce

Finely grated zest and juice of 1 lemon, plus more as desired

1 teaspoon hot sauce (such as Cholula or Crystal), plus more as desired

½ teaspoon hot paprika or your favorite Cajun spice blend

Potato chips or crackers, for serving

Fresh crudités, such as carrot, cucumber, or celery sticks, and wedges of chilled radish, for serving

Along the Gulf Coast of Alabama and Florida, smoked fish dip made with tuna or even mullet is a summer staple. In seafood shacks, salty oyster bars, and restaurants, the dip is usually served with saltines or tortilla chips and toppings like chopped onions, tomatoes, and slices of pickled jalapeños, and a bottle of hot sauce. Every spring, when my family vacations in Pensacola, Florida, we buy tuna dip at Joe Patti's, a massive, convivial seafood market on the water (and maybe my favorite place to shop ever?), and slather it on sturdy crackers like Triscuits. (It's also indulgently delicious on Zapp's potato chips.) When I can't be at the beach, the smoky flavor of this rich, luscious spread takes me there.

Prepare a charcoal grill for two-zone cooking and build a medium-high fire, or heat a gas grill to high.

When the coals are glowing red and covered with a fine gray ash, use tongs to remove the cooking grate and place a drip pan with 1 inch (2.5 cm) of warm water on the side with no coals, and add your smoke source (chips, chunks, or log). Return the cooking grate to its position, allow it to preheat, and then carefully wipe the preheated grill grates with a lightly oiled paper towel. Using a grill brush, scrape the grill grates clean, then carefully wipe with a lightly oiled towel again.

While the grill heats, place the tuna on a plate, drizzle with enough olive oil to lightly coat, and season both sides generously with salt, pepper, and thyme. Use your hands to rub the seasonings evenly over the fish and set it aside.

When the fire begins to produce a steady stream of smoke, place the tuna over indirect heat, close the grill, vent the grill for smoking, and smoke for 25 minutes, until firm and slightly darkened. Set aside to cool for 10 minutes.

Slice the tuna into ½-inch (1.3 cm) cubes and place them in a mixing bowl along with the onion, green onions, jalapeño, mayonnaise, sour cream, mustard, Worcestershire, lemon zest and juice, hot sauce, and paprika. Use two forks to shred the mixture into a coarse puree (or for a smoother texture, gently pulse the ingredients in a food processor).

Taste and adjust the seasonings, adding more lemon juice, hot sauce, salt, and pepper as desired. Transfer the dip to a serving bowl and, for the best results, cover and refrigerate for a few hours to allow the flavors to develop. Serve with crackers and crudités.

SMOKY LOBSTER TAILS
with Bay Leaves

SERVES 2 TO 4

4 uncooked lobster tails

Extra-virgin olive oil,
for brushing

Kosher salt and freshly
ground black pepper

4 to 8 fresh bay leaves

Lemon wedges, for serving

Grilled bread, for serving

Lobster tails offer the rich, tender meat you love, but they're much easier to prepare than a whole lobster. There are different ways to prep a lobster tail for the grill. The soft tissue underneath the tail shell can be removed (poultry shears work well for this task), or the entire tail can be split in half lengthwise. My favorite approach is a hybrid of the two: using shears to cut the shell up to the tail, then using a knife to split the meat along the same line. Spread open the lobster to expose more of its luxurious meat to aromatics and smoke. The results need nothing more than a drizzle of olive oil and a squeeze of lemon. My favorite flavor with lobster is also the easiest to prepare: I insert fresh fragrant bay leaves into the flesh. Round out the meal with a cold, crisp Belgian-style ale and garlicky roast potatoes (or buttery boiled new potatoes) served on a bed of arugula.

To prepare the lobster tails, use poultry shears to cut the shell up to the tail, then use a knife to split the meat along the same line as the shell cut, being careful not to slice all the way through the lobster.

Use the knife to gently spread open the lobster, exposing more of its meat (the remaining soft membrane will hold the sections intact). Brush the meat with olive oil and season with salt and pepper. Insert a bay leaf or two in the slit of the meat. Set the tails aside to marinate at room temperature while you heat the grill.

Prepare a charcoal grill for two-zone cooking and build a medium fire, or heat a gas grill to medium-high.

When the coals are glowing red and covered with a fine gray ash, add your smoke source (chips, chunks, or log). Carefully wipe the preheated grill grates with a lightly oiled paper towel. Using a grill brush, scrape the grill grates clean, then carefully wipe with a lightly oiled towel again.

When the fire begins to produce a steady stream of smoke, place the tails shell side down directly on the grates over direct heat, close the grill, vent the grill for smoking, and smoke for 5 minutes. Use tongs to flip the tails and cook for 3 to 4 minutes more, until the meat is cooked through and the internal temperature reads 135°F (60°C) on an instant-read thermometer.

Remove the lobster from the grill, cool for 5 minutes, and then serve in large, shallow bowls with plenty of napkins, lemon wedges, and grilled bread, if desired.

PAPPARDELLE
with Smoked Anchovy Butter & Herbs

The salty simplicity and burst of fresh herbs in this recipe is wonderful with fresh pasta (but you can also use dried noodles like linguine or bucatini). Twirled around a fork and generously seasoned with salt and pepper, the buttery noodles are delicious on their own, but for added crunch, top them off with rustic (not finely ground) bread crumbs toasted in olive oil.

Bring a large pot of generously salted water to a boil over high heat. Add the pasta and cook, stirring occasionally, until al dente (tender but still firm), about 3 minutes for fresh pasta or according to the package instructions for dried pasta. Drain the pasta in a colander (do not rinse) and return it to the pot off the heat.

Add the anchovy butter and toss well. Add the warm stock and Parmesan and toss to coat; allow the noodles to rest for a minute and toss again. Add the fresh herbs, season with salt and pepper to taste, add the red pepper flakes, and toss again.

Divide the pappardelle among bowls and top each with a sprinkling of flaky salt. Serve warm, with Parmesan on the side.

SERVES 4 TO 6

1 pound (450 g) fresh pappardelle or your favorite dried pasta

6 tablespoons (85 g) Smoked Anchovy Butter (page 27), cut into cubes, at room temperature

¾ cup (175 ml) warm Smoked Chicken Stock (page 161) or regular chicken stock

½ cup (50 g) freshly grated Parmesan, plus more for serving

Handful of lightly chopped fresh herbs (any combination of basil, chives, chervil, tarragon, and dill)

Kosher salt and freshly ground black pepper

Pinch of red pepper flakes or crumbled chile pequin

Flaky salt, for garnish

SMOKED SALMON
with Wild Pepper

SERVES 6 TO 8

One 4-pound (1.8 kg) skin-on side of salmon, pinbones removed

Extra-virgin olive oil

Kosher salt

1 tablespoon Voatsiperifery peppercorns or other peppercorns, coarsely ground

5 or 6 sprigs rosemary, thyme, or dill, as desired for fragrance

3 handfuls watercress, cleaned and trimmed

1 handful sunflower sprouts

3 tablespoons Pickled Mustard Seeds (page 24)

2 tablespoons white wine vinegar

Flaky salt, for garnish

Lemon wedges, for serving

Smoking a side of salmon leads to countless great meals. It's delicious on its own (eaten with your fingers and a squeeze of lemon), served in a salmon salad, or with deviled eggs, pasta, and more. You can season this salmon with any type of peppercorn, but the fragrance of an exotic variety like Akesson's Voatsiperifery "Wild" Pepper (available at Akessons-organic.com) infuses the fish with an enticing woodsy flavor as well as bright citrus and floral aromas. This salmon is a natural star on a brunch menu—served with a peppery salad of watercress and Pickled Mustard Seeds.

Measure out two sheets of heavy-duty aluminum foil that are 12 inches (30 cm) longer than the salmon and place them on a rimless baking sheet. Place the salmon skin-side down on the foil, drizzle with enough olive oil to lightly coat, and generously season with salt, pepper, and herbs (use your fingers to spread the seasonings and oil evenly over the flesh). Set the salmon aside to marinate at room temperature while you prepare the grill.

Prepare a charcoal grill for two-zone cooking and build a medium-high fire, or heat a gas grill to high.

When the coals are glowing red and covered with a fine gray ash, use tongs to remove the cooking grate and place a drip pan with 1 inch (2.5 cm) of warm water on the side with no coals, and add your smoke source (chips, chunks, or log). Return the cooking grate to its position, allow it to preheat, and then carefully wipe the preheated grill grates with a lightly oiled paper towel. Using a grill brush, scrape the grill grates clean, then carefully wipe with a lightly oiled towel again.

When the fire begins to produce a steady stream of smoke, carefully slide the foil and fish off of the baking sheet and onto the grill over indirect heat. Close the grill, vent the grill for smoking, and smoke for 25 to 30 minutes; be sure to rotate the fish as needed to ensure even cooking. When the salmon is cooked (it will feel just firm and flake easily with a fork), carefully slide the foil and salmon back onto the baking sheet and let it rest for 10 minutes.

Meanwhile, combine the watercress and sunflower sprouts in a mixing bowl, add the Pickled Mustard Seeds, vinegar, and 3 tablespoons olive oil, and toss to combine. Taste and season with more salt and pepper as desired.

Garnish the salmon with a light sprinkling of flaky salt and serve with the watercress salad and lemon wedges. Refrigerate the leftover salmon in a sealed container for up to 4 days.

GRILL-SMOKED DUNGENESS CRAB

SERVES 4

3 cloves garlic, thinly sliced

2 serrano chiles, stemmed, seeded, and chopped

1½ teaspoons fennel seeds

½ teaspoon kosher salt

3 green onions, white and light green parts, thinly sliced

½ cup (20 g) chopped fresh flat-leaf parsley

½ cup (20 g) chopped fresh cilantro (leaves and tender stems)

½ cup (15 g) fresh mint leaves

¼ cup (60 ml) freshly squeezed lime juice

2 teaspoons fish sauce

¼ cup (60 ml) extra-virgin olive oil

¼ cup unsalted butter (60 g), at room temperature

4 pre-steamed Dungeness crabs (whole or sections), about 3 pounds (1.4 kg), thawed if frozen

With its sweet, tender meat and often limited availability, eating fresh crab is a luxury. The West Coast has bragging rights to fresh Dungeness crab, while Maine peekytoe, Jonah, and blue crab are East Coast delicacies. Luckily, whole crab (or sections) that's steamed and frozen in its shell is widely available. Thaw frozen pre-steamed crab overnight in the refrigerator, or submerge them in a large container of cool water for a couple of hours. When thawed and lightly grilled, the meat retains its sweet, delicate flavor. All you need to do is give their shells a gentle whack to crack them slightly and submerge them in a marinade before grilling. Then it's time to roll up your sleeves—eating crab this way is messy and fun. If you aren't coated with herb butter by the time you're done, you've done something wrong.

Place the garlic, serranos, fennel seeds, and salt in the bowl of a food processor and pulse into a coarse paste. Add the green onions, parsley, cilantro, mint, lime juice, and fish sauce and pulse to combine. With the processor running, drizzle in the olive oil until the mixture pulls together into an even puree, stopping to scrape down the sides of the bowl with a rubber spatula as needed. Use a rubber spatula to transfer the mixture to a large mixing bowl, add the butter, and fold together. Add the crabs and toss to combine, using your hands to coat the surface of each crab or section and work the herb mixture into the cracks. Set the crabs aside to marinate while you heat the grill.

Prepare a charcoal grill for two-zone cooking and build a medium fire, or heat a gas grill to medium-high.

When the coals are glowing red and covered with a fine gray ash, add your smoke source (chips, chunks, or log). Carefully wipe the preheated grill grates with a lightly oiled paper towel. Using a grill brush, scrape the grill grates clean, then carefully wipe with a lightly oiled towel again.

When the fire begins to produce a steady stream of smoke, place the crabs directly on the grates over direct heat and close the grill, vent the grill for smoking, and smoke until the edges of the shell begin to char, 2 to 3 minutes per side (use a big metal spatula to flip the crabs). Remove the crabs from the heat and let them cool for 5 minutes. Serve in large shallow bowls (or on newspapers) with plenty of napkins.

SCALLOP SPAGHETTI
with Charred Lemons & Crème Fraîche

Two layers of lemon (grated zest and smoky, charred juice) create a flavor that's both bright and complex. This recipe calls for Thai basil, but feel free to swap in tarragon, dill, or chives. The final cooking process is brief, and this dish comes together quickly, so get organized before you start cooking by warming the serving bowls, chilling the white wine, and getting a salad ready to toss.

Place the scallops in a bowl and drizzle them with enough olive oil to lightly coat. Season the scallops generously with salt and pepper, add the red pepper flakes and use a rubber spatula to gently combine.

Prepare a charcoal grill for two-zone cooking and build a medium-high fire, or heat a gas grill to high.

When the coals are glowing red and covered with a fine gray ash, add your smoke source (chips, chunks, or log). Carefully wipe the preheated grill grates with a lightly oiled paper towel. Using a grill brush, scrape the grill grates clean, then carefully wipe with a lightly oiled towel again.

While the grill heats, bring a large pot of generously salted water to a boil over high heat on the stovetop. Place the scallops in a bowl, drizzle with enough olive oil to coat well and generously season with salt and pepper; set aside. Warm four pasta bowls in a low 200°F (95°C) oven or on an upper rack of your grill, if it has one.

Add the pasta to the pot and cook according to the package instructions until al dente (tender but still firm). Drain the pasta in a colander (do not rinse), reserving ½ cup (120 ml) of the cooking water.

Place a 15-inch (38 cm) paella pan or large cast-iron skillet over direct heat for 10 minutes to warm. While the pan heats, finely grate the zest from the lemons into a small bowl, add the crème fraîche, and stir to combine. Halve the lemons, brush the cut side of each lemon with olive oil, and grill the lemons over direct heat, cut side down, until nicely charred, 3 to 4 minutes. Remove the lemons from the heat and set them aside to cool briefly. Squeeze the juice from all 4 halves into a small bowl.

When the fire begins to produce a steady stream of smoke, pour a couple tablespoons of olive oil in the pan, place the scallops in a single layer, and cook until nicely browned on one side, about 2 minutes. Use a fish spatula to flip the scallops and cook again until browned on the second side, 1½ to 2 minutes

continued

1 pound (450 g) dry-packed sea scallops

Extra-virgin olive oil, for drizzling

Kosher salt and freshly ground black pepper

Pinch of red pepper flakes or crumbled chile pequin

1 pound (450 g) best-quality dried spaghetti

2 lemons (preferably organic)

8 ounces (120 g) crème fraîche

Handful of Thai basil leaves

Flaky salt, for garnish

more. Carefully move the pan to indirect heat. Add the drained pasta, the charred lemon juice, the basil, and the crème fraîche mixture and toss until the pasta is evenly coated. Close the grill for about 30 seconds, then open and toss again. Close the grill for 1 minute more, then remove the pan from the heat. Divide the pasta and scallops among the warm bowls and garnish with a drizzle of olive oil, a grinding of pepper, and a sprinkling of flaky salt.

SMOKED TROUT

**ABOUT 1 POUND; SERVES
4 TO 8**

1 skin-on side of steelhead
 or arctic char (about
1¼ pounds/570 g), or
2 skin-on trout fillets (about
8 ounces/225 g each),
pinbones removed

Extra-virgin olive oil,
for drizzling

Kosher salt and freshly
ground black pepper

3 or 4 sprigs rosemary,
thyme, or dill (enough to
cover the fish)

Flaky salt, for garnish

Lemon wedges, for serving

Having smoked fish on hand is a luxury that inspires easy meals and impromptu snacks at any time of day. The moist, flaky fish is delicious with scrambled eggs, for instance, or on toasted rye bread in the morning, in green or potato salads for lunch, or as an appetizer (with crackers and lemon). What follows is my basic method for smoking trout, which gives you a feast of smoked fish for brunch, pâté, or a serious spread inspired by Minnesota flavors (see the sidebar, opposite page). While you can use any variety of trout with this recipe, I usually opt for copper-colored varieties with a higher oil content, like steelhead or arctic char, which helps keep them moist. Don't forget to account for carryover heat during cooking, meaning the fish will continue to cook as it cools. To avoid overcooking, pull the trout off the heat when the fat begins to bead on the surface and the fish just begins to flake when tested with a fork.

Measure out two sheets of heavy-duty aluminum foil that are 12 inches (30 cm) longer than the trout and place them on a rimless baking sheet. Place the trout skin-side down on the foil, drizzle with enough olive oil to lightly coat, generously season with salt and pepper (use your fingers to spread the seasonings and oil evenly over the flesh), and top with herb sprigs. Set the trout aside to marinate at room temperature while you prepare the grill.

Prepare a charcoal grill for two-zone cooking and build a medium-high fire, or heat a gas grill to high.

When the coals are glowing red and covered with a fine gray ash, use tongs to remove the cooking grate and place a drip pan with 1 inch (2.5 cm) of warm water on the side with no coals, and add your smoke source (chips, chunks, or log). Return the cooking grate to its position, allow it to preheat, and then carefully wipe the preheated grill grates with a lightly oiled paper towel. Using a grill brush, scrape the grill grates clean, then carefully wipe with a lightly oiled towel again.

When the fire begins to produce a steady stream of smoke, carefully slide the foil and fish off of the baking sheet and onto the grill over indirect heat. Close the grill, vent the grill for smoking, and smoke for 20 to 30 minutes; be sure to rotate the fish as needed to ensure even cooking. When the trout is cooked (it will feel just firm to the touch and flake easily with a fork), carefully slide the foil and trout back onto the baking sheet and let it rest for 10 minutes. Garnish with a light sprinkling of flaky salt and serve with lemon wedges.

"Up North" Smoked Trout Spread

Every summer, my family escapes the Texas heat to spend a couple of months with my folks in Minnesota. Among the many things I look forward to (in addition to the magical sound of loons—truly a religious experience—and cooking from my mom's herb garden) are long, lazy smoked fish brunches—an up north tradition. To serve your smoked trout Minnesota-style, round out the table with dill mustard, a wild rice salad (mine usually includes green onions, drained canned chickpeas, golden raisins, and a white wine vinaigrette), salty cheese curds, capers, onions, and crackers. Beef or venison sticks, a pitcher of Bloody Mathildas (page 42), and shots of cold aquavit are essential. In the spirit of lake culture, don't plan much beyond a rousing match of cornhole for the remains of the day.

SMOKED TROUT GRATIN
with Potatoes, Spinach & Cream

SERVES 4 TO 6

2 tablespoons olive oil

2 shallots, halved and thinly sliced

2 cloves garlic, thinly sliced

Pinch of red pepper flakes or crumbled chile pequin

1 sprig thyme

2 fresh bay leaves

Kosher salt and freshly ground black pepper

Splash of dry white or rosé wine (optional)

4 cups (950 ml) heavy cream

1 tablespoon Creole mustard or other spicy whole-grain mustard

A few gratings fresh nutmeg

3 large Yukon gold potatoes (about 2 pounds/900 g), peeled and thinly sliced

1 large bunch spinach (10 ounces/280 g), cleaned and coarsely chopped

1 pound (450 g) Smoked Trout (page 140), broken into large flakes

¾ cup (45 g) toasted fresh bread crumbs, for topping

¾ cup (85 g) freshly grated Gruyère or Emmental, or ¾ cup (75 g) Parmesan, for topping

Bubbly and warm from the oven, this rich, creamy gratin is the ultimate comfort food on a cold night, especially when its served with sweet, slow-roasted tomatoes and a bottle of red wine. For the best flavor, avoid baby spinach and opt for a local variety (that you'll likely need to stem and wash yourself); it will give the dish more character. You can use any variety of smoked trout, but I prefer richly colored steelhead or artic char, which has more fat than other varieties.

Note: Use a light hand with seasonings, because the salted smoked trout will infuse the dish with plenty of flavor.

Preheat the oven to 350°F (175°C) and butter a 9 by 13-inch (23 by 33 cm) baking dish.

In a Dutch oven, heat the olive oil over medium-high heat. Add the shallots, garlic, red pepper flakes, thyme, and bay leaves and lightly season with salt and pepper. Cook, stirring often, until the shallots are fragrant and softened, 4 to 5 minutes. If the shallots begin to stick to the pan, add a splash of wine and continue to cook for a few minutes more. Whisk in the cream, mustard, and nutmeg, and then stir in the sliced potatoes. Turn the heat to medium-high and cook, stirring now and then, just until the mixture begins to bubble, about 8 minutes. Remove the pan from the heat and discard the herbs. Add the spinach in large handfuls, letting them wilt before adding more, and cook until the greens are tender, about 4 minutes total.

Spoon half of the potato-spinach mixture into the prepared baking dish and top with the smoked trout in a single, even layer. Spoon the rest of the potatoes over the trout and pour any remaining cream over the dish. Combine the toasted bread crumbs and cheese in a small bowl, then scatter the mixture over the top of the gratin.

Place the baking pan on a rimmed baking sheet and bake until the potatoes are tender and the mixture is bubbly, 55 to 60 minutes (for a crisper crust, give the dish a final 1 to 2 minutes under the broiler). Remove the pan from the oven and let the gratin cool for at least 15 minutes before serving (this will allow the potatoes to absorb the creamy liquid). To serve, cut the grain into generous squares and serve warm. Refrigerate leftovers in a sealed container for up to 4 days.

SMOKY SHRIMP
with Lemony Orzo, Green Olives & Feta

When it comes to grilling shrimp, I don't like to futz around with skewers because flipping them can be tricky. Instead, I prefer to grill shrimp in a preheated grill basket (with small vents that minimize moisture loss) or better yet, a cast-iron skillet or paella pan that retains all of the flavorful juices. I pour marinated shrimp onto a preheated surface, then use long-handled tongs to shake the skillet every now and then, flip the shrimp, and move the pan away from the heat to avoid flare-ups. The main objective is to keep the shrimp moving so they cook quickly and evenly. This lightly charred shrimp is a natural partner for orzo flavored with lemon zest, grilled lemons, crumbled feta, and olives.

If you prefer to grill directly on the grates, use jumbo shrimp so they're easier to turn.

Place the shrimp in a large mixing bowl, drizzle with enough olive oil to lightly coat, season generously with salt and pepper, and toss to combine. Add the oregano, thyme, and red pepper flakes and toss again, then set aside to marinate at room temperature while you prepare the grill.

Prepare a charcoal grill for two-zone cooking and build a medium-high fire, or heat a gas grill to high.

When the coals are glowing red and covered with a fine gray ash, add your smoke source (chips, chunks, or log). Carefully wipe the preheated grill grates with a lightly oiled paper towel. Using a grill brush, scrape the grill grates clean, then carefully wipe with a lightly oiled towel again and place a cast-iron skillet or grill basket over direct heat.

While the grill heats, bring a large pot of generously salted water to a boil over high heat. Add the orzo and cook according to the package instructions until al dente (tender but still firm). Drain the orzo in a colander, rinse it briefly, then transfer it to a mixing bowl. Drizzle the pasta with enough olive oil to lightly coat and toss to combine (this will help prevent the pasta from sticking).

Finely grate the zest from 1 lemon and add it to the orzo. Halve both of the lemons horizontally (from stem end to the blossom end).

When the fire begins to produce a steady stream of smoke, pour the shrimp into the preheated skillet and cook, flipping the shrimp and rotating the pan

continued

SERVES 4 TO 6

2 pounds (900 g) large shrimp, peeled and deveined, without tails

Extra-virgin olive oil

Kosher salt and freshly ground black pepper

2 tablespoons chopped fresh oregano or marjoram

2 teaspoons chopped fresh thyme

Pinch of red pepper flakes

12 ounces (340 g) orzo

2 lemons

½ bunch green onions, white and light green parts, thinly sliced, or ½ chopped red onion

½ cup (45 g) green olives (any variety), kalamata olives, or oil-cured olives

8 ounces (225 g) crumbled feta cheese

around the heat (closing the lid in between to make the most of the wood smoke) until just cooked (they will turn opaque and be firm and springy to the touch), 5 to 6 minutes total. Remove the pan from the heat and let the shrimp cool briefly.

Brush the cut sides of the lemons with olive oil and grill the citrus cut-side down over direct heat until dark char marks appear, 2 to 3 minutes.

Add the warm shrimp and any juices to the orzo and toss to combine. Add about ⅓ cup (80 ml) olive oil, the green onions, olives, and feta and toss gently to combine. Taste and adjust the seasonings, adding more salt or pepper as desired. Divide the pasta and shrimp among bowls and serve warm or at room temperature with the grilled lemon halves. Refrigerate any leftovers in a sealed container in the fridge for up to 4 days.

TIPSY MUSSELS & CLAMS
with Grilled Bread

SERVES 4

2 pounds (900 g) mussels

2 dozen littleneck clams

2 tablespoons extra-virgin olive oil

1 shallot, minced

4 cloves garlic, thinly sliced

2 dried arbol chiles

2 sprigs thyme

1 cup (240 ml) pale ale

2 tablespoons unsalted butter

½ cup (20 g) chopped fresh flat-leaf parsley

Finely grated zest of 1 lemon

Grilled bread, for serving

Cooked over a wood-infused fire in a fragrant garlic- and shallot-beer broth, these mussels and clams come together quickly and make for a fun and memorable meal. Plenty of grilled bread (to sop up the flavorful cooking liquid) and your favorite pale ale (you'll want to drink the same beer that you cook the shellfish in) are essential. This dish can be cooked in a deep cast-iron skillet, a 15-inch (38 cm) paella pan, or a French-style crock that can hold up to the heat.

Prepare a charcoal grill for two-zone cooking and build a medium-high fire, or heat a gas grill to high.

While the grill heats, scrub the mussels and clams under running water to remove any grit.

When the coals are glowing red and covered with a fine gray ash, add your smoke source (chips, chunks, or log). Carefully wipe the preheated grill grates with a lightly oiled paper towel. Using a grill brush, scrape the grill grates clean, then carefully wipe with a lightly oiled towel again and place a skillet over direct heat.

When the fire begins to produce a steady stream of smoke, combine the oil, shallot, garlic, chiles, and thyme sprigs in the preheated skillet and cook, stirring occasionally, until the vegetables are fragrant (but not browned), 4 to 5 minutes. Add the clams and beer to the skillet, close the grill, vent the grill for smoking, and smoke for 5 minutes. Open the grill and stir in the mussels, then move the pan to indirect heat, close the grill, and smoke 10 minutes more, or until all of the shells have opened.

Transfer the shellfish to a serving bowl (or serve directly from the paella pan, if using). Add the butter, parsley, and lemon zest and toss to combine. Serve immediately with slices of grilled bread.

SMOKY SEAFOOD
with Green Rice

Strange as it may sound, a frozen block of shelled seafood (shrimp, squid, and mussels) spotted at my local Whole Foods was the muse for this dish. The colorful mix of ready-to-go seafood was so appealing that I was determined to find a way to use it. I quickly thought of a hot grill (duh) and spicy, herbaceous *arroz verde,* or green rice, cooked paella-style. To create a deep green cooking liquid, I pureed poblano and jalapeño chiles, cilantro, and parsley with chicken and fish stock, and pulled in a few other favorite flavors.

When it comes to pulling this dish together, organization is everything (you don't want to be prepping ingredients while the fire burns down or your fish is overcooking). Read through the recipe a time or two before you get started, and make sure you have everything ready before you even light the fire. Toward the end of the cooking time, you want the fire low enough that the rice can rest and finish (and ideally develop a *socarrat,* the browned, crunchy crust that defines a great paella) in the closed grill.

Combine the chicken and fish stocks, the coarsely chopped onion, the poblanos, jalapeño, garlic, cilantro, parsley, spinach, and 1 teaspoon salt in a blender and puree until smooth, 3 to 4 minutes. Set aside.

Place the seafood in a large mixing bowl, drizzle with enough olive oil to lightly coat, season generously with salt and pepper, and toss to combine. Set aside.

Prepare a charcoal grill for two-zone cooking and build a medium-high fire, or heat a gas grill to high.

When the coals are glowing red and covered with a fine gray ash, add your smoke source (chips, chunks, or log). Carefully wipe the preheated grill grates with a lightly oiled paper towel. Using a grill brush, scrape the grill grates clean, then carefully wipe with a lightly oiled towel again and place a 15-inch (38 cm) paella pan or large skillet over direct heat.

When the fire begins to produce a steady stream of smoke, drizzle ¼ cup (60 ml) olive oil into the preheated pan and add the finely chopped onion and oregano and cook, stirring often, until the mixture is fragrant and just starting to brown, 3 to 4 minutes.

continued

SERVES 6 TO 8

4 cups (950 ml) chicken stock

2 cups (475 ml) fish stock or clam broth

½ white onion, coarsely chopped, plus 1 white onion, finely chopped

2 poblano chiles stemmed, seeded, and chopped

1 or 2 jalapeño or serrano chiles, stemmed, seeded, and chopped, as desired for heat

2 cloves garlic, lightly crushed and peeled

1 bunch cilantro (leaves and tender stems)

½ cup (15 g) fresh flat-leaf parsley leaves

Handful of fresh spinach or watercress, leaves and tender stems

Kosher salt

2½ pounds (1.1 kg) mixed seafood (such as peeled and deveined shrimp, shelled mussels, and squid parts), thawed if frozen

¼ cup (60 ml) extra-virgin olive oil, plus more for drizzling

Freshly ground black pepper

2 tablespoons chopped fresh oregano or marjoram, or 1 teaspoon dried Mexican oregano

2¼ cups (415 g) Bomba
or Calasparra rice

Handful of haricots verts,
stem ends timmed

¾ cup (100 g) green olives

Hot sauce (such as Cholula),
for serving

Lemon or lime wedges, for
serving

Add the rice and cook, stirring until the rice is evenly coated in the oil. Add 4 cups (950 ml) of the green stock mixture to the rice and stir once to ensure it is evenly combined. Close the grill, vent the grill for smoking, and cook without stirring (rotate the pan as needed for even cooking) until half of the liquid is absorbed, about 15 minutes. Add the remaining green stock and nestle the haricots verts, olives, and the seafood into the rice. Cook until all of the liquid is absorbed, about 20 minutes more, rotating and/or moving the pan to direct heat, as needed, to maintain a gentle simmer and even cooking.

When all the liquid has been absorbed, remove the pan from the heat and let the dish stand for 10 to 15 minutes to allow the flavors to meld. Serve warm, straight from the pan, using a large metal spoon to scrape up any *socarrat* (crunchy crust) from the bottom. Pass the hot sauce and lemon wedges at the table.

CHAPTER EIGHT

POULTRY & PORK

For most of us, dinner means chicken or pork several nights per week, whether it's crispy, juicy chicken thighs (my favorite meat to grill), a pair of Berkshire chops, or a pork tenderloin sizzled over the grates until deeply browned.

We love these meats for many reasons: they're affordable, endlessly adaptable, and absolutely shine with just a hint of char from a hot grill. After a long day, I'm happy to give simple herbed chicken breasts a quick spin on the grill, and then serve them over my favorite salad. On weekends, when I have more time to make dinner a production, I will gladly babysit a jalapeno-marinated pork roast for a few hours.

For special occasions and when you have even more time to spend around the fire, check out the longer smokes (identified by ✪). These recipes are perfect for holidays, birthdays, and any other festive event. The time investment is highly enjoyable and leads to some serious bragging rights when you serve a salad kicked up with your own homemade bacon, a gorgeous bronzed duck smoked over creamy white beans, or a show-stopping holiday ham.

This chapter teaches you to harness the potential of a wood-infused fire to create one-of-a-kind, satisfying meals that you just can't duplicate indoors.

DONENESS TEMPERATURE GUIDELINES

Chicken, Turkey, and Duck
Breasts and other boneless pieces: 165°F (74°C)

Bone-in pieces: 175°F (79°C) to 180°F (82°C)

Pork
Chops/Roast: 160°F (71°C) to 165°F (74°C)

Cured: 140°F (60°C)

GRILLED HERBED CHICKEN BREASTS
with Radicchio

SERVES 4

¼ cup (60 ml) good-quality balsamic vinegar

¼ cup (60 ml) good-quality sherry vinegar

½ medium red onion, chopped

1 tablespoon honey

¾ cup (175 ml) extra-virgin olive oil, plus more for drizzling

2 heads radicchio

4 boneless, skinless chicken breast halves

Kosher salt and freshly ground black pepper

2 tablespoons chopped fresh oregano or marjoram

1 tablespoon chopped fresh thyme

Pinch of red pepper flakes

¾ cup (100 g) coarsely grated or finely chopped Parmesan

⅓ cup (45 g) oil-cured black olives

If you're not already a radicchio fan, this salad will make you one. This recipe is inspired by a salad served at Toro restaurant in Boston that I discovered on Food52. In addition to a wonderful sweet-tart dressing (that begins as quick-pickled red onions), the brilliant trick here is soaking the radicchio in ice water to remove some of its bitterness. The result is a sweeter, crisper version of its former self, with just enough peppery bite. I add oil-cured olives, plenty of Parmesan, and a lightly grilled chicken breast to create the kind of simple—yet incredibly satisfying—meal that I could eat a couple of times a week. The dressing keeps for up to a week in the fridge, so consider prepping the components in advance.

Combine the vinegars, onion, and honey in a glass jar and macerate for 30 minutes, or up to 1 hour, at room temperature. Whisk in the olive oil and set aside.

Cut out the radicchio cores and discard, then chop the heads into 1-inch (2.5 cm) pieces and place them in the basket of a salad spinner. Fill the base of the spinner with ice water, submerge the basket, and chill the radicchio for 15 minutes. Drain the water and spin the radicchio until dry. Refrigerate until you're ready to serve.

Prepare a charcoal grill for two-zone cooking and build a medium-high fire, or heat a gas grill to high. When the coals are glowing red and covered with a fine gray ash, add your smoke source (chips, chunks, or log). Carefully wipe the preheated grill grates with a lightly oiled paper towel. Using a grill brush, scrape the grill grates clean, then carefully wipe with a lightly oiled towel again.

While the grill heats, use a meat pounder to pound the chicken breasts to an even ½-inch (1.3 cm) thickness. Place them in a glass baking dish, drizzle with enough olive oil to lightly coat, and season generously with salt and pepper. Sprinkle the chopped herbs and red pepper flakes over the chicken and use your hands to distribute the seasonings over each piece.

When the fire begins to produce a steady stream of smoke, place the chicken breasts over direct heat and grill, flipping every minute or so, until lightly charred, 6 to 7 minutes total. Transfer the breasts to a plate and let rest for 5 minutes. Place the radicchio in a bowl, top with a generous drizzle of the dressing, half of the Parmesan, and the olives and toss well. Taste the salad and add additional salt, pepper, or dressing as desired. Divide the salad among four plates and top with the remaining Parmesan and a whole or sliced chicken breast.

WILD WINGS
with Smoked Arbol Honey

3 pounds (1.4 kg) chicken wing drumettes

Extra-virgin olive oil, for drizzling

Kosher salt and freshly ground black pepper

¼ cup (60 ml) Smoked Arbol Honey (page 25)

2 tablespoons chopped fresh oregano

2 tablespoons freshly squeezed tangerine, orange, or lime juice (or a combination of both)

When I fell in love with cooking over fire, I discovered that I also adore chicken wings—when they're grilled. The direct heat of the hot grates renders the fat and creates crispy browned skin and tender, juicy meat enhanced with a wonderful charcoaled flavor that's worlds apart from the sports bar variety. Hot off the grill, the wings are delicious on their own or tossed with any number of sauces that suit the occasion or whatever you're craving (e.g., herb butter, hot sauce, or sambal-spiked mayo). In this version, Smoked Arbol Honey, one of my larder staples, creates a sweet and spicy glaze that's brightened with fresh oregano and a squeeze of citrus juice. Serve these wings as a party appetizer (they're easy to cook while you sip a beverage and chat with friends), as a snack while you're waiting on a Longer Smoke, or a roll-up-your-sleeves dinner on game night—with plenty of napkins and cold cans of your favorite local brew.

Place the drumettes in a large bowl, drizzle with enough olive oil to lightly coat, generously season with salt and pepper, and toss to combine.

Prepare a charcoal grill for two-zone cooking and build a medium fire, or heat a gas grill to medium-high.

When the coals are glowing red and covered with a fine gray ash, add your smoke source (chips, chunks, or log). Carefully wipe the preheated grill grates with a lightly oiled paper towel. Using a grill brush, scrape the grill grates clean, then carefully wipe with a lightly oiled towel again.

While the grill heats, in a separate bowl, whisk together the arbol honey, oregano, and citrus juice.

When the fire begins to produce a steady stream of smoke, place the drumettes over direct heat and cook, flipping and rotating them around the fire as needed for even cooking, until they're nicely charred on all sides, 5 to 7 minutes. Then move the chicken to indirect heat (you can even stack them up, if needed, for space), close the grill, and smoke, turning the drumettes every few minutes (and closing the grill lid in between), until they're cooked through and the juices run clear (if you're uncertain, cut into one to check), about 20 minutes more. Place the hot drumettes in the bowl with the honey mixture and toss vigorously. Taste and add more salt and/or citrus juice, if desired, and serve warm. Refrigerate leftovers in a sealed container for up to 4 days.

154 · THANK YOU FOR SMOKING

TORTILLA SOUP
with Smoked Chicken

The tomato base for this iconic soup is an elegant puree that showcases the complex flavor of smoked broth. The bowl becomes significantly more substantial—and the texture of the soup thickens—after you add the garnishes: crunchy strips of fried tortillas, grated Cheddar, avocado, cilantro, and lime. The Smoked Chicken Stock can be made well in advance and adds tremendous depth. In a pinch, you can use store-bought stock instead, and the results will still be delicious. Make this soup even more luxurious by topping each bowl with a drizzle of Mexican crema.

Note: Most dried chiles already have a smoky flavor, but you can enhance their earthy, complex flavors by toasting the chiles (try ancho, New Mexico, or guajillo) in a dry skillet over medium heat (or directly on the grill grates over a medium fire), until puffed and a shade darker.

In a large heavy skillet, heat ½ inch (1.3 cm) of frying oil over medium-high heat. When the oil is hot and shimmering, add half of the tortilla strips and fry until golden, about 1 minute (stirring a couple times to keep them from clumping). Remove with a slotted spoon and drain on paper towels; repeat with the remaining strips.

Drain all but 3 tablespoons of the oil and reduce the heat to medium. Add the onion, carrot, garlic, oregano, cumin, coriander, and a sprinkle of salt and cook, stirring frequently, for 5 minutes. Add the stock, tomatoes, bay leaves, and dried chile and bring to a boil. Turn the heat to low and simmer for 25 minutes, stirring occasionally.

Discard the bay leaves and dried chile stem, then transfer the soup to a blender (in batches if necessary) and puree until very smooth. (When blending hot liquids, remove the cap in the blender top and replace it with a kitchen towel to allow steam to release.) Alternately, use an immersion blender right in the pot. Return the puree to the pot, add the smoked chicken, and let it return to a simmer. Cook for 15 minutes more, until the chicken begins to soften and yield to the broth. Taste and adjust the seasonings, adding salt and pepper as desired.

To serve, ladle the soup into bowls and garnish with the tortilla strips, avocado, cheese, cilantro, and a squeeze of fresh lime. Refrigerate leftover soup in sealed containers for up to 1 week.

SERVES 6 TO 8

Peanut or vegetable oil, for frying

8 corn tortillas, halved and cut crosswise into ¼-inch (6 mm) strips

1 large white onion, chopped

1 large carrot, peeled and diced

2 cloves garlic, coarsely chopped

1½ teaspoons dried Mexican oregano

2 teaspoons ground cumin

1 teaspoon ground coriander

Kosher salt

2 quarts (1.9 L) Smoked Chicken Stock (page 161) or regular chicken stock

One 28-ounce (794 g) can crushed tomatoes (preferably organic)

2 fresh bay leaves

1 dried chile (see Note)

4 cups (600 g) chopped smoked chicken (see page 158)

Freshly ground black pepper

1 avocado, thinly sliced or cut into ½-inch (1.3 cm) dice, for garnish

½ cup (55 g) grated sharp Cheddar cheese, for garnish

Chopped fresh cilantro, for garnish

Lime wedges, for serving

CHICKEN THIGHS
with Smoked Green Olive Tapenade

Chicken thighs are my favorite meat to grill. They're inexpensive, forgiving (rich dark meat is less likely to dry out over the heat), and incredibly satisfying. Your goal is to crisp the skin over direct heat, and then allow the thighs to finish cooking to juicy perfection over indirect heat. Olives and lemons are natural allies with chicken. Here, a piquant tapenade made with smoked olives brings savory brightness to the luscious meat (you'll want to have bread on hand to sop up everything on the plate). I prefer an equal mix of regular and smoked olives, but feel free to adjust the ratio as you see fit. You can serve the thighs over a schmear of the tapenade (thin it as desired with additional olive oil) and a handful of feathery frisée leaves, or serve the olive puree on the side as a condiment.

Place the thighs in a large bowl, drizzle with enough olive oil to lightly coat, season generously with salt and pepper and the herb sprigs and toss to combine. Set aside at room temperature while you prepare the grill.

Prepare a charcoal grill for two-zone cooking and build a medium-high fire, or heat a gas grill to high.

When the coals are glowing red and covered with a fine gray ash, add your smoke source (chips, chunks, or log). Carefully wipe the preheated grill grates with a lightly oiled paper towel. Using a grill brush, scrape the grill grates clean, then carefully wipe with a lightly oiled towel again.

Place the thighs over direct heat, skin-side down and top with the herb sprigs. Close the grill, vent the grill for smoking, and smoke the chicken for about 4 minutes, until nice char marks form. Flip the thighs (use your tongs to reposition the herbs on top of the chicken, or discard) and smoke for about 3 minutes more, until you have nice char marks on both sides. Move the thighs to indirect heat, close the grill, and continue to cook for about 25 minutes more, flipping and rotating the thighs around the heat every 5 minutes or so, until the chicken is a rich mahogany and the meat feels firm but not dry to the touch. Transfer the thighs to a cutting board to rest for 10 minutes before serving with the tapenade and frisée. Refrigerate leftover chicken in a sealed container for up to 5 days.

SERVES 4

8 bone-in, skin-on chicken thighs

Extra-virgin olive oil, for drizzling

Kosher salt and freshly ground black pepper

4 sprigs fresh thyme, rosemary, or marjoram

½ cup (75 g) Green Olive Tapenade (page 26), or more as desired

Handful of frisée or other greens for serving (optional)

TWO SMOKED BIRDS

**MAKES 2 SMOKED
CHICKENS**

Two 4- to 4½-pound (1.8 to
2 kg) chickens

Extra-virgin olive oil,
for drizzling

Kosher salt and freshly
ground black pepper

1 small yellow onion,
quartered

1 lemon, quartered

4 sprigs thyme

4 fresh bay leaves

2 rosemary sprigs

My approach to most things in life is "more is more." Why buy one kind of fruit when you can fill the bowl with an abundant still life? When you discover a perfectly dry cava, why not get a case so you can be prepared? If you're going to build a fire to smoke a chicken, why not smoke two? That way, you have a sumptuous, juicy bird for dinner, plus extra for tacos, sandwiches, salads, or two of my favorites—tortilla soup (see page 155) and crispy flautas (see page 164)—for another night. As much as I adore the flavor of smoked chicken, the real star here is the rich, smoky pan drippings and the smoked carcass that provides the foundation for incredible Smoked Chicken Stock (page 161).

My grill retains heat exceptionally well, so if I begin with one chimney of coals and a couple of chunks of wood or a log nestled against the coals—I usually don't need to add more fuel to smoke two chickens (which usually takes just over an hour, plus resting time) at 350° (175°C). If the temperature does start to dip to 300°F (150°C) toward the end, I simply add another wood chunk or two or a couple more chunks of lump charcoal (they ignite quickly) or adjust the vents to kick up the fire with more oxygen.

The nice thing about grill-roasting at a moderate temperature is that you can actually use your hands to handle what you're cooking, which is handy when you want to move the chickens around for even cooking. I typically slide a fish spatula (or any large flat metal spatula) under the chicken (being careful not to lose the crispy skin that's been created) and use my hand to flip the chickens and rotate them. I find that if you get too caught up in only using tools, you're more likely to lose balance and pierce the meat or tear the skin. To avoid overcooking the breast meat, finish cooking with the chicken legs positioned closest to the fire.

Drizzle the chickens with enough olive oil to lightly coat and generously season the inside and outside of the chickens with salt and pepper. Insert 2 onion quarters, 2 lemon quarters, 2 thyme sprigs, 2 bay leaves, and 1 rosemary sprig inside the cavity of each chicken.

Position the chickens on a work surface, breast side up, with the legs pointing toward you. Center a 2-foot (60 cm) piece of butcher's twine under the back of a bird and bring both sides around the wings (securing them to the carcass) and up and around the legs (securing them together). Repeat with the second chicken, then set aside at room temperature for at least 30 minutes, or up to 1 hour.

Meanwhile, prepare a charcoal grill for two-zone cooking and build a medium-high fire, or heat a gas grill to medium-high.

When the coals are glowing red and covered with a fine gray ash, use tongs to remove the cooking grate and place a drip pan with 1 inch (2.5 cm) of warm water on the side with no coals (see Step Up Your Pan Drippings, page 160) and add your smoke source (chips, chunks, or log). Return the cooking grate to its position, allow it to preheat, and then carefully wipe the preheated grill grates with a lightly oiled paper towel. Using a grill brush, scrape the grill grates clean, then carefully wipe with a lightly oiled towel again.

When the fire begins to produce a steady stream of smoke, place the chickens, breast-side up, over the drip pan, close the grill, vent the grill for smoking, and smoke for 35 minutes, maintaining a grill temperature between 325°F (165°C) and 350°F (175°C). (This is a good time to refill and light your charcoal chimney so you have hot coals ready if you think you'll need them.) Using your tongs and your hands, carefully flip the chickens and rotate them from back to front. Close the grill and continue to smoke, maintaining a steady temperature, until the meat is cooked through and an instant-read thermometer inserted into the thickest part of the chicken leg reads 175°F (79°C), 35 to 40 minutes more.

Depending on the size of your birds and the temperature and model of your grill, the chickens might not take on a beautiful browned color when cooked over indirect heat. To achieve a darker, crisper skin, move them over direct heat during the last 10 to 20 minutes of cooking, carefully flipping and turning the chickens as needed for even coloring.

Transfer the chickens to a cutting board to rest for at least 15 minutes, or up to 30 minutes, before carving. Use a knife to quarter or carve the chicken as desired, and serve immediately. Store the second bird (whole or sectioned, as you prefer) and any leftovers in the refrigerator for up to 5 days.

continued

Step Up Your Pan Drippings

While the chickens roast, smoky juices collect in the drip pan, which is already filled with 1 inch (2.5 cm) of water. Since these juices heat for about an hour, why not flavor them to create a sauce for your chicken or build a base for stock (see Smoked Chicken Stock, opposite page)? To do this, add the chicken neck you pulled from the bird (along with any necks or backs that you've been saving in the freezer), a crushed garlic clove or two, herb sprigs, a few raw onion quarters, and a dried chile. While the cooked chicken rests, strain the liquid from the drip pan through a fine-mesh sieve and cook it in a small saucepan on the stove over medium heat until it thickens to your desired consistency.

SMOKED CHICKEN STOCK

This rich, smoky stock made from the carcass of a smoked chicken (or two) might be my favorite recipe in this book. The deeply flavored results are so satisfying and elevate countless meals, including soups, gumbo, chicken and dumplings, risotto, and more. It's also a delicious base for cooking dried beans (think smoky pintos or creamy white beans to serve with a pork roast).

When I smoke chickens with the intention of making stock (which is pretty much all the time), I put the drip pan to work. Since it catches all the delicious seasoned drippings and heats for more than an hour, I infuse that liquid with additional aromatics, just as I would when simmering stock. It's smart to get in the habit of stockpiling flavor enhancers—whenever I ask a butcher to spatchcock or split chickens for me, I save the backbone and freeze it for these occasions. When I know that I'm going to use the pan drippings for cooking, I take extra care to keep them free of ash. I clean the grates *before* I place the pan on the grill, and I use a light hand when moving the hot embers or adding more fuel so I don't send a flurry of ash into my pan. Because a few black flecks of ash do inevitably end up in the liquid, I strain it through a fine-mesh sieve before serving or adding to stock.

Adjust the amount of water to your other ingredients and the size of your pot (you want the carcasses to be floating and mostly covered with water). I usually end up with about 2 quarts (1.9 L) of stock.

Place the carcass in a large stockpot. Spear the cloves into 2 of the onion quarters and add them to the pot along with the remaining onion quarters, the carrot, celery, garlic, parsley, bay leaves (to taste), peppercorns, salt, and enough of the water so the carcass is floating and mostly covered by water. Bring the mixture to a boil over high heat, then immediately turn the heat to low and simmer very gently for 4 to 6 hours (as long as you have time for), skimming as necessary.

Once the stock has reached your desired concentration, remove the pan from the heat and let it cool for 10 minutes. Discard the solids and strain the liquid through a fine-mesh sieve into a glass container. Refrigerate the stock for at least 2 hours or overnight, then skim the fat from the top. Store in a sealed container in the refrigerator for up to 1 week or freeze for up to 4 months.

MAKES ABOUT 2 QUARTS (1.9 L)

1 smoked chicken carcass, plus additional chicken parts from the drip pan (such as smoked chicken backs and necks)

2 whole cloves

1 white or yellow onion, quartered

1 carrot, peeled and chopped

2 stalks celery, chopped

2 cloves garlic, peeled and crushed

3 or 4 stems fresh flat-leaf parsley, to taste

3 or 4 fresh bay leaves, torn

6 black peppercorns

2 teaspoons kosher salt

8 to 10 cups water (1.9 to 2.4 L)

GINGER-GARLIC CHICKEN

For a marinade that's whisked together in minutes, this one delivers incredible ginger, garlic, and umami flavor and creates a beautiful lacquered crust. To make prep even easier, ask your butcher to split the chicken for you, and save the backbone for stock (see page 161). The radiant heat of the grill cooks the chicken halves evenly, crisps the skin, and adds a wonderful charcoaled flavor. For this recipe, it's important to maintain a moderate temperature of 325°F (165°C) to 350°F (175°C) so the ginger and garlic paste skin don't burn. Japanese whisky is delicious, and thematically fun here, but you can use any variety. Serve this chicken with sautéed Asian greens, grilled broccolini, and steamed jasmine rice.

In a mixing bowl, whisk together the tamari, whisky, ginger, garlic, brown sugar, gochujang, and salt to make a marinade. Place the chicken halves in a baking dish. Pour three-quarters of the marinade over the chicken and reserve the rest. Use your hands to coat the entire surface of the chicken pieces with the marinade (flipping them three or four times as you go). Let the chickens marinate at room temperature for 30 minutes.

Prepare a charcoal grill for two-zone cooking and build a medium fire, or heat a gas grill to medium-high.

When the coals are glowing red and covered with a fine gray ash, use tongs to remove the cooking grate and place a drip pan with 1 inch (2.5 cm) of warm water on the side with no coals, and add your smoke source (chips, chunks, or log). Return the cooking grate to its position, allow it to preheat, and then carefully wipe the preheated grill grates with a lightly oiled paper towel. Using a grill brush, scrape the grill grates clean, then carefully wipe with a lightly oiled towel again.

When the fire begins to produce a steady stream of smoke, place the chicken halves, skin-side down, over direct heat, close the grill, vent the grill for smoking, and smoke for about 35 minutes, flipping the chickens every 7 to 8 minutes and brushing on more marinade after each turn. The chickens are done when they are very juicy, the meat pulls easily away from the bone, and an instant-read thermometer inserted into the thickest part of the chicken leg reads 175°F (79°C).

Transfer the chickens to a cutting board to rest for 10 minutes, then cut into serving portions and serve immediately.

SERVES 4

½ cup (120 ml) tamari

2 tablespoons Japanese whisky

2 tablespoons finely grated fresh ginger

3 cloves garlic, finely grated

2 tablespoons light brown sugar

1 tablespoon fermented Korean red chile paste (gochujang)

1 teaspoon kosher salt

One 4- to 4½-pound (1.8 to 2 kg) chicken, split in half lengthwise

SISSY'S FLAUTAS
with Avocado Crema

SERVES 4

Avocado Crema

1 cup (220 g) Mexican crema

1 ripe avocado

3 or 4 pickled jalapeño slices

1 tablespoon pickled jalapeño brine, plus more as desired

1 serrano chile (fresh or charred on the grill), stemmed, halved, and seeded

2 tablespoons coarsely chopped fresh cilantro (leaves and tender stems)

Flautas

Peanut or vegetable oil, for frying

About 4 cups (520 g) lightly shredded smoked chicken (page 158)

Kosher salt

16 best-quality 6-inch (15 cm) corn tortillas

½ small napa cabbage, very thinly sliced (about 3 cups/210 g), for garnish

6 to 8 radishes, thinly sliced, for garnish

½ cup (20 g) chopped fresh cilantro (leaves and tender stems), for garnish

½ cup (50 g) grated Cotija cheese, for garnish

Red salsa, for serving

When my family moved to Texas, I fell in love with flautas, snug cylinders of corn tortillas (*flauta* is Spanish for "flute") rolled around a meat filling (typically beef or chicken) and fried until crisp. In restaurants, they're a guilty pleasure, but they're often greasy, and the accoutrements can be uninspired. The first time my friend Melissa Garnett (aka Sissy) prepared them for me, served with a pile of thinly sliced cabbage, radishes, a dusting of grated Cotija cheese and drizzle of spicy crema, I swooned. When I get effusive and tell her they're my favorite thing (and annual birthday dinner request), she shakes her head and laughs because they're so simple. But when all the other elements come together and they're made with great ingredients (like smoked chicken), flautas are the perfect home-style meal for family and friends, and better than anything you'll find in a restaurant. Once you get your rhythm down, you'll be able to fry several of them at once.

To make the avocado crema, combine the crema, avocado, jalapeño and its brine, serrano, and cilantro in a blender or the bowl of a food processor and blend until very smooth. Taste the crema and add more jalapeño brine, if desired, then transfer to a serving dish and set aside.

To make the flautas, in a large heavy skillet (preferably cast iron), heat ½ inch (1.3 cm) of frying oil. Place a wire cooling rack on a rimmed baking sheet and preheat the oven to 200°F (95°C).

Lightly season the chicken with salt. Wrap the tortillas in a damp kitchen towel and microwave until softened and pliable, about 20 seconds. Working with 1 tortilla at a time, place about 2 tablespoons of the chicken in the middle of a tortilla and wrap it into a snug cylinder. Using tongs or your fingers, carefully place the flauta, seam-side down, into the hot oil and fry until the tortilla is golden brown and melds with the filling, about 45 seconds. Use tongs to flip the tortilla and cook the other side until golden brown, about 45 seconds more. Remove the flauta from the oil, allowing excess oil to drain back into skillet, then place it on the wire rack in the warm oven. Repeat with the remaining chicken and tortillas (once you get the rhythm down, you'll be able to cook 3 or 4 at once).

Serve the flautas warm, on top of the cabbage, radishes, cilantro, a generous drizzle of the avocado crema, a sprinkling of Cotija, and your favorite red salsa on the side.

✪ SOUTH TEXAS–STYLE TURKEY

SERVES 10 TO 12

One 12- to 15-pound (5.4 to 6.8 kg) turkey

Extra-virgin olive oil, for drizzling

Kosher salt and freshly ground black pepper

¼ cup (50 g) packed light brown sugar

2 tablespoons ground cumin

2 tablespoons ground coriander

2 teaspoons dried Mexican oregano

2 teaspoons sweet paprika

2 teaspoons pure ground chile powder (such as New Mexico or ancho)

2 tablespoons white wine vinegar

The swoon-worthy results and surprising ease of cooking a whole turkey over a wood-infused fire just might make you rethink your traditional Thanksgiving menu. Two things bring this method together: Butterflying the turkey creates a broad, flat surface that cooks more quickly and evenly. And to address the perennial quandary of how to cook the turkey through without drying out the breast meat, the coals are arranged in a crescent shape that allows both parts of the bird reach the ideal temperatures at the same time.

You can ask your butcher to spatchcock the turkey for you, or you can wrangle it yourself with poultry shears (be sure to reserve the backbone, neck, and giblets for making turkey stock or gravy). It's important to maintain the grill at a medium heat of 325°F (165°C) to 350°F (175°C) so the skin doesn't get too dark while the meat cooks through. To account for carryover cooking (which is more significant with a large bird), I pull the turkey off the grill at the lower end of the doneness range. Slathered with warm spices, this turkey is delicious on its own, with gravy, in tacos, and sliced for sandwiches.

At least 1 hour before cooking, spatchcock the turkey. Rinse the carcass under cold water, pat it dry with paper towels, and place it on a rimmed baking sheet. Drizzle both sides of the bird with oil and season generously with salt and pepper.

In a small bowl, stir together the brown sugar, cumin, coriander, oregano, paprika, chile powder, and vinegar until it forms a thick paste. Use your hands to slather the mixture over both sides of the turkey and set it aside to marinate while you prepare the fire.

Prepare a charcoal grill for two-zone cooking and build a medium-high fire, or heat a gas grill to high.

When the coals are glowing red and covered with a fine gray ash, use your tongs to arrange them into a crescent moon shape and add your smoke source (chips, chunks, or log). Carefully wipe the preheated grill grates with a lightly oiled paper towel. Using a grill brush, scrape the grill grates clean, then carefully wipe with a lightly oiled towel again.

continued

When the fire begins to produce a steady stream of smoke, place the turkey on the grill, skin-side down, with the turkey legs and thighs situated over the direct heat of the coals and the breast toward indirect heat. Close the grill, vent the grill for smoking, and smoke for 2 to 2½ hours, until an instant-read thermometer inserted into the thickest part of the thigh reads between 175°F (79°C) and 180°F (82°C) and the breast reads between 160°F (71°C) and 165°F (74°C). Add additional hot coals or wood chunks as needed to maintain a steady temperature between 325°F (165°C) and 350°F (175°C).

Transfer the turkey to a cutting board to rest for at least 20 minutes, then slice it into portions and serve immediately.

FIVE-SPICE DUCK BREASTS

The intoxicating fragrance of Chinese five-spice powder (made with fennel, clove, star anise, cinnamon, and Sichuan pepper) is an easy ally to the rich flavor of duck. Many people are intimidated to prepare duck at home, but with attention to a few key details, grilling duck breasts couldn't be easier and yields crispy, impressive results. Scoring the skin allows the fat to render and crisp. You don't want a scorching fire here—a moderate flame will cook the meat evenly and help avoid flare-ups that can burn the exterior of the meat. Despite its fatty skin, duck meat is actually quite lean and tends to dry out if you cook it past medium-rare, so pay attention to doneness toward the end of the process. Serve the sliced, grilled meat atop a slather of smoked almond butter or a pile of frisée with a sprinkling of pomegranate seeds.

SERVES 4 TO 6

Four 10-ounce (280 g) Muscovy duck breast halves, with skin

Kosher salt and freshly ground black pepper

2 teaspoons Chinese five-spice powder

Smoked Marcona Almond Butter (page 86), for serving (optional)

Handful of frisee, for serving (optional)

Pomegranate seeds, for garnish (optional)

Using a sharp knife, score the skin of each breast in a crosshatch pattern, making sure that you don't cut into the meat. Generously season both sides the breasts with salt, pepper, and the five-spice powder. Set aside while you prepare the grill (the breasts can also be seasoned and refrigerated a day in advance; just bring them to room temperature before cooking).

Prepare a charcoal grill for two-zone cooking and build a medium fire, or heat a gas grill to medium-high.

When the coals are glowing red and covered with a fine gray ash, add your smoke source (chips, chunks, or log). Carefully wipe the preheated grill grates with a lightly oiled paper towel. Using a grill brush, scrape the grill grates clean, then carefully wipe with a lightly oiled towel again.

When the fire begins to produce a steady stream of smoke, place the duck breasts over direct heat, skin-side down, close the grill, vent the grill for smoking, and smoke until lightly charred and crisp, about 4 minutes. Use tongs to flip the breasts and cook for 4 to 5 minutes more, until an instant-read thermometer inserted into the thickest part of the breast reads 125°F (52°C) for medium-rare. Transfer the duck to a cutting board to rest for 10 minutes.

To serve, slice the meat thinly across the grain on a diagonal and arrange on a platter over the nut butter or a pile of frisée, and garnish with pomegranate seeds. Refrigerate leftovers in a sealed container for up to 4 days.

✪ SMOKED DUCK
with Chateau Salt & White Beans

Duck

One 4½- to 5-pound (2 to 2.3 kg) duck, thawed if frozen

1½ teaspoons black peppercorns

1 teaspoon pink peppercorns

1 teaspoon fennel seeds

1 teaspoon allspice berries

1 tablespoon plus 1 teaspoon kosher salt

1 small onion, quartered

3 or 4 fresh bay leaves

White Beans

1 pound (450 g) dried white beans (preferably Marcella)

2 cups (475 ml) Smoked Chicken Stock (page 161) or regular chicken stock

2 cups (475 ml) water

1 white or yellow onion, chopped

3 cloves garlic

3 or 4 fresh bay leaves

4 or 5 sprigs marjoram, oregano, or thyme

1 duck neck (included with the carcass)

1 or 2 dried arbol chiles, as desired for heat

Kosher salt and freshly ground black pepper

Sherry vinegar

Smoking a seasoned duck over a pan of white beans creates a cassoulet-style feast of deep flavors and buttery textures. My favorite beans for this recipe are Marcella beans, which are available online from Rancho Gordo. The thin-skinned beans don't require soaking and have a creamy texture. Depending on how long it takes for your duck to cook, you might need to finish off the beans on the stovetop, but they'll be well on their way and intensely flavored.

To prep the duck, remove any organ meats from the carcass (reserve the neck for the beans), rinse it under cold water, pat dry with paper towels, and place on a rimmed baking sheet. In a small bowl, combine the peppercorns, fennel seeds, allspice, and salt. Season the inside and outside of the duck with the spice mixture. Insert the onion quarters and bay leaves inside the cavity.

To make the beans, combine the beans, stock, water, onion, garlic, bay leaves, herbs, duck neck, and chile in a disposable aluminum pan.

Prepare a charcoal grill for two-zone cooking and build a medium-high fire, or heat a gas grill to high. When the coals are glowing red and covered with a fine gray ash, add your smoke source (chips, chunks, or log). Carefully wipe the preheated grill grates with a lightly oiled paper towel. Using a grill brush, scrape the grill grates clean, then carefully wipe with a lightly oiled towel again.

When the fire begins to produce a steady stream of smoke, use tongs to remove the cooking grate and place the pan of white beans on the side with no coals. Return the cooking grate to its position and place the duck, breast-side up, directly on the grate over the beans. Close the grill, vent the grill for smoking, and smoke for about 1½ hours, until an instant-read thermometer inserted into the thickest part of the thigh reads between 160°F (70°C) and 170°F (80°C) and the breast reads between 145°F (62°C) and 150°F (68°C). Add hot coals or wood chunks as needed to maintain a steady temperature of around 300°F (150°C). Transfer the duck to a cutting board to rest for at least 20 minutes.

Remove the beans from the grill and taste. If they aren't quite done, transfer them to a pot and simmer over medium-low heat on the stovetop. When the beans are creamy and tender, discard the onion, bay leaves (to taste), herbs, duck neck, and chile. Season to taste with salt and pepper and a splash of sherry vinegar.

To serve, slice the duck into portions and serve it alongside the warm beans. Refrigerate leftovers in a sealed container for up to 5 days.

✪ JALAPEÑO PORK SHOULDER

SERVES 8 TO 10

2 cloves garlic, lightly crushed and peeled

2 jalapeño chiles, stemmed, halved, and seeded

2 tablespoons fresh thyme leaves

2 tablespoons fresh oregano leaves

2 tablespoons kosher salt

1 tablespoon pink peppercorns

1 tablespoon freshly ground black pepper

Finely grated zest of 2 oranges

⅓ cup (80 ml) freshly squeezed orange juice

2 tablespoons extra-virgin olive oil

One 5- to 6-pound (2.2 to 2.7 kg) bone-in pork shoulder

4 cups (280 g) Red Cabbage Slaw (see page 98), for serving

8 to 10 ciabatta rolls, split, for serving

Slathered with spicy marinade, this richly flavored roast is both succulent and brightly flavored, thanks to fresh jalapeño, thyme, and oregano. The marinade comes together in minutes, so it's easy to prepare the meat in the morning, or the night before a backyard party. The meat requires about three hours of cooking time, so depending on your grill (and how well it holds heat), you'll need to add hot coals every hour or so. I love to serve this roast with a mustardy red cabbage slaw and crackly ciabatta rolls, but it's also delicious alongside white beans (simmered with a Parmesan rind) or steamed rice. The availability of pork shoulder varies from week to week at my market. Sometimes the shoulders have smallish bones; other times they're boneless. You can absolutely use either one for this recipe, just keep in mind that the boneless cut may take a bit longer to cook. Regardless, let the internal temperature of the meat and the feel (it should be fork-tender when it comes off the grill) be your guide.

Combine the garlic, jalapeños, thyme, oregano, salt, peppercorns, and pepper in the bowl of a food processor and pulse into a coarse puree. Add the orange zest, orange juice, and olive oil and process until combined.

Place the pork in a baking dish. Using a paring knife, make small incisions about ½ inch (1.3 cm) deep on all sides of the pork shoulder. Pour the jalapeño mixture over the meat and use your hands to coat all sides, gently working the mixture into the incisions. Cover the meat with plastic wrap and refrigerate for at least 2 hours, or up to 1 day.

About 1 hour before smoking, remove the pork from the refrigerator.

Prepare a charcoal grill for two-zone cooking and build a medium-high fire, or heat a gas grill to high.

When the coals are glowing red and covered with a fine gray ash, use tongs to remove the cooking grate and place a drip pan with 1 inch (2.5 cm) of warm water on the side with no coals, and add your smoke source (chips, chunks, or log). Carefully wipe the preheated grill grates with a lightly oiled paper towel. Using a grill brush, scrape the grill grates clean, then carefully wipe with a lightly oiled towel again.

When the fire begins to produce a steady stream of smoke, place the pork (with the marinade still clinging to it) over indirect heat, close the grill, vent the grill for smoking, and smoke for about 3 hours, until an instant-read thermometer inserted into the center of the roast reads 170°F (80°C). Add additional hot coals or wood chunks as needed to maintain a steady temperature of 325°F (165°c) to 350°F (175°C).

Remove the pork from heat and allow it to rest in a baking dish (to capture its juices) for at least 15 minutes, or up to 30 minutes, before slicing. You can cut the meat into thick or thin slices, or use to forks to shred it. Either way, drizzle the pork with the meaty juices before serving a generous portion on the rolls with ½ cup (35 g) or so of slaw on top.

RED RIVER RIBS

SERVES 4 TO 6

3 tablespoons kosher salt

1 tablespoon plus 1 teaspoon sweet paprika

1 tablespoon garlic granules

1 tablespoon ground coriander

1 tablespoon freshly ground black pepper

2 teaspoons Korean red pepper flakes (gochugaru)

2 racks St. Louis-style spare ribs (about 4¼ pounds/2 kg), trimmed

Hot sauce or barbecue sauce, for serving (optional)

Rib lovers are a passionate bunch, with strong opinions about their favorite cut and style. I love a dry rub that relies on warm red spices—a style that's associated with Memphis. After the ribs have absorbed smoke for a couple of hours, I finish them in the oven (you could also finish them on the grill if you maintain the fire). The low heat allows the meat to gently braise in the seasoned juices, resulting in tender, fragrant ribs that will disappear from the table quickly.

In a small bowl, combine the salt, paprika, garlic granules, coriander, black pepper, and Korean red pepper flakes. Sprinkle the mixture over both sides of each rib rack, then use your hands to coat the surfaces evenly with the seasoning. Place the racks on a platter and let them rest at room temperature for 30 minutes, or wrap them well with plastic and refrigerate for up to 2 days. (Let the meat come to room temperature before grilling.)

Prepare a charcoal grill for two-zone cooking and build a medium-high fire, or heat a gas grill to high. When the coals are glowing red and covered with a fine gray ash, use tongs to remove the cooking grate and place a drip pan with 1 inch (2.5 cm) of warm water on the side with no coals, and add your smoke source (chips, chunks, or log). Carefully wipe the preheated grill grates with a lightly oiled paper towel. Using a grill brush, scrape the grill grates clean, then carefully wipe with a lightly oiled towel again.

When the fire begins to produce a steady stream of smoke, place the ribs over indirect heat (if a portion of the rack stretches over the coals, it's okay), close the grill, vent the grill for smoking, and smoke for 30 minutes, using the vents to maintain a temperature of 275°F (135°C) to 300°F (150°C). Use tongs to flip and rotate the ribs, so the opposite side is stretching over the coals. Close the grill and smoke for 1½ hours more, flipping and rotating the ribs every 30 minutes, adding more coals and wood as needed to maintain a steady temperature and smoke flow, until the ribs are deeply fragrant and have a nice crisp crust.

Preheat the oven to 225°F (108°C). Cover a rimmed baking sheet with a piece of heavy-duty aluminum foil and top the foil with two layers of parchment paper. Stack the racks on top of each other on the baking sheet. Wrap the racks tightly in the paper and foil packet, and cook in the oven for 2 hours. Remove the racks from the oven and let them rest in the packet for at least 10 minutes and up to 30 minutes.

To serve, unwrap the racks, slice into individual ribs, and serve with your favorite sauce on the side.

LUXEMBOURG-STYLE FRISÉE SALAD

SERVES 4

Croutons

Two 1-inch (2.5 cm)-thick slabs miche or levain bread, cut into 1-inch (2.5 cm) cubes

Extra-virgin olive oil, for drizzling

Kosher salt and freshly ground black pepper

2 teaspoons chopped fresh thyme, or 1½ teaspoon dried herbes de Provence, for seasoning

Salad

4 thick strips Cowgirl Bacon (page 182), cut into ½-inch (1.3 cm) cubes

1 clove garlic, finely chopped

Kosher salt

2 tablespoons finely chopped shallots

1 tablespoon red wine vinegar

1 tablespoon freshly squeezed lemon juice

1 generous tablespoon Dijon mustard

¼ cup plus 2 tablespoons (90 ml) extra-virgin olive oil

Freshly ground black pepper

2 heads frisée, cored and cut into 2-inch (5 cm) pieces

1 cup (75 g) crumbled blue cheese

2 tablespoons snipped fresh chives or chervil

Back when I lived in New York, my friend Chip and I often ended late nights on the town at Café Luxembourg, where we'd sip Côtes du Rhône and nibble frites at the bar, look for celebrities, and watch the circus of Lincoln Center roll in. And eventually, we'd both dig into the "country" French salad—a tumble of frisée lettuce, chewy lardons, croutons made with a hearty, country-style French bread, and blue cheese—without a doubt, the most inspired combination to ever grace a salad menu. To this day, whenever feathery, pale green and white heads of frisée appear in the market, I know exactly what's for dinner. To make this salad even more satisfying, top it off with a soft-poached egg.

To make the croutons, preheat the oven to 400°F (200°C). Place the bread cubes on a rimmed baking sheet, drizzle them with enough olive oil to lightly coat, and season generously with salt, pepper, and thyme. Toss to combine, then bake the croutons for 9 to 11 minutes, until golden (flip them one or two times while they bake). Remove from the oven and set aside.

To make the salad, heat a skillet over medium-high heat. Add the bacon and fry until browned and crisp but still moist, about 8 minutes. Transfer to a paper towel–lined plate to drain and set aside.

On a cutting board, use the flat side of a chef's knife to mash the garlic with a pinch of salt until a paste forms. In a large salad bowl, whisk together the garlic paste, shallots, vinegar, lemon juice, and mustard. Whisk in the olive oil and season with salt and pepper.

Place the frisée in the bowl with the dressing and toss until evenly coated. Add the bacon, blue cheese, chives, and croutons and toss again. Serve immediately.

✪ HOLIDAY HAM
with Red Boat Salt

Moist and slightly sweet, spiral-cut hams—the ones that most of us serve for the holidays—can be flavored more dramatically and given a deeper smoke flavor on the grill. In this version, Red Boat salt (essentially a dehydrated version of the brand's popular fish sauce), bourbon, and other aromatics infuse the meat with umami notes that play beautifully with pork's inherent sweetness. For the best results, seek out an artisanal ham from a heritage breed like Berkshire, Duroc, or Red Wattle.

Note: If you are using a spiral-cut ham, place it in the roasting pan cut side down so the ham slices are parallel to the grill grate. The weight of the ham compresses the slices and reduces moisture loss.

Combine the bourbon, brown sugar, mustard, Red Boat salt, soy sauce, fennel seeds, coriander seeds, and cayenne in a saucepan and cook over medium heat just until the sugar dissolves, 3 to 4 minutes. Remove the pan from the heat and let the glaze cool.

Using a sharp knife, score the ham in a crosshatch pattern, about 1 inch (2.5 cm) apart and ½ inch (1.3 cm) deep on all sides except the cut side. Place the ham, cut side down, in a roasting pan or large disposable aluminum pan. Brush some of the glaze over the top (don't use all of it; you'll be repeating this process on the grill). Loosely tent the ham with aluminum foil and set aside.

Meanwhile, prepare a charcoal grill for two-zone cooking and build a medium-low fire, or heat a gas grill to medium.

When the coals are glowing red and covered with a fine gray ash, use tongs to remove the cooking grate and place a drip pan with 1 inch (2.5 cm) of warm water on the side with no coals, and add your smoke source (chips, chunks, or log). Carefully wipe the preheated grill grates with a lightly oiled paper towel. Using a grill brush, scrape the grill grates clean, then carefully wipe with a lightly oiled towel again.

When the fire begins to produce a steady stream of smoke, place the ham over indirect heat, close the grill, vent the grill for smoking, and smoke for 2 to 2½ hours, brushing the ham with additional glaze every 30 minutes, until an instant-read thermometer inserted into the thickest part of the ham

continued

SERVES 16 TO 20, WITH DELICIOUS LEFTOVERS

1 cup (240 ml) bourbon

½ cup (100 g) packed dark brown sugar

2 tablespoons Creole mustard, or other spicy whole-grain mustard

2 tablespoons Red Boat salt, or ⅓ cup fish sauce

2 tablespoons soy sauce

1 tablespoon fennel seeds, lightly crushed

1 tablespoon coriander seeds, lightly crushed

½ teaspoon cayenne

One 7- to 8-pound (3.2 to 3.6 kg) fully cooked smoked bone-in ham (but not touching the bone) registers 120°F (49°C). Add additional hot coals or wood chunks as needed to maintain a steady temperature between 325°F (165°C) and 350°F (175°C). Remove the foil and continue to cook the ham until the glaze is bubbling and caramelized and an instant-read thermometer inserted into the thickest part of the ham reads 135°F (58°C), about 30 minutes more.

Transfer the ham to a cutting board, tent it with foil, and let it rest for about 20 minutes before carving. Pour any remaining glaze into the roasting pan and heat the mixture on the grill or stove over medium-low heat, gently whisking, until everything that is baked onto the pan dissolves into the glaze. Simmer until syrupy, 4 to 5 minutes.

Carve the ham as desired and arrange on a platter. Serve with the pan juices.

CRISPY LEMONGRASS CHOPS
with Charred Green Beans & Noodles

SERVES 4 TO 6

⅓ cup plus 2 tablespoons (100 g) packed light brown sugar

4 stalks lemongrass, white and light green parts, thinly sliced

2 shallots, thinly sliced

One 1-inch (2.5 cm) piece ginger, peeled and coarsely chopped

4 cloves garlic, thinly sliced

⅓ cup (80 ml) fish sauce (preferably Red Boat)

2 tablespoons soy sauce or mushroom soy sauce

2 tablespoons canola oil

1 tablespoon cornstarch

10 to 12 thin-cut pork chops (1¾ to 2 pounds/795 to 900 g)

One 14-ounce (400 g) package flat (linguine-shaped) rice noodles

1 pound (450 g) haricots verts or regular green beans

1 handful (about ¾ cup/30 g) lightly chopped fresh herbs (preferably a mix of mint, cilantro, and Thai basil)

1 cup (105 g) thinly sliced Persian cucumbers

½ cup (60 g) Curry-Chile Peanuts (page 73) or salted roasted peanuts, coarsely chopped

Lime wedges, for serving

I don't think I've ever met a Vietnamese-style noodle salad I didn't like. However, there's a big difference between mediocre takeout and the stellar creations you can make at home when you seek out the best, freshest ingredients and add a hot, smoky grill. In this recipe, a fragrant lemongrass marinade is whizzed together in minutes and infuses pork chops and green beans with a sweet-and-spicy flavor. By the time you've prepared the fire, the meat and green beans are ready to be quickly charred and served with a heap of chilled rice noodles, fresh herbs, and vegetables. *Nuoc cham*, a Vietnamese dipping sauce, pulls all the flavors together. Rather than using the skinny "stick" vermicelli, I like the wider, linguine-size rice noodles that can hold up to all the ingredients.

Place the brown sugar, lemongrass, shallots, ginger, and garlic in the bowl of a food processor and process into a rough paste. Use a rubber spatula to transfer the paste to a bowl and whisk in the fish sauce, soy sauce, canola oil, and cornstarch. Place the pork chops in a large sealable plastic bag, pour in three-quarters of the marinade, press out excess air, and seal. Marinate the meat at room temperature for 30 minutes, or refrigerate for up to 12 hours (remove the pork from the refrigerator 30 minutes before grilling). Set the remaining marinade aside.

Prepare a charcoal grill for two-zone cooking and build a medium-high fire, or heat a gas grill to high.

When the coals are glowing red and covered with a fine gray ash, add your smoke source (chips, chunks, or log). Carefully wipe the preheated grill grates with a lightly oiled paper towel. Using a grill brush, scrape the grill grates clean, then carefully wipe with a lightly oiled towel again.

To make the *nuoc cham*, in a small bowl, whisk together the lime juice, fish sauce, sugar, 6 tablespoons (90 ml) of the water, the garlic, and bird's-eye chile. The dressing will taste very pungent (add additional water, if desired), but the noodles and other ingredients will balance the sharp edges. Set the dressing aside.

Bring a large pot of generously salted water to a boil over high heat. Add the noodles and cook according to the package instructions until tender but not mushy. Immediately drain the noodles in a colander, rinse them briefly with cold water, and set aside to drain again.

When the fire begins to produce a steady stream of smoke, place the chops over direct heat and grill for 3 to 4 minutes, turning the chops frequently and shifting them to the cooler side of the grill if there are excessive flare-ups, until they are charred and just cooked through. Remove the chops from the heat and let the meat rest.

Place a grill basket over direct heat for 5 minutes. Place the green beans in a bowl, drizzle them with the remaining marinade, and toss to coat. Add the beans to the hot grill basket and cook, shaking the basket or tossing the beans with tongs for 2 to 3 minutes, until nicely charred. Remove the basket from the heat.

Place the noodles on a large serving platter and top with the pork (and any of its juices) and the charred green beans. Sprinkle the herbs, cucumber, and peanuts over the top, then drizzle everything with *nuoc cham* and serve with lime wedges.

Nuoc Cham

½ cup (120 ml) freshly squeezed lime juice

⅓ cup (80 ml) fish sauce (preferably Red Boat)

2 tablespoons light brown sugar

6 to 8 tablespoons (90 to 120 ml) water

1 clove garlic, minced

1 Thai bird's-eye or pequin chile, stemmed and finely chopped

✪ COWGIRL BACON

MAKES 2 POUNDS (900 G)

2 pounds (900 g) fresh pork belly, sliced in half

4 cups (800 g) kosher salt

¾ teaspoon curing salt (see Note)

2¼ cups (450 g) granulated sugar

1¾ cups (350 g) lightly packed light brown sugar

2 tablespoons pink peppercorns, crushed

1 tablespoon juniper berries, lightly crushed

1 tablespoon fennel seeds, lightly crushed

Although it would give me some serious street cred in regions of southwest Louisiana, smoking pork belly isn't the kind of thing I do on a weekly basis (after all, it has to cure for ten days). So, when I do prepare it, I invest in the best-quality pork available—from humanely raised hogs or a heritage breed like Duroc or Berkshire (also known as Kurobuta). Restaurants smoke whole pork bellies weighing from 10 to 12 pounds (4.5 to 5.4 kg). Luckily, Whole Foods sells pork bellies by the pound, so I smoke 1-pound (450 g) pieces that yield enough for a few favorite dishes, and then freeze the rest for later.

For best results, slice the bacon when it's cold (room-temperature bacon is soft and flabby). I like the chewy texture and meaty bite of thick, slightly undercooked slices that showcase the flavor of the pork; however, thinner slices will crisp up better in a skillet.

Note: Curing salt typically contains sugar, nitrates, and curing agents that help preserve meat and prevent the flesh from turning drab and gray. Regular salt cannot be used as a substitute.

Pat the pork belly with paper towels to remove any excess moisture.

Combine the kosher salt, curing salt, the sugars, peppercorns, juniper berries, and fennel seeds in a mixing bowl. Place the pork in a baking dish or a large plastic container. Cover the top of the pork with a layer of the salt mixture, then flip it over and top with the remaining salt, using your hands to gently pack and nestle the pork into the seasoning.

Cover the container with plastic wrap and refrigerate for 10 days. This process will "cure" the belly, and you'll have salt pork or unsmoked bacon.

Remove the pork from the salt and rinse each piece under cold water, then pat dry with paper towels. Place the pork on a wire rack inserted into a rimmed baking sheet and refrigerate overnight, uncovered. (Air-drying the bacon allows a dry, slightly tacky skin to form for the smoke to adhere to—a surface that's essential to create the deeply bronzed color that makes bacon so crave-worthy.)

Prepare a charcoal grill for two-zone cooking and build a medium fire, or heat a gas grill to medium-high. When the coals are glowing red and covered with a fine gray ash, use tongs to remove the cooking grate and place a drip pan with 1 inch (2.5 cm) of warm water on the side with no coals, and add your smoke source (chips, chunks, or log). Carefully wipe the preheated grill grates with a lightly oiled paper towel. Using a grill brush, scrape the grill grates clean, then carefully wipe with a lightly oiled towel again.

When the fire begins to produce a steady stream of smoke, place the pork over indirect heat, close the grill, vent for smoking, and smoke the pork for about 2 hours, maintaining a steady temperature between 150°F (68°C) and 160°F (70°C). Add additional hot coals or wood chunks as needed to maintain the temperature until an instant-read thermometer inserted into the thickest part of the bacon reads 150°F (68°C). Transfer the bacon to a wire rack and let it cool to room temperature. Tightly wrap the bacon in plastic and refrigerate it overnight to let the flavor and texture develop. The bacon is now ready to slice and cook. Store it, tightly wrapped, in the refrigerator for up to 5 days or in the freezer for up to 4 months.

PORK TENDERLOIN
with Olive-Anchovy Vinaigrette

SERVES 4 TO 6

Two 8-ounce (225 g) pork tenderloins

Extra-virgin olive oil, for drizzling

Kosher salt and freshly ground black pepper

Olive-Anchovy Vinaigrette

1 clove garlic, minced

3 anchovy fillets, drained and finely chopped

Pinch of red pepper flakes or crumbled chile pequin

1 generous tablespoon Creole mustard, or other spicy whole-grain mustard

Finely grated zest and juice of 1 lemon

2 teaspoons sherry vinegar

¼ cup (60 ml) extra-virgin olive oil

½ cup (65 g) chopped pitted kalamata olives

½ cup (65 g) chopped pitted green olives (such as Castelvetrano, Lucques, or Picholine)

1 tablespoon chopped fresh thyme

1 tablespoon chopped fresh marjoram or oregano

Kosher salt and freshly ground black pepper

About 6 ounces (170 g) arugula

½ cup (50 g) shaved Parmesan or Pecorino Romano

The easiest way to infuse pork tenderloin with some serious personality is to give it a spin over a smoky fire and pair it with a zippy olive dressing and a pile of fresh, peppery greens. This dish is back porch dinner at its easiest and most satisfying. Consider serving the pork alongside roasted potatoes, or slabs of grilled bread.

Place the tenderloins in a baking dish, drizzle them with enough olive oil to lightly coat, and generously season with salt and pepper. Use your hands to rub the oil and seasonings all over the meat.

Prepare a charcoal grill for two-zone cooking and build a medium-high fire, or heat a gas grill to high.

While the grill heats, make the vinaigrette. In a small bowl, whisk together the garlic, anchovies, red pepper flakes, mustard, lemon zest and juice, and vinegar and then whisk in the olive oil oil. Whisk in the olives, thyme, and marjoram and season to taste with salt and pepper.

When the coals are glowing red and covered with a fine gray ash, add your smoke source (chips, chunks, or log). Carefully wipe the preheated grill grates with a lightly oiled paper towel. Using a grill brush, scrape the grill grates clean, then carefully wipe with a lightly oiled towel again.

When the fire begins to produce a steady stream of smoke, place the pork over direct heat, close the grill, vent for smoking, and smoke for 10 to 12 minutes, using your tongs to roll the meat every couple of minutes (be sure to close the grill each time), until the tenderloin is cooked to medium (150°F/70°C) and deeply browned on all sides. Transfer the meat to a cutting board to rest for 5 to 7 minutes.

To serve, place the arugula on a large platter. Thinly slice the pork (warm or room temperature) and place it over the greens, drizzling any of its juices over the meat. Top with the vinaigrette and Parmesan. Refrigerate any leftovers (the sliced pork makes a great sandwich) for up to 5 days.

CHAPTER NINE

BEEF & LAMB

For carnivores, few aromas are more seductive than the mingling of a charcoal fire and the dripping, sizzling fat of well-marbled steak. Growing up in the Midwest, any celebratory occasion (like a Saturday evening in late June, for instance) meant a grilled steak, usually served with a side of "Homer" potatoes (thinly sliced potatoes and onions fried in butter that my grandfather used to prepare). To this day, the smell of red meat on the grill conjures up happy memories of clanging horseshoes, fireflies, rhubarb pie, and those meals.

A meal made with grilled beef or lamb still feels like a special occasion (partly because I don't eat it as often as I used to). In that spirit, the recipes in this chapter range from casual dinners like burgers or tacos that make the most of inexpensive cuts, to splurges like a porterhouse steak or prime rib worthy of a celebration.

I admit that I'm a bit cavalier when it comes to gauging the doneness for, say, a strip steak. But cooking prime cuts is an investment, so pay close attention to the temperature of the grill (adjusting the air vents as necessary to maintain a steady temperature) and use a thermometer to check the internal temperature of the meat to ensure it's done to your liking. To account for carryover cooking, or the residual heat that continues to cook the meat once you remove it from the heat, pull the meat off the grill when the temperature reads about 5 degrees lower than your target doneness.

Some of the cuts in this chapter, like short ribs and chuck roast, are associated with long braises and other forms of indoor cooking. You'll be surprised at how easy it is to transfer the process outdoors and delighted at how a wood-infused fire elevates a dish.

When you have time to make the meal an event, try one of the longer smokes (identified by ✪) that require a bit more planning and cooking time. The end result is an incredible meal and memories for everyone at the table.

DONENESS TEMPERATURE GUIDELINES

Rare: 125°F (52°C)

Medium-rare: 130°F (55°C)

Medium: 135°F (57°C)

Medium-well: 145°F (63°C)

Well done: 155°F (68°C)

COWBOY BURGERS

SERVES 4

1 pound (450 g) freshly ground beef chuck

1 pound (450 g) freshly ground pork

1 jalapeño or serrano chile, stemmed, seeded and finely chopped

½ cup (20 g) chopped fresh cilantro (leaves and tender stems)

Kosher salt and freshly ground black pepper

4 slices sharp white Cheddar or shaved Manchego cheese

4 burger buns, split

Beet Ketchup, for serving (recipe follows)

Pickled Red Onions, for serving (recipe follows)

When I ask my kids what they want for dinner, there's a good chance that my son, Wyatt, will suggest cheeseburgers. I am usually a purist when it comes to burgers, and I prefer the patties to be made with nothing more than the best-quality meat and salt and pepper. But the Texas tradition of cowboy burgers (the premade patties are sold in most grocery stores) is just plain fun. Kicked up with fresh jalapeños and cilantro, the spicy, belt-busting creations are delicious with sweet and tangy condiments like beet ketchup and pickled red onions (both can be made in advance).

Combine the beef, pork, jalapeño, and cilantro in a large bowl and use your hands to combine the mixture, being careful not to overwork the meat. Divide into four portions. Form each portion into a patty that's about 1 inch (2.5 cm) wider than your burger buns, pressing gently until they hold together. Form a slight dimple in the center of each patty. Season the top and bottom sides liberally with salt and pepper. Refrigerate for up to 4 hours.

Prepare a charcoal grill for two-zone cooking and build a medium-high fire, or heat a gas grill to high.

When the coals are glowing red and covered with a fine gray ash, add your smoke source (chips, chunks, or log). Carefully wipe the preheated grill grates with a lightly oiled paper towel. Using a grill brush, scrape the grill grates clean, then carefully wipe with a lightly oiled towel again.

When the fire begins to produce a steady stream of smoke, place the burgers over direct heat and cook for 10 to 12 minutes, flipping and rotating as needed for even cooking (move the patties away from direct heat if flare-ups occur or if they're browning too fast), until an instant-read thermometer inserted into the burgers reads 130°F (55°C) for medium-rare or 135°F (57°C) for medium. Top the burgers with cheese slices during the last minute of cooking (the cheese will continue to melt as the meat rests).

Transfer the burgers to a large plate to rest for about 5 minutes. Meanwhile, toast the buns over direct heat until golden brown, 1 to 2 minutes. Spread the bottoms of the buns with Beet Ketchup, slide the burgers on the buns, and top each with the Pickled Red Onions. Serve immediately.

Beet Ketchup

Combine the beets, vinegar, shallots, brown sugar, and ginger in a saucepan and cook over high heat. Bring the mixture to a boil, then turn the heat to low and simmer until thickened and the vegetables are very tender, about 12 minutes. Remove the pan from the heat, let the mixture cool slightly, then pour it into the bowl of a food processor. Add the salt, coriander, allspice, and pepper to taste and puree until very smooth (add a little water as needed to reach your desired consistency). Store the ketchup in an airtight container in the refrigerator for up to 2 weeks.

MAKES ABOUT 3 CUPS (720 G)

1 pound (450 g) cooked, peeled, and diced red beets

1 cup (240 ml) apple cider vinegar

¼ cup (40 g) chopped shallots

¼ cup (50 g) packed light brown sugar

3 tablespoons grated fresh ginger

1 teaspoon kosher salt

½ teaspoon ground coriander

Pinch of ground allspice

Freshly ground black pepper

Pickled Red Onions

In a skillet, heat the oil over medium heat. Add the garlic, arbol chile, coriander, bay leaves, thyme, and salt and cook, stirring occasionally, until the spices and herbs are fragrant and the garlic is golden, about 3 minutes. Stir in the onions and honey and cook for 2 minutes more. Stir in the vinegar, turn the heat to high, bring the mixture to a boil, then immediately remove the pan from the heat. Carefully transfer the mixture to a lidded glass jar to cool to room temperature, then refrigerate for at least 2 hours, until the pickled onions are cold. The onions will crisp as they chill. Store the sealed jar in the refrigerator for up to 3 weeks.

MAKES ABOUT 3½ CUPS (800 G)

2 tablespoons olive oil

2 cloves garlic, lightly crushed and peeled

1 dried arbol chile, stemmed

1 teaspoon coriander seeds

2 fresh bay leaves

1 or 2 sprigs thyme, or ½ teaspoon dried thyme

1½ teaspoons kosher salt

2 red onions, thinly sliced

1 tablespoon honey

½ cup plus 2 tablespoons (150 ml) red wine vinegar

HOT LUCK TRI-TIP
with Fresh Herbs

SERVES 4 TO 6

One 2½-pound (1.1 kg) tri-tip (about 2 inches/5 cm thick)

Vegetable oil, for drizzling

Kosher salt and freshly ground black pepper

2 cloves garlic, finely chopped or grated on a Microplane

2 tablespoons finely chopped fresh ginger

2 teaspoons Spicy Curry Salt (page 26)

12 Bibb lettuce leaves

1 cup (30 g) fresh Thai basil leaves

½ cup (20 g) lightly chopped fresh cilantro

½ cup (20 g) lightly chopped fresh mint

Pickled Carrots and Radishes (recipe follows), for serving

Hot sauce (such as sambal oelek), for serving

Tri-tip is a relatively inexpensive cut with a deep, beefy flavor that can stand up to punchy marinades and bold spices. To keep it moist on the grill, brush it with an extra coating of oil just before grilling and don't cook it past medium-rare. The spicy meat is delicious served with crisp Bibb lettuce leaves, fragrant fresh herbs, and Pickled Carrots and Radishes.

Place the steak on a baking sheet and use a paring knife to make several ½-inch (1.3 cm) incisions on both sides of the meat; drizzle it with enough oil to lightly coat, and generously season with salt and pepper. Combine the garlic, ginger, and Spicy Curry Salt in a small bowl and then rub the mixture over the entire surface of the meat. Let the meat marinate at room temperature for 1 hour.

Prepare a charcoal grill for two-zone cooking and build a medium fire, or heat a gas grill to medium-high. When the coals are glowing red and covered with a fine gray ash, add your smoke source (chips, chunks, or log). Carefully wipe the preheated grill grates with a lightly oiled paper towel. Using a grill brush, scrape the grill grates clean, then carefully wipe with a lightly oiled towel again.

When the fire begins to produce a steady stream of smoke, place the steak over direct heat and grill for 5 to 6 minutes, then flip the meat and cook it for an additional 15 to 17 minutes (flipping every 4 to 5 minutes), until an instant-read thermometer inserted into the thickest part of the meat reads 125°F (52°C); carryover heat will take it to 130°F (55°C) for medium-rare as it rests.

Transfer the steak to a cutting board to rest for 5 minutes. Thinly slice the meat against the grain and arrange the slices on a serving platter with the lettuce, herbs, pickled vegetables, and hot sauce.

Pickled Carrots and Radishes

MAKES ABOUT 1 QUART (950 G)

1 large carrot, peeled and cut into thin matchsticks

15 radishes, thinly sliced

½ cup sugar

1 tablespoon kosher salt

1 cup water

½ cup rice wine vinegar

Combine the carrot, radishes, sugar, and salt in a large bowl and use your fingers to gently massage the seasonings into the vegetables until dissolved. Transfer the vegetables and their liquid to a clean quart-size jar, add the water and rice vinegar and stir to combine. You can use the pickles immediately, but they'll be crisper and have more flavor if you refrigerate them overnight (they'll last for up to 1 week).

BEEF TENDERLOIN
with Smoked Garlic Aioli

SERVES 6 TO 8

One 3½-pound (1.6 kg)
beef tenderloin

Extra-virgin olive oil,
for drizzling

Kosher salt and freshly
ground black pepper

2 tablespoons herbes de
Provence

2 or 3 bunches watercress,
as desired

Smoked Garlic Aioli (page 33),
for serving

The simple perfection of this meal—tender beef, creamy aioli, and French herbs—always whisks me back to a memorable picnic on our ranch. We placed an iron table high up on a hill, so the view of the rolling hills stole the show—until we tasted the meat. The intoxicating aroma of herbes de Provence (the French seasoning that typically includes rosemary, thyme, fennel, summer savory, and lavender) infuses the beef with a delicate perfume, and a rich, smoky aioli and bed of fresh, peppery greens round out the meal. No one would complain if you wanted to serve roasted new potatoes or root vegetables on the side. Charring over direct heat, then finishing over a more moderate temperature gives the beef a crusty exterior and rosy, tender middle. Allowing larger pieces of meat like a tenderloin to come to room temperature before grilling helps them cook more evenly. Letting the meat rest before slicing is essential for allowing the meat's juices to be reabsorbed.

Place the tenderloin in a large baking dish, drizzle it with enough oil to lightly coat, and generously season with salt and pepper. Sprinkle the herbes de Provence over the meat, and then use your hands to rub the seasonings over the entire cut.

Prepare a charcoal grill for two-zone cooking and build a medium fire, or heat a gas grill to medium-high.

When the coals are glowing red and covered with a fine gray ash, add your smoke source (chips, chunks, or log). Carefully wipe the preheated grill grates with a lightly oiled paper towel. Using a grill brush, scrape the grill grates clean, then carefully wipe with a lightly oiled towel again.

When the fire begins to produce a steady stream of smoke, place the beef over direct heat and grill for 5 to 7 minutes, using tongs to roll the tenderloin every couple of minutes, until it's nicely charred on all sides. Move the meat to indirect heat, close the grill, vent the grill for smoking, and smoke for 15 to 20 minutes, until an instant-read thermometer inserted into the thickest part of the tenderloin reads 125°F (52°C); carryover heat will take it to 130°F (55°C) for medium-rare as it rests. Check on the meat every 5 minutes or so and flip it for even browning.

Transfer the meat to a cutting board to rest for 15 minutes. Meanwhile, arrange the watercress on a platter. Thinly slice the beef against the grain and arrange the slices over the greens. Serve with the aioli on the side.

SAN ANTONIO–STYLE TACOS

Throughout Texas, the best beef tacos are typically made with skirt or flank steak—tougher "flat" cuts that are best enjoyed lightly grilled and sliced across the grain. Flank steak is slightly leaner than skirt (you can use either one in this recipe), but it has a rich, satisfying flavor. In my mind, the best way to prepare flank steak is to marinate it with a spicy rub (piercing the meat with a paring knife helps the flavors permeate the entire cut) and cook it to medium-rare. After slicing, pile the steak onto warm corn tortillas with fresh cilantro, sliced avocado, lime wedges, and Green Chile Salsa.

Place the flank steak in a shallow dish and use a paring knife to make several ½-inch (1.3 cm) incisions on both sides; drizzle it with enough oil to lightly coat.

To make the rub, in a small dry skillet over medium heat, toast the chiles, peppercorns, coriander seeds, fennel seeds, and cumin seeds until fragrant and slightly darkened, 2 to 3 minutes. Allow the spices to cool, then add them to the bowl of a food processor with the garlic and salt. Pulse the mixture into a coarse paste, then add the brown sugar and vinegar and pulse again until evenly combined.

Use a rubber spatula to spread the chile rub over the meat, and then use your hands to evenly coat the seasonings over the entire cut, pressing the rub into the holes you created with the knife. Cover the meat with plastic wrap and set aside to marinate for 1 hour at room temperature.

Prepare a charcoal grill for two-zone cooking and build a medium fire, or heat a gas grill to medium-high.

When the coals are glowing red and covered with a fine gray ash, add your smoke source (chips, chunks, or log). Carefully wipe the preheated grill grates with a lightly oiled paper towel. Using a grill brush, scrape the grill grates clean, then carefully wipe with a lightly oiled towel again.

When the fire begins to produce a steady stream of smoke, place the steak over direct heat and grill for about 4 minutes, then flip the meat and cook it for 3 to 4 minutes more, until an instant-read thermometer inserted into the center of the steak reads 125°F (52°C); carryover heat will take it to 130°F (55°C) for medium-rare as it rests.

Transfer the steak to a cutting board to rest for 5 minutes. Meanwhile, warm the corn tortillas on the grill. Thinly slice the meat against the grain and arrange the slices on a platter. Serve with the warm corn tortillas, cilantro, sliced avocados, lime wedges, and salsa.

SERVES 4 TO 6

3 pounds (1.4 kg) flank steak

Extra-virgin olive oil, for drizzling

Red Chile Rub

3 dried arbol chiles

2 tablespoons smoked pink peppercorns (see page 18)

1 tablespoon coriander seeds

1 teaspoon fennel seeds

½ teaspoon cumin seeds

2 cloves garlic, sliced

2 teaspoons kosher salt

1 tablespoon dark brown sugar

3 tablespoons white wine vinegar

Twelve 6-inch (15 cm) best-quality corn tortillas, for serving

1 bunch cilantro, chopped (leaves and tender stems), for serving

2 avocados, thinly sliced, for serving

Lime wedges, for serving

Green Chile Salsa (page 29) or hot sauce, for serving

CROSS-CUT SHORT RIBS
with Herb Sauce

SERVES 4

Eight ½-inch (1.3 cm)-thick flanken-style bone-in short ribs

½ cup (120 ml) extra-virgin olive oil, plus more for drizzling

Kosher salt and freshly ground black pepper

3 tablespoons fresh oregano or marjoram leaves

1 tablespoon fresh thyme leaves

2 cloves garlic, peeled and lightly crushed

½ teaspoon red pepper flakes or crumbled chile pequin

Finely grated zest and juice of 1 lemon

2 teaspoons capers

I always thought short ribs required hours of braising, until I spotted flanken-style short ribs (short ribs cut crosswise in thin slices against the bone) at my local Asian market. The bone-in cut is also known as *kalbi*, and it has a cult following among Korean barbecue enthusiasts. Because my local market takes their meat seriously (they were made from Wagyu beef), I grabbed a couple of packages of the well-marbled cuts and went home to fire up the grill.

Over a smoky fire, the well-marbled cuts develop a crusty edge and intense beefy flavor that rival rib eye—in a fraction of the cooking time. Attention to a few key details delivers great results. Grill over a moderately hot fire and cook the ribs to medium-rare, when the fat yields and the meat becomes very juicy. A garlicky herb sauce that can be whizzed together in minutes balances the rich ribs.

Place the ribs in a large baking dish, drizzle them with enough oil to lightly coat, and season generously with salt and pepper. Allow the meat to marinate at room temperature for at least 30 minutes, or up to 1 hour.

Meanwhile, place the oregano, thyme, garlic, red pepper flakes, and 1 teaspoon salt in the bowl of a food processor and pulse to combine. Add the lemon zest and juice and the capers and pulse into a course paste. With the processor running, slowly drizzle in ½ cup (120 ml) oil and process until smooth. Use a rubber spatula to transfer the herb sauce to a bowl. Season to taste with pepper and set aside.

Prepare a charcoal grill for two-zone cooking and build a medium-high fire, or heat a gas grill to high.

When the coals are glowing red and covered with a fine gray ash, add your smoke source (chips, chunks, or log). Carefully wipe the preheated grill grates with a lightly oiled paper towel. Using a grill brush, scrape the grill grates clean, then carefully wipe with a lightly oiled towel again.

When the fire begins to produce a steady stream of smoke, place the ribs over direct heat, close the grill, vent the grill for smoking, and smoke for 6 to 8 minutes, turning frequently, until the ribs are crusty and charred on both sides and an instant-read thermometer inserted into the thickest part of a rib reads 125°F (52°C). Brush the ribs with the herb sauce just before taking them off the grill, and then transfer the meat to a cutting board to rest for about 10 minutes. Serve warm with the remaining herb sauce on the side.

TOGARASHI PORTERHOUSE

You might think of a porterhouse as the luxurious cousin to the T-bone. Both steaks have the iconic T-shaped bone that imparts flavor and divides the sirloin and tenderloin—the most premium cuts of beef available. But a porterhouse is cut from the rear end of the short loin, so it has a bigger section of luscious tenderloin. The meat is so extraordinary that you don't want to do too much to it. Here I give it a subtle heat with shichimi togarashi, a peppery Japanese condiment, and a quick turn in a garlic-soy marinade that enhances the beef's umami.

Keep in mind that the meat along the bone will cook more slowly than the rest of the steak, so a porterhouse can actually hold two different temperatures (say, from rare to medium-rare) when it's ready to serve. Allowing the meat to rest briefly before slicing helps even out the doneness.

In a small bowl, combine the soy sauce, oil, togarashi, and garlic. Pour three-quarters of the marinade into a baking dish and reserve the rest. Lay the steaks in the marinade and flip them a few times to generously coat. Set aside to marinate for 10 minutes.

Prepare a charcoal grill for two-zone cooking and build a medium-high fire, or heat a gas grill to high.

When the coals are glowing red and covered with a fine gray ash, add your smoke source (chips, chunks, or log). Carefully wipe the preheated grill grates with a lightly oiled paper towel. Using a grill brush, scrape the grill grates clean, then carefully wipe with a lightly oiled towel again.

When the fire begins to produce a steady stream of smoke, place the steaks over direct heat, close the grill, vent the grill for smoking, and smoke for 2 minutes. Move the steak to indirect heat, close the grill, and smoke for 4 to 5 minutes. When juices appear on the top of the meat, flip the steak and repeat the whole process, starting on direct heat for 2 minutes, then moving to indirect heat for 4 to 5 minutes, until the meat is nicely charred and glossy and an instant-read thermometer inserted into the thickest part of the steak reads 125°F (52°C), 15 to 20 minutes total; carryover heat will take it to 130°F (55°C) for medium-rare as it rests. Transfer the meat to a cutting board to rest for 10 minutes.

Using a sharp knife, cut the meat off the bone, then cut the sections into thin slices. Serve with the remaining marinade on the side.

**SERVES 6 TO 8
(OR 4 STEAK LOVERS)**

¼ cup (60 ml) soy sauce

2 tablespoons olive oil

2 tablespoons shichimi togarashi

2 cloves garlic, grated on a Microplane

Two 1½-inch (4 cm)-thick porterhouse steaks, about 3½ pounds (1.6 kg) total

✪ BACKYARD PRIME RIB

SERVES 6 MEAT LOVERS

One 6-rib prime rib roast (about 12 pounds/5.4 kg), fat trimmed to lean (preferably dry-aged)

Extra-virgin olive oil, for drizzling

Kosher salt and freshly ground black pepper

1 bunch thyme

1 bunch rosemary

3 fresh bay leaves (optional)

Flaky salt, for serving

A prime rib roast is the ultimate special occasion meal, perfect for holidays and other milestone events. If you're going to splurge on this luxury cut, it's worth planning ahead to make the most of the experience. To achieve the fullest taste and texture, season the beef a day in advance, allowing the salt to fully permeate the cut. Grill-roasting the meat fat side up allows the rendered fat to baste the meat as it cooks (and the bottom of the roast to crisp), which creates an exceptionally flavorful browned crust.

My friend Aaron Franklin, the acclaimed pit master at Franklin Barbecue (I think of him as the Elvis of barbecue), has taught me a lot about cooking over fire. Most important, our families have shared back-porch pumpkin carving, Easter egg hunts, Father's Day fish tacos, and plenty of laughs. I follow Aaron's method for cooking this substantial piece of meat—cooking it slowly over indirect heat. Then after a resting period (a good time for you to shake cocktails and prepare appetizers), the roast is seared over a very hot fire, which makes for good dinner theater.

Place the roast on a rimmed baking sheet lined with parchment paper. Drizzle it with enough oil to lightly coat and generously season with salt and pepper. Place half of the herb sprigs and leaves under the roast, and place the other half on top of the meat. Set aside to marinate at room temperature for 1 to 2 hours (as time allows).

Prepare a charcoal grill for two-zone cooking and build a medium fire, or heat a gas grill to medium-high.

When the coals are glowing red and covered with a fine gray ash, add your smoke source (chips, chunks, or log). Carefully wipe the preheated grill grates with a lightly oiled paper towel. Using a grill brush, scrape the grill grates clean, then carefully wipe with a lightly oiled towel again.

When the fire begins to produce a steady stream of smoke, place the roast (rib bones down and fat side up) over indirect heat, close the grill, vent the grill for smoking, and smoke for about 2 hours, rotating the meat every 30 minutes, until an instant-read thermometer inserted into the thickest part of the roast reads 125°F (52°C); carryover heat will take it to 130°F (55°C) for medium-rare as it rests. Add additional hot coals or wood chunks as needed to maintain a steady temperature of around 325°F (165°C). Transfer the roast to a cutting board to rest for at least 30 minutes, or up to 1 hour. Discard the herbs.

Add another chimney of hot coals to the grill to raise the heat to high. Place the roast over indirect heat, close the grill and smoke for 6 to 8 minutes, until deeply browned. Transfer the beef to a cutting board.

Holding a sharp knife parallel to the bones, cut between the bones to create six portions. Transfer the meat to a serving dish, drizzle it with the pan juices, and sprinkle with flaky salt before serving.

ROSEMARY LAMB KEBABS
with Smoky Eggplant

SERVES 4 (MAKES 4 KEBABS)

4 sturdy rosemary sprigs, each about 8 inches (20 cm) long

1½ pounds (680 g) boneless lamb shoulder or leg, cut into 1½- to 2-inch (4 to 5 cm) cubes

¼ cup (60 ml) extra-virgin olive oil, plus more for drizzling

Kosher salt

1 tablespoon Sichuan peppercorns

2 teaspoons cumin seeds

2 teaspoons coriander seeds

3 tablespoons chopped fresh oregano

2 teaspoons Korean red pepper flakes (gochugaru)

2 cloves garlic, finely chopped

2 large eggplants

2 tablespoons tahini

2 teaspoons freshly squeezed lemon juice

Freshly ground black pepper

Pomegranate seeds, for garnish (optional)

Toasted pine nuts, for garnish (optional)

Lemon wedges, for serving

Grilled pita bread, for serving

Perfumed with warm spices and fresh oregano, skewers of charred lamb make a striking and satisfying weeknight dinner (just add olives and a cold bottle of dry pink wine). In terms of a game plan here, it's best to coal-roast the eggplant first, so you have time to drain its excess moisture before pureeing (you can cook the eggplant up to two days in advance). While the eggplant rests, you'll have time to pull together the other elements and then grill the lamb over direct heat. Your grill should be able to hold its temperature during the process, but if it dips, just add a few wood chunks before you cook the meat. The smoky eggplant puree, a scattering of tart pomegranate seeds, pine nuts, and lemon are complements to the rich, spicy meat. Serve with grilled pita bread.

Remove all the rosemary leaves from the branches except 2 inches (5 cm) at the top of each sprig. Using a sharp knife, cut the leafless end of each branch at an angle to make a point, which will make it easier to skewer the lamb. Save the rosemary leaves you removed for another use. Place the lamb in a large mixing bowl, drizzle with enough oil to coat, season generously with salt, and toss to combine.

In a small dry skillet over medium heat, toast the peppercorns, cumin, and coriander until fragrant and slightly darkened, about 3 minutes. Remove the pan from the heat and allow the spices to cool, then coarsely grind them in a coffee grinder or mortar and pestle. Add the ground spices, the oregano, Korean red pepper flakes, and garlic, followed by ¼ cup (60 ml) oil to the lamb and toss to combine. Set the meat aside to marinate at room temperature for at least 30 minutes, or up to 1 hour.

Prepare a charcoal grill for two-zone cooking and build a medium-high fire, or heat a gas grill to high.

When the coals are glowing red and covered with a fine gray ash, add your smoke source (chips, chunks, or log).

Place the eggplants directly on the coals (if cooking on a gas grill, place the eggplants directly on the grates) and cook, using tongs to turn them occasionally, until the skins are blackened and tender and the eggplants have collapsed, 10 to 15 minutes. Transfer the eggplants to a rimmed baking sheet to cool slightly, and

continued

then slice them open lengthwise. Use a spoon to scrape out the tender insides, discarding the charred skin and stems. Place the eggplant flesh in a colander and let the excess moisture drain for 15 to 30 minutes (as time allows).

Meanwhile, skewer the lamb onto the rosemary skewers and place them on a rimmed baking sheet.

Return the cooking grate to its position, allow it to preheat, and then carefully wipe the preheated grill grates with a lightly oiled paper towel. Using a grill brush, scrape the grill grates clean, then carefully wipe with a lightly oiled towel again.

When the fire begins to produce a steady stream of smoke, place the kebabs over direct heat, close the grill, vent the grill for smoking, and smoke for about 4 minutes, or until medium-rare, turning the kebabs often. Keep the lamb warm on an upper tier rack of your grill, if it has one, or transfer the kebabs to a cutting board and tent with aluminum foil while you finish the eggplant.

Place the drained eggplant in the bowl of a food processor with ½ teaspoon salt and pulse into a coarse puree. Add the tahini and lemon juice and process until smooth. Transfer the puree to a serving bowl and season to taste with salt and pepper.

Serve the lamb kebabs over a slather of eggplant puree drizzled with olive oil. Garnish with pomegranate seeds and pine nuts and serve with lemon wedges and grilled pita bread.

✪ SMOKY CHUCK ROAST
with Coffee & Whiskey

Two ranch staples, coffee and whiskey, are among my favorite flavors with slow-cooked beef. With its rich, beefy flavor, chuck roast is at its best when slowly braised in a small amount of liquid, a process that melts its tougher connective tissues and creates the fall-apart tender texture we all love. Here the meat is cooked over a gentle wood-infused fire, and then doused with whiskey and finished in a foil wrap that preserves its flavorful juices. The smoky, flavorful meat is perfect for tacos, crusty ciabatta rolls, or on its own with mashed potatoes or soft rolls to soak up the flavorful juices.

Place the roast on a rimmed baking sheet lined with parchment paper and generously season the entire surface with salt and pepper. In a small bowl, combine the chile powders and espresso powder, and then use your hands to rub the seasonings over the entire roast. Set aside to marinate at room temperature for 1 hour.

Prepare a charcoal grill for two-zone cooking and build a medium fire, or heat a gas grill to medium-high.

When the coals are glowing red and covered with a fine gray ash, add your smoke source (chips, chunks, or log). Carefully wipe the preheated grill grates with a lightly oiled paper towel. Using a grill brush, scrape the grill grates clean, then carefully wipe with a lightly oiled towel again.

When the fire begins to produce a steady stream of smoke, place the roast over indirect heat, close the grill, vent the grill for smoking, and smoke for about 2 hours, rotating the meat every 30 minutes and adjusting the vents to maintain a temperature between 250° (120°C) and 275°F (135°C), until an instant-read thermometer inserted into the thickest part of the roast reads 160°F (70°C).

Use tongs and a two-pronged fork to transfer the meat to two large sheets of heavy-duty aluminum foil. Crimp the edges of the foil upward to create a rim to hold the juices. Pour the whiskey over the meat, and then tightly wrap the meat in the foil. Return the roast to the grill over indirect heat and cook for about 45 minutes more, until an instant-read thermometer inserted into the thickest part of the roast reads 205°F (98°C). Remove the roast from the heat, carefully open the foil to allow the hot steam to escape, and let the meat rest for 30 minutes, or up to 1 hour. Transfer the meat to a cutting board and slice or shred as desired, then serve topped with its juices.

SERVES 6 TO 8

One 3-pound (1.4 kg) boneless chuck roast

Kosher salt and freshly ground black pepper

1 tablespoon pure ground ancho chile powder

2 teaspoons pure ground chipotle chile powder

1 tablespoon instant espresso powder

¼ cup (60 ml) whiskey

✪ HERB-STUFFED LEG OF LAMB
with Tapenade

SERVES 6 TO 8

1 boneless leg of lamb
(about 4 pounds/1.8 kg)

2 tablespoons extra-virgin
olive oil, plus more for
drizzling

Kosher salt and freshly
ground black pepper

3 tablespoons chopped
fresh rosemary

2 tablespoons chopped
fresh thyme

4 cloves garlic, minced or
grated with a Microplane

Finely grated zest and juice
of 1 lemon

½ cup (110 g) Black Olive
Tapenade (recipe follows)

A quick bit of mincing is all that's required to create an aromatic rub made with lamb's best allies—rosemary, thyme, garlic, and lemon—that perfumes this roast with extraordinary flavor. A slather of Black Olive Tapenade provides a salty, savory aroma that brings out the best in the meat and the herbs. The great thing about a boneless leg of lamb is that it's easy to season both sides of the meat, allowing the flavors to permeate every bite. Consider serving the warm lamb slices (crusty on the outside, rosy in the middle) alongside roasted new potatoes and buttery haricots verts.

Note: The interior of a lamb leg has a large vein structure that should be removed before cooking (ask a butcher to do this for you). If you want to cut the lamb into thin slices, let the roast rest for the full hour so the meat holds together better.

Place the lamb on a rimmed baking sheet lined with parchment paper. Drizzle the lamb with enough oil to lightly coat and generously season both sides of the meat with salt and pepper. Set aside to marinate at room temperature for at least 1 hour, or up to 2 hours if time allows.

In a small bowl, combine the rosemary, thyme, garlic, lemon zest and juice, and the 2 tablespoons oil. Rub an even layer of herb paste over one side of the meat, and then top with an even layer of tapenade.

Cut long pieces of butcher's twine. Starting in the middle of the leg, center the meat on the string and tie up the meat tightly. Working your way toward both ends of the roast, tie two or three more pieces of butcher's twine around the leg to bind it. Cut one more piece of butcher's twine to run the length of the roast. (It should resemble a tight cylinder.) Season the exterior of the meat generously with salt and pepper.

Prepare a charcoal grill for two-zone cooking and build a medium fire, or heat a gas grill to medium-high.

When the coals are glowing red and covered with a fine gray ash, use tongs to remove the cooking grate and place a drip pan with 1 inch (2.5 cm) of warm water on the side with no coals and add your smoke source (chips, chunks, or log). Carefully wipe the preheated grill grates with a lightly oiled paper towel. Using a grill brush, scrape the grill grates clean, then carefully wipe with a lightly oiled towel again.

When the fire begins to produce a steady stream of smoke, place the lamb over indirect heat, close the grill, vent the grill for smoking, and smoke for 1 hour 45 minutes, rolling and rotating the meat every 30 minutes, until an instant-read thermometer inserted into the thickest part of the lamb reads 130°F (55°C) for medium-rare. Add additional hot coals or wood chunks as needed to maintain a steady temperature of around 325°F (165°C). Transfer the roast to a cutting board to rest for at least 30 minutes, or up to 1 hour.

When you're ready to serve, snip and discard the butcher's twine and thinly slice the roast crosswise into rounds. Transfer to a serving dish and serve warm or at room temperature.

Black Olive Tapenade

My favorite tapenade is made with a combination of rich oil-cured black olives and bright brine-cured kalamatas. You only need half of this recipe for the lamb. Serve leftovers on grilled bread, on mozzarella and tomato sandwiches, or spooned onto deviled eggs.

Combine the garlic, thyme, salt, and red pepper flakes in the bowl of a food processor and pulse into a coarse paste. Add the olives, capers, anchovies, and cognac and pulse until combined. With the processor running, slowly drizzle in the oil and process until very smooth. Season with pepper to taste and store in a sealed container in the refrigerator for 2 weeks.

MAKES 1 CUP (220 G)

1 clove garlic, sliced

1 teaspoon chopped fresh thyme, rosemary, or winter savory

½ teaspoon kosher salt

Generous pinch of red pepper flakes or chile pequin

½ cup (65 g) pitted oil-cured black olives

½ cup (65 g) pitted kalamata olives

2 teaspoons capers

2 or 3 anchovy fillets, to taste, rinsed and chopped

1 tablespoon Cognac or brandy

½ cup (120 ml) olive oil

Freshly ground black pepper

CHAPTER TEN

THE SWEET SIDE OF SMOKE

When smoke drifts into the realm of sweet dishes, classic desserts (from bar cookies to apple pie) become more complex and sophisticated. The process is not unlike how a marshmallow transforms over flames. As the sugar heats, the marshmallow turns from toasted and tan to bubbly and black, each stage and color offering its own complex flavors and textures.

The recipes in this chapter celebrate the timeless allure of those toasted marshmallows (with reimagined Krispie squares!), as well as smoke in more subtle appearances. Lightly smoked ingredients are deployed to perfume pastry crust, enhance the caramel quality of dates, intensify chocolate, and create deeper, savory notes (via smoked nuts) in tarts, bars, and brittles.

BURNT MARSHMALLOW KRISPIES

**MAKES ABOUT
16 SQUARES**

1½ pounds (600 g)
marshmallows

¾ cup (170 g) unsalted butter

1 teaspoon pure vanilla
extract

1 teaspoon kosher salt

7 cups (560 g) crispy rice
cereal, such as Rice Krispies

½ cup (110 g) toffee bits

½ cup (60 g) dried
cranberries or dried cherries

When I first tasted the brilliant Krispie squares made with "burnt" marshmallows at the Larder, a stylish grab-and-go food shop at Hotel Emma in San Antonio, I felt like dancing. In chef John Brand's recipe, he browns half of the butter for richness. My version uses straight-up butter to allow the Proustian flavor of burnt marshmallows to shine, and dried cranberries (feel free to use cherries) for a sweet-tart pop. These bars will taste quite salty right after you make them, but the flavor settles in upon standing, resulting in irresistible treats that both kids and grown-ups love. Note: You'll need nonstick cooking spray and eight to ten metal skewers for this recipe.

Prepare a charcoal grill for two-zone cooking and build a medium fire, or heat a gas grill to medium-high.

When the coals are glowing red and covered with a fine gray ash, add your smoke source (chips, chunks, or log). Carefully wipe the preheated grill grates and a grill basket with a lightly oiled paper towel.

Spray an 8-inch (20 cm) square baking dish with cooking spray (or coat it with butter). Spray 8 to 10 skewers with cooking spray and slide 8 to 10 marshmallows on each skewer, leaving 1½ inches (4 cm) bare on each end from which you will suspend the skewers.

When the fire begins to produce a steady stream of smoke, suspend the skewers over the oiled grill basket and place the basket over direct heat. (Or go old-school and remove the cooking grate and hold the skewers directly over the coals.) Toast the marshmallows until one side of the marshmallows is puffed and blackened. (If you try to toast both sides of the marshmallows, you'll likely have multiple casualties.) Remove the basket from the heat and immediately scrape the marshmallows into a Dutch oven.

Place the Dutch oven on the stovetop over medium-low heat, add the butter, and stir until melted. When the mixture is mostly smooth, stir in the vanilla and salt. Remove the pot from the heat and use a rubber spatula to fold in the cereal, toffee bits, and dried cranberries. Transfer the mixture to the prepared baking dish, pressing gently to compress and smooth the surface. If you can't wait, you can dig in immediately, but for the best texture and flavor, cover with plastic wrap and let the flavors to meld for at least 3 hours before serving. Store the bars, covered, at room temperature for up to 5 days.

SMOKED CASHEW & POPCORN BRITTLE

Warning: This salty, smoky, crunchy brittle is extremely addictive. The mix of cashews, popcorn, and pepitas looks beautiful suspended in the luxurious caramel and broken into big, irregular shards. It's a no-brainer for holiday gifts, but don't wait until then—it's also delicious for dessert, alongside vanilla ice cream, perhaps, or with your favorite nightcap.

Line two baking sheets with silicone baking mats or generously coat with cooking spray.

In a large saucepan, combine the corn syrup with the water, then add the sugar without stirring. Cook the mixture, uncovered, over medium-high heat and do not stir until a candy thermometer inserted into the mixture reads 260°F (127°C) degrees.

Gently add the cashews, pepitas, popcorn, and butter without splashing the caramel (it will scald your skin). Turn the heat to medium and stir constantly until the temperature reaches 300°F (150°C) to 305°F (152°C), 8 to 10 minutes.

Remove the pan from the heat and add the baking soda, vanilla, and salt, stirring to combine. (It will bubble up and increase in volume.) Pour the mixture onto the prepared baking sheets. (If possible, ask someone to help you scrape the pot.) Using a rubber spatula, spread the mixture as thinly as possible and let it cool and set up for about 30 minutes. Break the brittle into pieces and store in a sealed container at room temperature (it will get sticky if left out in the humidity) for up to 1 month.

MAKES ABOUT 3 POUNDS (1.4 KG)

1½ cups (355 ml) light corn syrup

1 cup (240 ml) water

3 cups (600 g) sugar

2 cups (260 g) smoked roasted and salted cashews (see page 72)

½ cup (70 g) smoked pepitas (see page 72)

4 cups (45 g) popped popcorn (no salt, no butter)

3 tablespoons unsalted butter, cut into pieces

1 tablespoon baking soda

1½ teaspoons pure vanilla extract

4 teaspoons flaky salt

STICKY TOFFEE PUDDING
with Smoked Dates

Pudding

1 cup (250 g) smoked Medjool dates (see page 18)

1 cup (240 ml) boiling water

¾ cup plus 2 tablespoons (110 g) all-purpose flour

⅓ cup plus 1 teaspoon (75g) demerara sugar

⅓ cup plus 1 teaspoon (80 g) packed dark brown sugar

2 eggs

3 tablespoons cold unsalted butter, cut into cubes

1 teaspoon pure vanilla extract

1 teaspoon baking soda

½ teaspoon instant espresso powder

¼ teaspoon fine sea salt

Sticky Toffee Topping

5 tablespoons (70 g) unsalted butter

1 cup (240 ml) heavy cream

6 tablespoons (75 g) packed dark brown sugar

⅛ teaspoon fine sea salt

The first time I served this dessert at a dinner party, a deep silence fell around the table. Women who thought they'd have "just a bite" cleaned their bowls. It's not exaggerating to say that the men seemed more lighthearted, and possibly amorous. Using Simon Hopkinson's sticky toffee pudding method (the English chef is revered throughout Europe) as a starting point, this recipe incorporates smoked dates, which hold their own beautifully on the smoker, where their intense sweetness becomes more caramel-like and complex. A whiff of espresso powder deepens the sultry flavors. Is the extra sauce necessary? Absolutely.

Preheat the oven to 350°F (175°C) and grease 8 cups in a muffin tin with nonstick spray.

To make the pudding, pit and chop the dates, place them in a bowl and cover with the boiling water. Set aside to soften for at least 5 minutes.

Combine the flour, demerara sugar, brown sugar, eggs, butter, vanilla, baking soda, espresso powder, and salt in the bowl of a food processor and pulse until just combined. Drain the dates, reserving the water. Add the softened smoked dates and ½ cup (120 ml) of the warm date water to the mixture and pulse until nearly smooth (specks of dates should remain visible).

Divide the mixture among the muffin cups and bake for 24 to 26 minutes, until just firm to the touch. When the pudding has finished baking, remove the pan from the oven. Position the oven rack about 4 inches (10 cm) from the heat source and turn on the broiler.

Meanwhile, to make the topping, melt the butter in a small saucepan over medium heat. Slowly add the cream, brown sugar, and salt, whisking continuously until the mixture bubbles gently and comes together to form a smooth mixture, about 4 minutes. Remove from the heat.

To make the extra sauce, melt the butter in another small saucepan over medium heat, then slowly add the cream, brown sugar, and salt, whisking continuously until the mixture bubbles gently and comes together to form a smooth mixture, about 4 minutes. Remove from the heat and cover to keep warm.

Invert the individual puddings into a glass baking dish. Pour the topping over the cooked puddings and place the dish under the broiler until the topping bubbles and looks sticky, 1 to 2 minutes (watch it closely).

To serve, place the puddings in bowls (with a spoonful of topping from the bottom of the dish) and cover with the extra sauce. Serve with whipped cream, if you like.

Extra Sauce

3 tablespoons unsalted butter

1¼ cups (300 ml) heavy cream, plus more for serving

3 tablespoons dark brown sugar

⅛ teaspoon fine sea salt

Whipped cream, for serving (optional)

SMOKED PISTACHIO SHORTBREAD

These crisp, buttery shortbreads melt in your mouth, and because they're both interesting (with the smoked nuts and subtle heat from white pepper) and fairly neutral, they go with everything from a mug of steaming tea to bowls of ice cream or grilled stone fruit (my favorite combination). Because this recipe makes a nice amount, it's also great for holiday cookie swaps or potlucks.

Combine the flour, confectioners' sugar, white peppercorns, and salt in the bowl of a food processor and pulse a few times to combine. Add the butter, pistachios, and egg yolk and pulse until the mixture forms a moist, sticky ball, 2 to 3 minutes. Transfer the dough to a work surface and use a bench cutter to divide the dough in half. Form each half into an 8 by 1½-inch (20 by 4 cm) log, then wrap the logs in plastic wrap and refrigerate for at least 4 hours, until firm, or up to 5 days in advance.

Preheat the oven to 325°F (165°C) and line two rimmed baking sheets with parchment paper. Slice the logs into ¼-inch (6 mm) rounds, rolling the log every few slices to retain the round shape. Place the rounds on the baking sheet, spacing them 1 inch (2.5 cm) apart. Bake the cookies 16 to 18 minutes, until they are lightly golden. Remove the baking sheet from the oven and cool the cookies on the sheet for 5 minutes. Transfer the cookies to a wire rack to cool completely. Repeat with the remaining dough. Store the cookies in a sealed container for up to 1 week.

MAKES ABOUT 45 COOKIES

1½ cups (190 g) all-purpose flour

½ cup plus 2 tablespoons (75 g) confectioners' sugar

¾ teaspoon white peppercorns

½ teaspoon fine sea salt

¾ cup (170 g) cold unsalted butter, cut into ½-inch (1.3 cm) cubes

¾ cup (105 g) smoked pistachios (see page 72)

1 egg yolk

ALMOND BUTTER & CHOCOLATE COOKIES

MAKES ABOUT
44 COOKIES

⅔ cup (165 g) Smoked Marcona Almond Butter (page 86)

½ cup (100 g) packed light brown sugar

¼ cup (50 g) granulated sugar, plus more for dipping

¼ cup (50 g) vegetable shortening

1 teaspoon pure vanilla extract

1 teaspoon baking soda

½ teaspoon kosher salt

1 large egg

1 cup (90 g) rolled oats (not instant)

⅔ cup (85 g) all-purpose flour

1½ cups (255 g) bittersweet chocolate chunks or disks

Flaky salt, for garnish (optional)

The confluence of two of my favorite flavors—bittersweet chocolate and creamy nut butter—creates a pretty irresistible cookie that's right at home in lunch boxes, for ice cream sandwiches, or paired with late-night movies and milk (or red wine). Using vegetable shortening gives the cookie a delightful crunchy texture that's reminiscent of the Girl Scouts' Do-Si-Dos. If you prefer, you can use an equal amount of butter, but consider chilling the dough overnight before baking so the cookies hold their shape better.

Preheat the oven to 350°F (175°C) and line two rimmed baking sheets with parchment paper.

Combine the almond butter, sugars, shortening, vanilla, baking soda, and salt in the bowl of a stand mixer fitted with the paddle attachment. Beat on medium speed until smooth, about 4 minutes. Add the egg and beat for 1 minute more, until combined. Turn the mixer to low speed, add the oats, flour, and chocolate chunks and mix until combined.

Drop the dough by the heaping teaspoonful (or use a teaspoon-size cookie scoop) onto the baking sheets, spacing them 1½ inches (4 cm) apart. Using the flat bottom of a drinking glass dipped in granulated sugar, flatten each cookie until it's ¼ inch (6 mm) thick and about 1½ inches (4 cm) in diameter. To give the cookies a salty edge, lightly sprinkle them with flaky salt.

Bake the cookies for 12 to 14 minutes, until richly golden. Remove the baking sheet from the oven and transfer the cookies to a wire rack to cool completely. Repeat with the remaining dough. Store the cookies in a sealed container for up to 1 week.

SMOKED PECAN-CHOCOLATE SQUARES

These rich, chewy bars combine the best qualities: buttery shortbread and gooey pecan pie. And while they look entirely familiar, there are a few secret weapons that elevate these squares: a thin layer of bittersweet chocolate, a pinch of cayenne in the cookie base, and a healthy amount of salt in the topping. Using smoked pecans in the caramel-like topping adds an entirely new level of sophistication—and creates the kind of after-dinner treat you'll want to have with a few sips of your favorite single-barrel beverage.

Position a rack in the middle of the oven and preheat the oven to 350°F (175°C).

To make the cookie base, combine the flour, butter, light brown sugar, cinnamon, salt, and cayenne in the bowl of a food processor and pulse about twenty times, until the mixture is well combined. Press the dough evenly into the bottom of a 9-inch (23 cm) square baking pan. Wipe out the processor bowl, but don't bother washing it.

Bake the cookie base until firm and lightly browned, about 25 minutes. Remove the pan from the oven and sprinkle the grated chocolate evenly over the cookie base. Set the pan aside and leave the oven on.

To make the pecan topping, place the smoked pecans in the bowl of a food processor and pulse until coarsely chopped. In a heavy saucepan, melt the butter over medium heat. Stir in the dark brown sugar, honey, cream, and salt and simmer for 1 minute, stirring occasionally. Remove the pan from the heat and stir in the smoked pecans.

Pour the pecan topping over the cookie base, spreading it evenly with a rubber spatula. Return the pan to the oven and bake until much of the topping is bubbling (not just the edges), 16 to 18 minutes. Remove the pan from the oven and place it on a wire rack to cool completely.

To serve, run a sharp knife around the rim of the bars to loosen them from the pan. Invert the pan onto a cutting board and bang the bottom a few times to release the bars. Use a chef's knife or metal bench scraper to cut the bars into 16 squares. Store the bars tightly covered at room temperature for up to 5 days (though they never last that long).

MAKES 16 SQUARES

Cookie Base

2 cups (250 g) unbleached all-purpose flour

¾ cup (170 g) cold unsalted butter, cut into ½-inch (1.3 cm) pieces

½ cup (100 g) packed light brown sugar

2 teaspoons ground cinnamon

½ teaspoon kosher salt

Pinch of cayenne

4 ounces (115 g) bittersweet chocolate, grated

Pecan Topping

3 cups (420 g) smoked pecans (see page 72)

½ cup (110 g) unsalted butter

1 cup (200 g) packed dark brown sugar

⅓ cup (80 ml) honey

2 tablespoons heavy cream

¾ teaspoon kosher salt

BERRY GALETTE
with Smoked Pink Peppercorn Crust

MAKES ONE 12-INCH (30 CM) GALETTE

Pink Peppercorn Crust

1 tablespoon granulated sugar

1 teaspoon smoked pink peppercorns (see page 18)

½ teaspoon kosher salt

1½ cups (190 g) all-purpose flour

½ cup plus 3 tablespoons (155 g) cold unsalted butter, cut into ½-inch (1.3 cm) cubes

1 egg yolk

4 to 5 tablespoons (60 to 75 ml) half-and-half

1 egg

2 tablespoons turbinado sugar

Berry Filling

Generous 3 cups (480 g) fresh blueberries, blackberries, or raspberries, or a combination

½ cup (100 g) granulated sugar

1 tablespoon all-purpose flour

2 teaspoons pure vanilla extract

1½ teaspoons elderberry vinegar or raw apple cider vinegar

½ teaspoon ground cinnamon

Generous pinch of kosher salt

3 tablespoons raspberry jam

Pretty pink peppercorns are one of my favorite ingredients to use desserts and with fresh cheeses like chèvre. They have a flavor that's brighter and more floral than black peppercorns. In this recipe, the peppercorns infuse a flaky crust with a subtle heat and enhance the bright flavor of fresh berries.

To make the crust, place the granulated sugar, smoked pink peppercorns, and salt in the bowl of a food processor and pulse until the peppercorns are lightly crushed. Add the flour and pulse to blend. Add the butter and pulse until the flour clumps together when you squeeze it. Break up any large clumps of butter with your fingers and pulse again for a few seconds. Add the egg yolk and 2 tablespoons of the half-and-half and process just until the dough pulls together, adding up to 1 additional tablespoon half-and-half as needed. Run a rubber spatula along the bowl to work in any ingredients stuck to the bottom.

Transfer the dough to a sheet of plastic wrap, shape the dough into a flattened rectangle, wrap tightly, and refrigerate for at least 30 minutes, or up to 3 days.

When you're ready to bake, preheat the oven to 400°F (200°C). Line a baking sheet with parchment paper.

To make the filling, in a mixing bowl, toss together the berries, granulated sugar, flour, vanilla, vinegar, cinnamon, and salt.

Remove the dough from the refrigerator and roll it into a rustic circle or rectangle, as you prefer, until the dough is ¼ inch thick, and transfer it to the prepared baking sheet. Spread a thin layer of jam over the center of the pastry, leaving a 1½-inch (4 cm) border. Pile the fruit on top of the jam and gently fold the pastry up and over the fruit, using your fingers to pleat the dough and seal the crust.

In a small bowl, use a fork to lightly beat the egg with the remaining 2 tablespoons half-and-half. Brush the pastry with the egg wash and sprinkle with turbinado sugar.

Bake the galette for 35 to 45 minutes, until the fruit is bubbly and the crust is deeply golden. Cool on a wire rack for at least 20 minutes, then serve warm or at room temperature.

NINE-APPLE PIE
with Smoked Peppercorn Crust

**MAKES ONE 9½ OR
10-INCH (24 OR 25 CM)
DEEP-DISH PIE**

Smoked Peppercorn Crust

2½ cups (315 g) all-purpose
flour, plus extra for dusting

1 tablespoon granulated sugar

1½ teaspoons smoked black
peppercorns (see page 18),
coarsely ground

1 teaspoon kosher salt

¾ cup (170 g) cold unsalted
European-style butter, cut
into cubes

2 teaspoons raw apple
cider vinegar

¼ cup plus 3 tablespoons
(105 ml) ice water

**There are two camps in apple pie baking—to cook the filling, or
not to cook the filling? Leaning toward the lazy side, I've always
used slices of uncooked apples. No one's complained if a few slices
were a little on the firm side—because, well, it's pie! But then my
friend Jess Maher, the pastry chef at Lenoir in Austin, told me she
partially cooks her fillings because the process allows you to add
more fruit. "Sometimes I use as many as nine apples in my pies," she
told me. The notion of more fruit definitely appealed to me, so the
challenge was on. I peeled and sliced nine apples, simmered them
into a fragrant, luscious filling, and then baked off my best pie ever—
packed to the brim with tender fruit, just how I like it. Perfuming
the crust with smoked black peppercorns gives this classic dessert
a sophisticated edge. Note that the apple filling needs to chill before
baking, so plan accordingly.**

To make the crust, combine the flour, granulated sugar, smoked peppercorns,
and salt in the bowl of a food processor and pulse about eight times to combine.
Add the butter and pulse about twenty times, until the mixture is coarse and
pebbly. While pulsing, add the vinegar and ice water, continuing just until the
mixture comes together.

Transfer the dough to a lightly floured work surface. Use your hands to knead
the dough together two or three times (turning the round after each knead)
just until it's smooth and supple, and then pat the dough into a square. Divide
the dough in half, wrap each half in plastic wrap, and refrigerate the dough for
at least 30 minutes, or up to 2 days in advance.

To make the filling, peel, core, and halve the apples lengthwise. Cut the apples in
half again widthwise, then cut the quarters into ¼-inch (6 mm) slices and toss
with the lemon juice in a bowl. Sprinkle the slices with the granulated sugar, flour,
vanilla, cinnamon, and salt and toss to combine. Transfer the filling to a heavy
saucepan over medium heat and cook, stirring occasionally, until the apples are
partially softened and the juices have thickened, about 10 minutes. Transfer the
filling to a container to cool for 10 minutes, and then cover with plastic wrap
and refrigerate until cold, about 2½ hours.

For smokier results, smoke the chilled apple filling before placing it in the crust. To do this, place the filling in a mixing bowl and cover with plastic wrap. Add a pinch of wood chips to the burn chamber of a smoking gun, place the hose in under the plastic wrap with the end sitting above the filling, and reseal the plastic wrap. Follow the manufacturer's instructions to ignite the wood chips and smoke for a few seconds, until the bowl is filled with a dense smoke. Remove the hose and reseal the plastic wrap. Let the smoke infuse for 3 minutes, then remove the plastic wrap. Taste, and if you want smokier results, repeat the process, stirring in between smoking to distribute the flavor.

When you're ready to bake, preheat the oven to 425°F (220°C).

On a lightly floured surface, roll out the first dough half into a 12-inch (30 cm) circle. Use the rolling pin to transfer the crust to a 9½- or 10-inch (24 or 25 cm) deep-dish pie plate. Pour the chilled filling over the crust. Roll out the second dough round as above and drape it over the fruit. Use your fingers or a fork to crimp the crust and make a few vents in the top with a sharp paring knife.

In a small bowl, use a fork to lightly beat the egg with the cream. Brush the top crust with the egg wash and sprinkle with turbinado sugar.

Place the pie on a baking sheet and bake until the top crust is golden, about 25 minutes. Rotate the pie, turn the oven to 375°F (190°C), and continue baking until the juices bubble and the crust is deep golden brown, 30 to 35 minutes more.

Transfer the pie to a wire rack to cool to room temperature before serving, at least 4 hours.

Apple Filling

2½ pounds (1.1 kg) large Granny Smith apples (about 5 apples)

1½ pounds (680 g) Opal Gold apples (about 4 apples) or another sweet variety

Juice of ½ lemon

¾ cup (150 g) granulated sugar

2 tablespoons all-purpose flour

1 teaspoon pure vanilla extract

1 teaspoon ground cinnamon

¼ teaspoon kosher salt

1 egg

1 tablespoon heavy cream

Turbinado sugar, for topping

VELVETY CHOCOLATE CAKE
with Smoked Pears

Ask your friends to guess the fruit in this sumptuous cake and you'll get a wide range of replies (bananas, figs, apples?). It took my family several guesses before they finally landed on pears. The smoky fruit puree is a quiet presence here that creates a moist, velvety texture—like a few notes from a familiar song that you can't quite recall.

I'm crazy about cocoa noir, the intensely chocolaty, unsweetened black cocoa powder used to make Oreos, but you can use Dutch-processed cocoa here as well. The pear puree can be made a day or two in advance, but you'll want to smoke it just before baking. Standard black peppercorns are fine, but this cake is also a good platform for using exotic varieties, like floral, cardamom-scented long peppers or Voatsiperifery "wild" peppers from Madagascar that have woodsy and citrus notes. You won't use all of the pear puree for the cake, so eat the leftovers or fold them into crème fraîche or sweetened whipped cream to serve alongside.

Preheat the oven to 350°F (175°C). Grease a 9-inch (23 cm) springform pan with butter and line it with parchment paper.

Combine the espresso powder and the boiling water in a large heatproof bowl and stir until dissolved. Add the butter and chocolate and gently whisk until the chocolate has melted and the mixture is smooth. Whisk in the granulated sugar until it dissolves. Add the eggs and vanilla and whisk again until thoroughly combined.

In a separate bowl, sift together the flour, cocoa powder, baking powder, ground peppercorns, and salt. Whisk the dry ingredients into the chocolate mixture until combined, then fold in the Smoked Pear Puree.

Pour the batter into the prepared pan and bake for 1 hour, until a cake tester inserted into the center comes out clean or with just a few dry crumbs attached (the top of the cake will likely form a crackly crust). Let the cake cool on a wire rack for 20 minutes before removing the sides from the pan, then let the cake cool completely on the wire rack. Dust the cake with cocoa noir before slicing and serving.

continued

MAKES ONE 9-INCH
(23 CM) CAKE

1½ teaspoons instant espresso powder

1½ cups (355 ml) boiling water

1 cup plus 1½ tablespoons (245 g) unsalted butter, cut into ¾-inch (2 cm) cubes, at room temperature

7 ounces (200 g) dark chocolate (at least 70 percent cocoa solids), coarsely chopped

1¼ cups (250 g) granulated sugar

2 eggs, lightly beaten

2 teaspoons pure vanilla extract

1¾ cups plus 2 tablespoons (235 g) all-purpose flour

⅓ cup (30 g) cocoa noir or Dutch-processed cocoa powder, plus more for dusting

2¾ teaspoons baking powder

1 teaspoon freshly ground Voatsiperifery peppercorns or other peppercorns

¼ teaspoon kosher salt

1 cup (240 ml) Smoked Pear Puree (recipe follows)

MAKES ABOUT 1¾ CUPS (415 ML)

2 large pears, peeled and chopped

¼ cup (50 g) turbinado sugar

2 tablespoons water

1½ tablespoons freshly squeezed lemon juice

Pinch of kosher salt

Smoked Pear Puree

To make the pear puree, combine the pears, turbinado sugar, water, lemon juice, and salt in a small heavy saucepan and cook over medium-high heat. Bring the mixture to a lively simmer, stirring occasionally. Turn the heat to low and simmer until the pears are tender and the liquid thickens and reduces by half, 7 to 9 minutes. Remove the pan from the heat and let the puree cool slightly. Pour the puree into a mixing bowl and refrigerate until the mixture is completely cool.

To smoke the puree, add a pinch of wood chips to the burn chamber of a smoking gun, place the hose in the mixing bowl with the end above the puree, and cover with plastic wrap. Follow the manufacturer's instructions to ignite the wood chips and smoke for a few seconds, until the bowl is filled with a dense smoke. Remove the hose and reseal the plastic wrap. Let the smoke infuse for 3 minutes, then remove the plastic wrap. Stir and taste, and if you want smokier results, repeat the process, stirring in between smoking to distribute the flavor.

SMOKED PECAN–WHISKEY HONEYCOMB

The crackly texture and toffee flavor of honeycomb candy whisks me back to London and the candy bars I used to snack on while waiting for the tube to arrive. Luckily, I discovered how easy this sweet treat is to make at home. Baking soda is the magical ingredient here—whisking it in at the end of cooking (after the syrup has reached a "hard crack" temperature) creates gas holes that give the candy its bubbly namesake appearance. In this Texas-inspired version, the bacony flavor of smoked pecans and a splash of whiskey balance the candy's intense sweetness. Nibble this sweet treat with your favorite single-barrel bourbon, serve it with ice cream, or pack it as a treat on camping trips.

Line a rimmed baking sheet with aluminum foil.

In a large heavy saucepan or Dutch oven, combine the sugar, corn syrup, honey, salt, pecans, whiskey, and vinegar. (The pan might seem too big for the ingredients, but the mixture increases in volume dramatically.) Cook over high heat, stirring constantly to make sure the bottom doesn't burn, until a candy thermometer inserted into the mixture reads 280°F (138°C).

Remove the pan from the heat and stir in the baking soda, mixing well. The mixture will double, if not triple, in size. Carefully pour the honeycomb onto the prepared baking sheet. Do not spread out the mixture or you'll lose the suspended gas bubbles that give honeycomb its characteristic shape. Once the mixture has cooled completely, about 30 minutes, break it into small pieces and store in a sealed container at room temperature for up to 1 month.

**MAKES ABOUT
1½ POUNDS (680 G)**

½ cup (100 g) sugar

¼ cup (60 ml) light corn syrup

¼ cup (60 ml) honey

¼ teaspoon kosher salt

1 cup (140 g) chopped smoked pecans (see page 72)

1 ounce (30 ml) whiskey

1½ teaspoons apple cider vinegar

1½ teaspoons baking soda

CHOCOLATE & RYE BREAD PUDDING
with Candied Orange Peel

**MAKES ONE
9 BY 13-INCH DISH**

1 pound (450 g) German-style rye bread

1 pound (450 g) bittersweet chocolate discs, or coarsely chopped bittersweet chocolate

3¼ cups (770 ml) heavy cream

¾ cup (150 g) granulated sugar

½ teaspoon ground cardamom

½ teaspoon ground cinnamon

½ teaspoon freshly ground black pepper

8 eggs

2 tablespoons coarsely chopped Candied Orange Peel (opposite page), or finely grated peel of 1 large orange

Flaky salt, for garnish

Whipped cream, for serving (optional)

This is not your grandmother's bread pudding: using a tangy toasted German-style rye and bittersweet chocolate creates a rich and rustic version of the traditional. Cardamom, cinnamon, black pepper, candied orange peel, and a whiff of smoke meld beautifully with the dark chocolate.

Preheat the oven to 400°F (200°C). Cut the bread into ½-inch (1.3 cm) slices, then cut the slices into 1-inch (2.5 cm) pieces. Place the bread on a rimmed baking sheet and bake until toasted and darkened somewhat, 8 to 10 minutes.

Butter a 9 by 13-inch (23 by 33 cm) baking dish and add the toasted rye cubes, overlapping as necessary. Sprinkle with half of the chocolate and set aside.

In a saucepan, combine the remaining chocolate, 1 cup (240 ml) of the heavy cream, and the sugar and cook over medium heat, stirring frequently, just until the chocolate is melted. Gradually stir in the remaining 2¼ cups (530 ml) cream, the cardamom, cinnamon, and pepper until smooth and combined. Remove the pan from the heat.

Combine the eggs and Candied Orange Peel in a very large bowl and whisk vigorously to blend. Continue to whisk while you slowly pour in the melted chocolate mixture.

Add a pinch of wood chips to the burn chamber of a smoking gun, place the hose in the bowl with the end above the chocolate, and cover the bowl with plastic wrap. Follow the manufacturer's instructions to ignite the wood chips and smoke for a few seconds, until the bowl is filled with a dense smoke. Remove the hose and reseal the plastic wrap. Let the smoke infuse for 3 minutes, then remove the plastic wrap. Stir the chocolate and taste, and if you want smokier results, repeat the process, stirring in between smoking to distribute the flavor.

After smoking, slowly pour the chocolate mixture over the bread in the dish, allowing the bread to absorb the liquid as you go (the dish will be very full). Cover with plastic wrap and refrigerate for at least 2 hours, or overnight.

When you're ready to bake, preheat the oven to 325°F (165°C) and line a baking sheet with aluminum foil. Uncover the bread pudding and place the baking dish on the prepared baking sheet. Sprinkle the top of the pudding with flaky salt and bake for 70 to 80 minutes, until the texture is firm and springy or an instant-read thermometer inserted into the center reads 160°F (70°C). Remove the dish from the oven and cool on a wire rack for at least 45 minutes. Serve warm topped with a generous dollop of whipped cream.

Candied Orange Peel

Making candied orange peel from scratch takes a bit of time, but after the simmering, you'll have a fragrant jar of peels for baking or snacking that will last for three months.

Note: If you live in a humid climate and are making this in the summer months, consider adding a food-grade silica desiccant pack (available online) to the jar to absorb humidity.

4 ripe oranges
(preferably organic)

4 cups (950 ml) water

2 cups (400 g) sugar

2 green cardamom pods

1 star anise pod

Place a wire rack on a baking sheet lined with parchment paper.

Using a vegetable peeler, remove the outer peel of each orange, working from stem end to blossom end. Lay each piece on a cutting board, pith side up, and use a paring knife to scrape off as much of the pith as possible (the more you remove, the less bitter it will be).

Place the peel strips and 2 cups (480 ml) of the water in a saucepan and bring to a boil over medium-high heat. Turn the heat to low and simmer for 15 minutes. Drain and return the peels to the pan.

Add the sugar, cardamom, star anise, and the remaining 2 cups (480 ml) water. Bring to a boil over medium-high heat, stirring every few minutes, until the sugar dissolves. Once the syrup boils, turn the heat to low and simmer for approximately 1 hour. (Since the syrup is going to slowly concentrate, you'll need to turn down the heat every now and then to maintain that simmer.) Stir every few minutes to ensure the peels are evenly coated.

After 50 minutes, the majority of the water will have evaporated and the syrup will be thick and bubbly. You'll know you're almost done when you feel grit at the bottom of the pan when you swipe the spatula across it. That means the syrup is "concentrated" and the sugar is falling out of solution. At this point, use an instant-read thermometer to start checking the temperature (there won't really be enough syrup left to use a clamp-on candy thermometer).

When the syrup hits 250°F (120°C), quickly remove the pan from the heat and pour the orange peels onto the wire rack, separating and straightening the pieces as quickly as you can with a couple of forks. Once the peels have cooled, shake off any excess sugar and cover them lightly with paper towels or a clean towel to rest overnight at room temperature.

Store the candied peels in a glass jar at room temperature for up to 3 months.

Recipe Course Index

Acknowledgments

Thanks to my intrepid agent, Janis Donnaud, for helping me hatch this book and demanding my best for so many years.

Deepest gratitude to my friend Amanda Hesser, her co-pilot Merrill Stubbs, and the team at Food52 for asking me to write *Any Night Grilling*. That delightful project ignited my passion for live fire cooking, and set me on a path that led to this book, and continues to unfold.

Thanks to the entire team at Ten Speed Press, especially Julie Bennett, Emma Campion, Lisa Ferkel, and Ashley Pierce for enthusiastically embracing this project, and improving it with their sharp filter and killer design.

Thanks to my stellar photo shoot team, who braved a week of triple digit temperatures to make this book so beautiful, including photographer Johnny Autry, his assistant Nick Iway, and the abundantly talented Ali Slagle.

Thanks to Keith and Courtnery Langford and David and Myrna Langford for the gracious gift of unfettered work time at the Camphouse. Muchas Gracias Rebecca Rather, for the same gift in Fredricksburg.

Thanks to the team at PK Grills, especially my friend (and partner in orange jumpsuits) Scott Moody.

Thanks to Stacy and Aaron Franklin, for generously sharing your expertise, friendship, and delicious meals that get to the heart of good food, family, and fun.

Thanks also to our friends who came for meals to offer feedback and support, especially Todd Duplechan and Jessica Maher, Amy Brotman, Greg Lane, Pat Sharpe, Charles Lohrmann, Amanda Eyre Ward and Tip Meckel, Claiborne Smith and Tomas Rivera. Nettie Patterson, Tammy and Eddie Young, Clayton Maxwell and Scott Sloan, Abigail King, Melissa and Craig Garnett, Danny and Celina Leskovar, Rachel Zindler, Paul Newman, Joshua and Jaime LaRue, Scott Foster, Nancy Mimms, and Rodney Gibbs.

Thanks to my parents, Mike and Julie Disbrowe, for always cheering me on, and for enduring the rollercoaster of recipe testing that my crazy profession requires.

Thanks to Fran Norman, Jana Norman, and Paul Turley for love and support from Pensacola and Adelaide.

Most of all, thanks to my family: My wonderful children, Flannery and Wyatt, for being so cool about all the time that mom spent racing through grocery stores, schlepping charcoal, and cooking out back. Thanks to my husband, David Norman, for being my most trusted sounding board and letting me take over the backyard shift. The moment when the three of you pull up a seat to our dinner table will always be the best part of any day.

Index

Library of Congress Cataloging-in-Publication Data
    Names: Disbrowe, Paula, author.
    Title: Thank you for smoking : fun and fearless recipes cooked with a whiff
        of wood fire on your grill or smoker / Paula Disbrowe.
    Description: California : Ten Speed Press, an imprint of the Crown
        Publishing Group, a division of Penguin Random House LLC, [2019] |
        Includes bibliographical references and index. |
    Identifiers: LCCN 2018038937 (print) | LCCN 2018039355 (ebook) | ISBN
        9780399582141 (ebook) | ISBN 9780399582134 (hardcover : alk. paper)
    Subjects: LCSH: Smoking (Cooking) | LCGFT: Cookbooks.
    Classification: LCC TX609 (ebook) | LCC TX609 .D57 2019 (print) |
        DDC 641.4/6—dc23
    LC record available at https://lccn.loc.gov/2018038937

Hardcover ISBN: 978-0-399-58213-4
eBook ISBN: 978-0-399-58214-1

Printed in China

Design by Lisa Ferkel
Food styling by Paula Disbrowe and Ali Slagle
Prop styling by Ali Slagle

10 9 8 7 6 5 4 3 2 1

First Edition